The Kabbalistic Visions

And the Secrets of the Phoenician Tradition

Karim El Koussa

ARS METAPHYSICA

an imprint of Sunbury Press, Inc.
Mechanicsburg, PA USA

ARS METAPHYSICA

an imprint of Sunbury Press, Inc.
Mechanicsburg, PA USA

For information about special discounts for bulk purchases, please contact Sunbury Press Orders Dept. at (855) 338-8359 or orders@sunburypress.com.

To request one of our authors for speaking engagements or book signings, please contact Sunbury Press Publicity Dept. at publicity@sunburypress.com.

FIRST ARS METAPHYSICA EDITION: June 2021

Set in Garamond | Interior design by Crystal Devine | Cover by Lawrence Knorr | Cover illustration and symbols by Maria Matta (https://www.behance.net/maria-matta) | Edited by Lawrence Knorr.

Publisher's Cataloging-in-Publication Data
Names: El Koussa, Karim, author.
Title: The kabbalistic visions : and the secrets of the phoenician tradition / Karim El Koussa..
Description: First trade paperback edition. | Mechanicsburg, PA : Ars Metaphysica, 2021.
Summary: This book is an esoteric work that may shed light on our true divine nature and our direct relationship with the Divine Archetype, the Universe, and Humanity, as well as our substantial duty toward the existence as a whole, our *Unitas* state. It delves into the *Initiatic* Secrets of Enoch's original Phoenician Tradition of the Kabbala and reveals differences with the Chaldean Kabbala incorporated by Jewish Kabbalists.
Identifiers: ISBN : 978-1-62006-478-8 (softcover).
Subjects: BODY, MIND & SPIRIT / Ancient Mysteries & Controversial Knowledge | BODY, MIND & SPIRIT / Mysticism | RELIGION / Ancient | RELIGION / Judaism / Kabbalah & Mysticism.

Product of the United States of America
0 1 1 2 3 5 8 13 21 34 55

Continue the Enlightenment!

To all Brothers and Sisters, Seekers of Truth, and Lovers of Light.

Also By
Karim El Koussa

~ ~ ~

The PHOENICIAN Code
Unveiling the Secrets of the Holy Grail
Metaphysical/Religious Mystery (Christianity)/Fiction Thriller
Sunbury Press, USA, 2011/2018
Rights to The PHOENICIAN Code optioned for TV by
Northern Star Pictures, Inc. USA, September 2018
Winner of the Sunbury Press SUNNY AWARD, USA, January 19, 2020

JESUS the Phoenician
Religious History/Christianity
Sunbury Press, USA, 2013

PYTHAGORAS the Mathemagician
Historical Fiction/Philosophical novel
Sunbury Press, USA, 2010
Receiver of two Official Citations for the first American edition
Cloonfad Press, USA, 2005
USA, October 17, 2005
Winner of the SAÏD AKL Prize for the Lebanese self-published edition
LEB, December 19, 2001

Contents

Foreword

There are traditions that have existed (and which continue to exist), which try and preserve sacred knowledge and history of earlier times, in which humanity was said to be closer to God, and inheritors of a wisdom that brought people greater security, health, and consequently, happiness.

This knowledge dealt with the mysteries of life and death and the secrets of stability on different planes of consciousness. It was an understanding of the power of language, number, shapes, and forms and how these can be utilized to guide people towards a greater connection with each other and the Universe around them. Out of this knowledge arose the great civilizations of antiquity, as well as the great leaders who provided law and order on both the material and spiritual planes of causation.

Fundamental to this history is the esoteric and kabbalistic traditions of the Phoenician civilization, from which many others have inherited so much. Being an extension of the traditions of Egypt but preserving doctrines unto themselves, the Phoenicians also provided the framework for what was to become the spiritual doctrines of the Hebrews, and they stand as the root of the Canaanite heritage and the tradition of Enoch.

For this reason, and many others, the term "kabbalistic" can be correctly utilized in this book. The word "kabbala" is generally accepted to be derived from the Hebrew word "qabal," meaning "to receive," and alluding to the receiving of special knowledge and interpretation of sacred texts. However, it is no mistake that the twenty-two letters of the Hebrew aleph-bet (alphabet) are themselves derived from the original Phoenician. Nor is it a coincidence that the Phoenician letters resemble, in form, similar shapes to the Egyptian hieroglyphs for the same letters. Likewise, it is not a coincidence that the Greeks, with their own doctrines of number and letter correspondences, resemble those of the Phoenicians, as they too had inherited much from this Phoenician civilization.

Until recently, the mysteries of the Phoenician civilization had only been whispered in occult and religious Orders, in the Orthodoxy of Judaism,

Christianity, and Islam, and academic and theological circles. The history of Western civilization has been completely shaped to resemble a narrative dictated by certain religious sects, which has largely been uncomfortable acknowledging the debt that it owes to this Phoenician source, and as a result, little information regarding the doctrines and initiation practices of the Phoenicians has made the light of day in the public domain.

Fortunately, Karim El Koussa has made it his life's work to bring an understanding of these doctrines to the world. His mastery of language and Phoenician history has finally opened a glimpse of what the Phoenician tradition has offered the world for ages. His understanding of this history and tradition brings a new perspective to the mysteries of the Holy Bible, as well as ideas preserved in more modern Orders.

Whether we look at the ancient rites of initiation alluded to in ancient texts and the Bible, or we attempt to make sense of the enigmas preserved by the Templars and their later expressions of Freemasonry, Rosicrucianism, and Theosophy, a full appreciation of what was being preserved can only be understood with the help of the Phoenician theological and cosmological understanding of things. Certainly, there have been others throughout history who have figured out this secret and have alluded to it in safe and tactful ways, but until now, the extent of the Phoenician doctrine has not been published in one place.

The following book must be digested thoughtfully and intentionally, sometimes requiring us to "relearn what we have learned," but with new eyes. *The Kabbalistic Visions* can provide a new understanding of the Pythagorean and Hermetic ideas that have been at the core of western civilization. It will explore the origin of names found in sacred texts, including locations, prophets, angels, and gods. Beyond this, it offers a fresh look at ideas passed down in kabbalistic traditions, and it illustrates the origin of these concepts. Likewise, many of the *mysteries of Initiation traditions* can only be understood with the keys provided in this book.

Any theologian or student of sacred texts will do themselves a great service by studying this book and understanding the root concepts within it, for it will shed light on many mysteries that have largely remained out of reach to the masses for centuries. Understanding the origin of the Phoenician alphabet letter meanings can likewise provide a framework for understanding the languages that later came out of it. In fact, I would argue that Biblical texts, in particular, cannot be properly understood without the key information provided in this book. Though other authors have alluded to such ideas in the past, Karim El Koussa unveils these concepts and illustrates them in a plain and easy to grasp fashion, citing the foundations of so many concepts.

If you wish to understand the mysteries of the Phoenicians, which were at the heart of their worship and practice, then read this book, and then read it again, many times, until you internalize the keys which will open the symbolic language of the ancients! The keys given in this book also provide perspective on more arcane subjects like the mysteries of the Holy Grail and alchemy, as well as Pythagorean concepts of number and form. Such perspective will validate the important role of the Phoenicians and their secret tradition that you have now received!

Timothy Warren Hogan
Grand Master of the Order of the Temple of Secret Initiates
and the Templar Collegia

Acknowledgments

I would like first to acknowledge a very special and extraordinary person, Father Dr. Youssef Yammine, for the many helpful sessions granted to realize two of my preceding books; the novel *The Phoenician Code* and its follow-up companion academic work *Jesus the Phoenician*. Although we may differ in opinion on specific points or few details in this book, Fr. Yammine opened my eyes to the ultimate reality that enabled me to understand that the authentic Kabbala could have started initially with Enoch in the ancient land of the Phoenicians.

I should like to express my indebtedness to the late Dr. Eddy Dib for his valuable comments and various advice on the subject matter dealt with here while considering all the important variations before actually presenting it and properly from the correct esoteric Kabbalistic approach.

I am also greatly honored to have Brother Timothy Hogan reviewing the book and presenting it with a beautiful Foreword. I also feel committed to giving my appreciation to both Esoteric Researcher Jonny Enoch and Dr. Jean-Marc Aractingi for reading the book and reviewing it on the back cover.

I also owe a great debt to all friends and acquaintances who have helped me write this book and have supported me, each in his/her different way, and who wish to remain anonymous.

I am also grateful to Mr. Lawrence Knorr, the publisher, who has given me another great opportunity to publish my fourth book in the USA. A special thanks also goes to the staff at Sunbury Press and its Ars Metaphysica imprint.

I should also express my appreciation to Maria Matta for the impressive cover illustration and for drawing the symbols used in Part II.

Finally, I would like to show my sincere gratitude to my growing readers around the world.

Karim El Koussa
Ehden, March 17, 2021

Introduction

Before we proceed with the Introduction, let us take a few minutes in silence and think about the following.

There are many things in life that might happen and many others that might not. Not everything or every idea thought about in our minds is destined to be manifested in the course of time and space that we are experiencing and perceiving here on earth, our *physical cube*.

We, who believe that God is merciful and compassionate, often wish for things to happen in our lives, good things of course, and when they do not transpire, we feel a bit sad and perhaps desperate. Our wishes then turn into prayers and adoration. Still, things remain unable, un-wanting, and unwilling to change for the better good in general or our betterment in life. They are meant to be or not to be, for as above, so is below!

Is God playing the dice? White or Black! Good or Bad!

Existence and life seem to be no more than statistical probabilities, where every act, every feeling, everything is shaped accordingly. There are certain religions in the world and some spiritual guides who do believe in reincarnation. They teach that we have the chance to live many lives, and somewhere along that elliptical spiral ascension and evolution, things start affirmatively to happen or may begin to happen. They begin to evolve for the better general good and our betterment. Then, our good wishes, and many loads of them, become true.

I mean, is this the right question we ask, or are we just making false assumptions about God shooting the dice on a dualistic basis? Yet God is One. This indeed compels us to make a multi-conceptual choice. Is this our human way to justify creation, evolution, and reincarnation plans figured by God, or justify our own belief in the final judgment according to our deeds? What is going on, really? What is more sublime than wishing to live in Love and Peace? Yet, we fail to grasp it!

Illusion or Reality is what is what. Is it a dilemma, a simple mathematical formula, or just the manifested world's natural behavior?

Alphabets, Numbers, and Symbols are surely diffused magically, say, *alchemically,* all through the entire scope of existence. There are truly no specific limitations in time and no determinate boundaries in the spatial fabric for things to occur. Every piece must fit its place in the Great Kosmic Puzzle. Make a wish, blow the candle, then eat a piece of the cake. Is it tasty or not? Draw a line within the circle, in your mind, or on a sheet of paper! Invisible or visible; what happens is what happens.

Leave . . . forget about it. Do not get attached to it, for it is not permanent. Nothing is, except the Truth. There is nothing higher than the Truth, and it is not for us to know It, as yet! Never can we reach It, can we? Can we do it, though, in our *union* with God? Through our perception of the Light? Must every one of us reach It separately! Alternatively, shouldn't we do it collectively, ultimately?

I am not an atheist, of course, nor agnostic for that matter, yet not a blind believer. I am a thinker, a Seeker of Truth, and a Lover of Light. I am what I am, a particle in space, a drop in the ocean, and a moment in time. For sure, I'm not a sheep that follows the whistle of the wrong shepherd. I keep on existing yet in a different shape and a more elaborate condition. There is no end, no beginning, but a continuous flow of energy, a quantum leap throughout the *eternal.*

~ ~ ~

Now, this book is an esoteric work of three Parts that may shed light on our true divine nature and our direct relationship with the Divine Archetype, the Universe, and Humanity, as well as our substantial duty toward the existence as a whole, our *Unitas* state. It delves high and deep into the *Initiatic* Secrets of the original Phoenician Tradition of the Kabbala that was first ever accepted by Enoch, the *seer* of visions on Mt. Hermon in the ancient land of Phoenicia, and reveals its essential differences with the Chaldean Kabbala incorporated by Jewish Kabbalists.

Part I primarily deals with the essential matters that will enlighten the readers about Enoch's *Acceptance of the Divine Laws* from the Angels of God, say, the Good Watchers, the authentic *Tradition of the Kabbala* he was entrusted to transmit to Phoenician Initiates first. Then, we would discover where *The First*

Initiation Temple was erected and how it was copied in the Canaanite-Phoenician Land before *Transmitting the Tradition primary to Egypt* along with the masonic operative work of the Temple and its gradual spread all across the world. We shall also tackle the undoubtedly Phoenician connection to the Christian Savior by revealing *The Sacerdotal Line to Jesus Christ*, before ending this exploratory and explanatory Part with the foundation of *The Babylonian Brotherhood* in Babylon through Persian influence, and that which stands as a deviated and corrupted form of the *Initiatic* Tradition from its often recognized—but systemically overlaid original—Phoenician/Egyptian system taught by the very few chosen adepts of the Great White Fraternity.

In Part II, we start by showing the visions of the Sacred Alphabet as per the esoteric and occult meanings of the Kabbalistic letters inspired by Enoch and described within the Authentic Enochian-Hermetic Tradition. Not only that, but this Part also focuses on the other two essential levels that will altogether awaken the human unconscious to become conscious of itself. The three levels are depicted in the following manner. First, *The Sacred Alphabet*: the 22 letters of the Alphabet's Occult Doctrine; the Enochian Kabbala[1], are the secret keys of the Universe and its absolute principles. If one knows how to use them by will, when one becomes knowledgeable of their codes, one will obtain wisdom and power. The twenty-two visions here presented are my personal experience with the occult meaning of the 22 Alphabetical letters inscribed in the Enochian Kabbala of the authentic Phoenician Tradition. Second, *The Occult Numbers*: "they are the Divine Powers that are in action within the Macrocosm and Microcosm. They are the movers of the Kosmos and rulers of all forms and ideas. They are gods! The Number is not an abstract quantity but indeed a real and active virtue of the Supreme One—Source of the Universal Harmony! Number[2] itself is also a factual and dynamic asset of the harmonious structure of the Psyche. It is the wisest!" Pythagoras taught.[3] Thence, the ten meditations later presented are in direct concordance with the ten numbers[4] (1 to 10) taken

---

1. We believe that the initial form of the *Sacred Alphabet* was kabbalistically encrypted by Enoch who received them from the Angels of El and slightly different from the shapes the letters took when they later appeared in Gebel (Byblos). In truth, we think they even had some magical resonance in their formation.

2. Numbers were formed in geometrical shapes, and we believe they were created in Gebel by the Sacred Builders. Each number is formed to reflect an angle. For example, Number 1 is made of one angle, number 2 is made of two angles, and that goes on until number 9. Number 10 was depicted in the form of a circle.

3. El Koussa, Karim, *Pythagoras the Mathemagician*, 294.

4. To Pythagoras and the Pythagoreans, Numbers are the essence; the measure of all things. The whole existence is naught but of a Mathemagical dimension; a real state of concatenation and an infinite frame of becoming! (*Pythagoras the Mathemagician*, 118). Each number has its own personality, whether it is masculine or feminine, complete or incomplete. (Pythagoras the Mathemagician, 258–259)

from Pythagoras' esoteric interpretation and occult teachings transmitted to his disciples. Last, *The Mystic Symbols*: the eight symbols herein presented carry deep mystical meanings that shall trigger one's primordial faculties of both intuition and inspiration. With every new mystical revelation, a flicker of light awakens the state of one's intuitive and inspirational knowledge for a higher understanding of the Kosmic secrets.

Part III starts by setting forth a knowledgeable apprehension *On God or Deity* in its global general form but focuses precisely on the Canaanite-Phoenician perception of the Divine Archetype and the concept of Monotheism, which had initially originated with Phoenician High Priests and Initiates. Although there was a Pantheon of divine beings in Phoenician theology, each playing their role, they were all actually part of the Assembly of Gods presided over by El (El-Elyon), regarded as their Father (the Creator God) and that of humanity. Then, we treat a chapter *On Creation and Man*, where we shall tackle the very concept of the creation of the universe, the physical manifestation of Man in its dual nature—Male and Female—which is not but a division from unity, the implication of such partition, and how can we restore *union* with the One. Followed by a chapter in which we reveal some of the mysteries *On the Secrets of Initiation*, naturally Phoenician Initiation, engaging other than Enoch himself, very well-known characters in the ancient *Initiatic* Circles, such as Tubal-Cain, Hiram Abif, Melki-Sedek, etc.! Finally, an introductory *On the Ancient and Primitive Phoenician Rite*!

Speaking of Phoenicians and their secrets, many people may not know how the Phoenicians worked and functioned. Their origin, existence, and importance have long been overlaid by a considerable amount of confusion and mystery and covered by a systematized plan, masterminded by those who tried to debunk them or even steal their accomplishments throughout history, mainly Persians, Hebrews, Greeks, and Romans. Phoenicians were, in fact, very secretive people, keeping everything they did or excelled at under total control and secrecy. Perhaps this has unfortunately made it more difficult to accurately document their outstanding achievements for the various things they were later better known for, such as religion, theology, philosophy, sciences and the art of masonry[5], etc.

Regardless, Phoenicians have made significant contributions to Mankind, such as the Phonetic alphabet, opening trade routes throughout the Mediterranean and beyond, sea navigation, manufacturing, and producing their famous

---

5. There is no doubt that they greatly excelled in the building of cities, structures, temples, etc., not only in the main Canaanite-Phoenician Land but also wherever their ships docked, all around the orb, say Earth.

Tyrian purple dye or imperial dye valued across the world for its distinctive color. Let's look back and see how the skillful Phoenicians used to produce the purple dye to beautifully create the "Royal Purple," for example. We will find that it was done in total secrecy by the artists involved in its creation. Every worker was fetched at the end of the day by a superior to see if the secrets of the trade are being betrayed. When found loyal, the superior will pay them their wages, and when found guilty, they will be expelled from the syndicate. And that goes for every Art or Craft they so elegantly practiced. Because of this desire for secrecy and what has been slightly left to us, at least orally, of the Great White Fraternity, they have been linked to secret societies like Freemasonry, etc., as we shall see later on and explain the nuances there is.

The same system was carried on by the "Sacred Builders," mainly from Gebel and Sūr. They became officially entrusted by the Great White Fraternity to build Temples to the deities the Phoenicians worshiped, mainly Temples dedicated to the God Ēl the Most High, the Elohim (Sons of El: Baal, Adon, Yām, and Šalim) and the Goddesses (Anat, Ashirai, Astarte). Sacred Builders erected Temples to host the Divine, fundamentally in concordance with the mysterious "triune" nature of man[6]. This was all done in total secrecy using sacred measurements.

One of the most reputed Architects of these "Sacred Builders" has been none other than Hiram Abiff, who commanded the Great Work by the power of the *Tau*! Egyptians, like their brothers, the Phoenicians, followed suit in the construction of their Temples and Pyramids. Fortunately, most Egyptian monuments stood still, and regrettably, most of the Phoenician monuments were destroyed and vanished forever. However, thanks to great Phoenician authors and historians like Sanchuniathon, Iamblichus, Philo of Byblos, etc., the crucial findings at archeological sites in many Canaanite-Phoenician cities like Gebel, Sūr, Ba'albek, Saydoun, Ugarit, etc., and the various accounts left to us by Egyptians and Greeks, that we have been successfully able to recuperate at long last many of the most essential Phoenician knowledge, religious practices and esoteric tradition, which if we compare to the Egyptians', we will undoubtedly find a great match.

Now, many people may ask legitimate questions about the authenticity of the Phoenician secret Order, meaning the Great White Fraternity, and these questions are mainly about the following three points:

---

6. The triune nature of man is his/her constituents of Body, Mind and Spirit. We may come to explain that in the last chapter of the book.

1. The existence of this ancient Fraternity in the past and the present;
2. Were there any Degrees practiced in that *Initiatic* system?;
3. Were there any Rituals?

The answer to question 1 is Yes. We will thoroughly explain this ancient Fraternity's religious and physical existence in the remote past in both Phoenicia and Egypt and throughout the world. Today, however, the Great White Fraternity is not organized. Still, we have already found parts of its *Initiatic* mysteries at the heart of certain religions and fraternities that we will present in the book. Some of these important groups and Orders are somehow focusing more than others on the Canaanite-Phoenician Tradition and may be working on reviving that ancient lore!

The answer to question 2 is Yes. Our extensive research led us to discover and understand that Phoenician adepts were divided into three main bodies, say, degrees. First, the *Listeners* who receive the teachings from Initiates, Masters, or High Priests, and that process could take many years of labor. Second, the *Initiates* who receive Divine teachings through Rituals (sacred practices, religious ceremonies, etc.). Last, the *Sacred Builders,* who were once Listeners then Initiates, and have become afterward builders of special consecrated sacred places worldwide. Thus, mystically speaking, the Great White Fraternity was initially conceived as a disciplinary esoteric system that builds and elevates humans, preparing them to receive the Divine in Temples it erects!

The answer to question 3 is Yes. We have learned that Initiates/High Priests performed rituals and were often perceived as supportive dramatic elements to the basic imparted Teachings Listeners gradually grasp during their development. However, rituals were left secret and only enacted in special consecrated sacred places such as Temples, Sanctuaries, etc., and which were called initially *Beth El,* meaning the "House of El."

Should we want to envision the most essential *Pillars* on which the revival of the Phoenician Council of the Great White Fraternity, say the *Phenokians,* could firmly stand and endure, it would thus be an *Initiatic* system divided into 5 degrees and based on the following Great Initiates: Enoch (Phenok); Melchizedek (Melki-Sedek); Hiram (Abiff); Pythagoras (Beth-agor); and Jesus Christ (Yāwshua Meshiha).[7]

---

7. We will therefore provide in the final chapter of this book some additional but introductory information on how these five Pillars are incorporated in our Ancient and Primitive Phoenician *Initiatic* system.

At any rate, for those who are curious to know about that Order or feel they belong to it in one way or the other, and hence desire to be part of this *Initiatic* journey, let us then begin. We are positive we may find great synchronicity in our souls, minds, and spirits, and we believe the time has come to start the transmutation, for the Time of Revelation is near. Eventually, the Great White Fraternity's revival will occur in due time, though we hope it transpires in this coming cycle. Amen!

~ PART I ~

1.

The Acceptance of the Divine Laws

Ēlim Šalam Likum,
Melki Rouh, Melki Šamaš, Melki Yām, Melki Aretz,
Berikoun-Berikoun-Berikoun . . .

Brothers and Sisters, Seekers of Truth and Lovers of Light.

First thing first, and before we proceed into developing and explaining what the Phoenician system of the Kabbala is, which we undoubtedly believe is the authentic tradition of the esoteric secret knowledge of what appeared later as in the form of religions, we feel responsibly committed to introducing the Great Man behind it all, the exact place where it all started and the lost Fraternity that held its beacon throughout the centuries; the Great White Fraternity.

It has nothing to do with the Great White Brotherhood (also known as the Great White Lodge), which was said to have appeared some long time ago in the East and talks about Ascended Masters. Both Orders may, however, have similar goals but not similar origins. Moreover, it is neither directly associated, connected, nor affiliated to the Freemasonic Brotherhood (Blue Lodge, Degrees or Grades, Rites), nor it has anything to do with the Templar Order (Priories, Commanderies) that have existed in the past or still existing now in the world, though it may look indirectly connected to Freemasonry and maybe to some form of Templarism, mainly Christian Templarism, the type we see in Europe, especially in Germany. This general direct disconnection and non-affiliation to Masonic and Templar doctrines are merely because it had preceded both organizations by thousands of years.

That being said, the Great White Fraternity is an ancient secret fraternity that may have been officially founded around 1500 BC or even a few hundred years earlier. However, it is much older than this date and might reasonably go back to a certain seer known as Enoch. In our historical understanding of the ancient past, and due to many factors, Enoch could not be the seventh Jewish Patriarch of the antediluvian period, as cited in the Hebrew Bible, being the ancestor of the mythical Noah, and born in Babylon, because we have proved in previous books, and will also explain some of the details here in this book, that Judaism came into existence at a much later period in time, in the 1st millennium BC.

The Old Testament had proven itself to be a non-historical book *per se*. The many narrations we have read there do not necessary reflect the history of the Hebrews or Jews as an ethnic group. Rather, it stands as a compilation of stories that happened in the lives of previous cultures, mainly the Canaanite-Phoenicians, Egyptians, and Mesopotamians. The lack of archeological evidence today to support the biblical narration proves the uncertainty of the Hebrews' historicity and adds to the confusion of the biblical texts that we believe were created by the Persian propagandists during the Achaemenid period!

We are mostly sure and believe that Enoch was a Canaanite-Phoenician prophet most probably originating from the ancient cities of Saydoun (Sidon) or Sūr (Tyre), and perhaps was living in the region of Galilee before he had his visions of the God El and his Angels on the top of Mt. Hermon overlooking the plains of Galilee. Enoch himself founded the Great White Fraternity a long time ago as a secret religious fraternity after *accepting the Divine Laws*—that is, receiving the *Word* from the Angels in his celestial visions. That could have transpired thousands of years before the official fraternity recognition in the 2nd millennium BC.

Following that line, we come to an eye-opening statement from the Old Testament about when Moses sent his people to spy out on the Canaanites[8] in the Land of Canaan. His spies informed him, Aaron, and all the congregation of the children of Israel on the goodness of the Land; it surely floweth with milk and honey amongst other fruitful things like a cluster of grapes, pomegranates, and figs, etc. They also reported that they saw the Children of

---

8. The Canaanite tribes they encountered there were the Jebusites and Amorites who dwelt in the mountains, and the Canaanites (better say the Phoenicians) who dwelt by the sea and by the coast of Jordan. There, they also found the Amalekites (probably the ancestors of the Edomites through Amalek, the son of Eliphaz, son of Esau, ancestor of the Edomites) who dwelt in the land of the south, and the Hittites, who were not Canaanites as well.

Anak there, and how strong are the people dwelling on the land, and their cities are walled and very great. These spies sent to search out the Land of Canaan added[9]—

> And there we saw the giants, the sons of Anak, which come of the giants: and we were in our own sight as grasshoppers, and so we were in their sight.

This Anak is undoubtedly identified as Enoch himself of the Land of Canaan. No matter how some writers or archeoastronomy researchers would like to interpret the above mentioning of the giants in a literal manner, we would instead prefer to give it a more Kabbalistic interpretation. Consequently, these giants, sons of Enoch, are rendered as the *Initiates*, the *Kabbirim* of the Land, whereas the followers of Moses represented the vulgarly small, less knowledgeable people standing in awe in front of them and bringing, therefore, proofs of the wisdom of the Canaanites.

In that respect, and as a supportive revelation to our above argument, the great 19th-century Russian occultist, philosopher, and author, H.P. Blavatsky, the founder of the Theosophical Society, described Enoch as such[10]—

> The Phoenix—called by the Hebrews Onech (from *Phenoch*, Enoch, symbol of a secret cycle and Initiation).

Even the Hebrews themselves, perhaps in their Rabbinical literature, consider Enoch belonging to the Phoenicians. That copes very well with our beliefs and understanding of this historical character. Enoch is thus associated with the Phenoch (Phenok) Council of Initiation, being the humanoid representation of the legendary bird, the Phoenix, an all-time sacred symbol of Phoenicia, who dies and resurrects after three days from its burned ashes during secret ritualistic ceremonies performed in the ancient city of *Enochia*, which is said to have been built by Cain or Kenan (introduced in the coming page), and of which we shall talk in Chapter 12 of this book. Enochia, *Henochia,* or Phenokia was later known as Ba'albek, the city of Ba'al, the city of the Sun. Such ceremonial performance was a religious ritual that may have been primarily introduced

---

9. Numbers 13 and Numbers 13:33.
10. Blavatsky, H.P, *The Secret Doctrine*, vol. 2, 617.

by Enoch himself and immediately adopted by his son Methusael and his first Enochian disciples on top of Mount Hermon.

The Great White Fraternity, the *Phenokian Tradition*, was a monotheistic religious community that began to function as an esoteric secret society in Phoenicia and was then immediately adopted by Egyptian Priests. There existed a great religious and spiritual connection between Egypt and Phoenicia, and especially between Memphis and Gebel (Byblos). Egyptian Priests also adopted the story of Adon[11] and Astarte that had occurred in Gebel and identified the names of these divinities with those of their own, Osiris and Isis. The death of Osiris and his resurrection is undoubtedly the Egyptian version of the death and resurrection of the Geblite Adon.

Also, the Phoenician's belief in the One Most High God "Al-Elyon" became the cornerstone at the Temple of Akhenaton in Egypt, who initiated the preaching of the One God, Aton[12]. Among the early prominent adepts of the Great White Fraternity were both Pharaohs Thutmose III, Akhenaton of Egypt, and the priest Osarsiph (who we shall introduce later on), as well as the Canaanite-Phoenician Kings; Melki-Sedek of Jerusalem, Ahiram of Gebel, and Hiram of Tyre.

The Divine Messenger of the Great White Fraternity stood then as Enoch-Taautus. Enoch (Anak) the Canaanite-Phoenician became a Metatron—the chosen one who stood before God. He is represented as the type of the dual man, meaning both terrestrial and spiritual, for it is said that he *walked with God* and *did not die*. Therefore, he typifies humanity in its utmost spirituality, going through intensive spiritual development of the flesh by means of the authentic Kabbala, of course.

In fact, esoterically speaking, the name it was given to him by his father and/or the one he took by himself as an *Initiate*, Enoch, Khanoch, Hanoch or Henoch means the "Teacher" or "Initiator," as well as the son of man, Enosh or Enos, of the lineage of Seth, which we shall see later on in the book. Enoch is very much perceived like Melki-Sedek (Melchisedech) or Jesus in the New Testament. It gives us an idea that he, like Jesus Christ, was a kind of "Son of Man - Son of God," very much like Cain or Kenan (Cainan), his son per the Sethite Line of Generation or his father in the Kenite Line of Generation, being the Son of the Lord, as we shall see later in Part III.

---

11. Adon was the real Phoenician name of this deity and he was one of the Elohim (one of the sons of the Most High God El) in the Phoenician Pantheon. He was referred to as Adonis by the Greeks.

12. Please note the similarity between the two names Adon and Aton.

On this very notion, Blavatsky wrote[13]—

> Cain leads the ascending line, or Macrocosm, for he is the Son of the
> "Lord," not of Adam. The "Lord" is Adam-Kadmon, Cain, the son of
> sinful thought, not the progeny of flesh and blood.

I always wondered why Blavatsky cited Cain as "son of sinful thought,"
although she considers him at the same time, Son of Lord and not the progeny
of flesh and blood! I genuinely don't understand this contradiction herein. I
will get back to that in Chapter 12.

Anyway, the *Father of Religions and Spiritual Laws* was also identified as Thot-
Taautus[14] in the Khemite-Egyptian religion. He was known by the name of
Mithra for the Hindus and Persians; Enki/Ea/Oannes in Mesopotamia; Nabū/
Nebo in the Babylonian mythology; Quetzalcóatl for the Mexican Aztecs; Thor
in the Scandinavian tradition; Hermes-Kadmos for the Greeks or Inachus in
Grecian mythology, and Mercury for the Romans. He was also Adam-Kadmon
for the Kabbalists, Edris for the Arabs and Muslims, and then Enoch for the
Druzes.

He was also the god of Wisdom, Science, and occult teachings.

~ ~ ~

When we mention Phoenician Tradition or Phoenician Initiation,
we thence first think of Enoch and second of the tradition of the
Authentic Kabbala that would refer directly to him—the *Father of Religions and
Spiritual Laws*. The Tradition was—in both its Phoenician and Egyptian essence—the same, much more ancient and authentic than the Chaldean-Judaic
Kabbalistic System that we shall explore in this chapter and show its essential
differences with the Enochian one.

---

13. Blavatsky, H.P, *Isis Unveiled*, vol. 2, 464.

14. Thot, the Egyptian Ibis-headed god, is known as *Djehuty* in the ancient Khemite language. It is said
that he has created himself through the power of the *Word*. With the *Was-Scepter* in his right hand, he brings
forth the powers of gods in worlds beyond for he is the great Councilor, and by his left hand he brings
life through the full circular energy of the *Ankh*. Behold, the Great Alignment has been balanced between
Heaven and Earth. He is the voice of wisdom, author of all works on every branch of knowledge, both
divine and human. He is the creator of magic, for he is the magician who knows all that is concealed under
the heavenly vault. He is the calculator of time who measures out the heavens and the stars and plans the
work on earth. His book, the *Book of Djehuty*, in which he inscribed all the secrets of the universe, was
secured in the library of the gods and that of men, down at *Per-Ankh*, the House of Knowledge, Life, and
Wisdom, inside the Lion in the desert, the Sphinx.

When we mention Enoch, we first think of the Book of Enoch (1 Enoch), which narrated the Meeting of Enoch with the Angels of God, whose names end by the suffix "el," like the most important ones: Michael, Gabriel, Raphael, Auriel, and, meaning they are the Angels of the Most High God El appearing on the top of Mt. Hermon—called *Jabal al-sheikh*, the Mountain of the Lord, and also known as the Mountain of Acceptance and the Meetings—in Phoenicia-Lebanon[15].

The book reported the visions of Enoch throughout the Heavenly realms. Electing him among all the sages of the Earth, the Angels had taught him the Tradition and asked him to convey it in secrecy, from *mouth to ear*, to a generation of Adepts. That had been his mission, and he had accomplished it. We will see that the further we turn the pages.

Enoch or Anak, the Canaanite-Phoenician, stood a *Metatron* before God, the Most High El. He dies not, but walks with God; he is the first possessor of the *mirific name* as per the Enochian Authentic Kabbala, the *Acceptance of the Divine Laws* taught by the Phenokians and as per some of the rituals of Freemasonry, known as the "Royal Arch of Enoch," which we believe goes back to the Great White Fraternity Tradition with some apparent alterations made by Freemasons.

We, the Phenokians who believe are descendants of that Initiatic lore; the Great White Fraternity—Phenok Council, proudly represent ourselves as *Keepers of the Lost Word* and consecrate Wednesday his holy day like it was in the old days. And, it seems that history repeats itself, for it was on top of Mt. Hermon from where God and his Angels took Enoch up—and not on mount Tabor, as traditionally and formerly believed—that Jesus' Transfiguration had occurred, observed by his three disciples: Peter, James, and John. It is also important to remember that the New Testament relates that Jesus actually claimed his divinity there, and there, it is said that Peter recognized him as the Son of God.

It is imperative at this precise moment during the development of this work to relate the Transfiguration[16] herein, for it has lots of meaning to us since it copes very well with the context of this book. We shall quote from Matthew[17]—

---

15. Please note that the name Hermes, given to him by the Greeks at a later stage, might be a derivative of Hermon! Hermes is described as the divine messenger in Greek mythology and is accredited for the writing of a major book known as *Corpus Hermeticum*, or the *Hermetica* (Egyptian-Greek) wisdom texts (of the 2nd century but it is certainly of a much earlier date) on the secret teachings of the gods, the universe, nature and on the divinity of man. He is known as Thrice Great Hermes—the Trismegistus.

16. Mark 9:2-8, Luke 9:28-36.

17. Matthew 17:1-8.

After six days,[18] Jesus took with him Peter, James, and John the brother of James, and led them up a high mountain by themselves. There he was transfigured before them. His face shone like the sun, and his clothes became as white as the light. Just then there appeared before them Moses and Elijah, talking with Jesus. Peter said to Jesus, "Lord, it is good for us to be here. If you wish, I will put up three shelters—one for you, one for Moses, and one for Elijah." While he was still speaking, a bright cloud covered them, and a voice from the cloud said, "This is my Son, whom I love; with him, I am well pleased. Listen to him!" When the disciples heard this, they fell facedown to the ground, terrified. But Jesus came and touched them. "Get up," he said. "Don't be afraid." When they looked up, they saw no one except Jesus.

Reading this text and both texts by Mark and Luke allows us to understand three main points, other than the supernatural or spiritual event happening on top of a high mountain, which we concluded was Mt. Hermon. When Peter spoke to Jesus about Moses and Elijah, Mark adds that Peter "did not know what to say, they were so frightened," and Luke adds that Peter "did not know what he was saying." It seems that Peter was perplexed and perhaps talking *nonsense*, because, secondly, as he was still speaking, a white cloud covered them, and a voice was heard, not that of one of the four Cardinal Angels we have already presented, but rather the voice of the Most High El, confirming Jesus as his Son, Immanuel, the *Christ* whom He loves; with him, He is well pleased and to whom they should listen! Therefore, thirdly, at this moment of great revelation, their faces down to the ground, petrified, Jesus raised them up, assuring them not to be afraid, and he was alone, for both Moses and Elijah had already disappeared. This unravels that with Jesus Christ alone, say, the New Testament spirit, the entirety of the Old Testament and its Prophets are unnecessary for the three disciples who witnessed and experienced that powerful divine moment and for Christianity thereafter.

Certainly, we have already stated our take about the Old Testament's veracity, a non-historical book, and we shall elaborate more on that idea throughout the pages of this work. At any rate, when the Transfiguration ended, Luke revealed that the sacred *initiatic* experience the three disciples had lived kept it secret to themselves and did not tell anyone at that time what they had seen.

---

18. It is eight days as per Luke.

Other than the above quote and John's famous opening of his gospel[19], another important passage that adds more value to our perception of Jesus' connection to Mt. Hermon and the Enochian Tradition of the Most High El—which we shall emphasize in Chapter 5—comes from the second epistle of Peter[20]—

> For we did not follow cleverly devised stories when we told you about the coming of our Lord Jesus Christ in power, but we were eyewitnesses of his majesty. He received honor and glory from God the Father when the voice came to him from the Majestic Glory, saying, "This is my Son, whom I love; with him, I am well pleased." We ourselves heard this voice that came from heaven when we were with him on the sacred mountain.

That said, Mt. Hermon stood as one of the most essential spiritual mountains in Canaan, and we think that everything started there as explained in the Book of Enoch. We will come to that in the third chapter when we talk about the *First Initiation Temple*, but now, before we find out next, in Chapter 2, what the Angels of El taught Enoch and what is the Tradition, the "Kabbala," from a bit more explanatory approach, yet eager to know at this point, we briefly give herein a quick glimpse about it, as well as on the Chaldean-Judaic Kabbala, that essentially differs from it.

The Kabbala—*accepted* by the first seer, Enoch-Taautus-Hermes, at the top of Mt. Hermon—is figuratively represented by the Caduceus that would lead true Kabbalists up, in spiral ascension, along yet beyond the dualistic principles, to finally reaching the wings of Liberty in the abode of the One.

The Tradition is divided into three parts. First, the *Divine Inspiration*, revealed to Enoch-Taautus by the Angels of God—the Exalted Beings or Higher Selves. It contained the *Omnific Word* that was never written, but rather, given in secret from *mouth to ear*, and in that case, divine whispers of Angels. Second, there is the *Emerald Tablet*, written down by Henoch on a piece of emerald stone with the purest of Gold. It contained the process of *Alchemy*, which focused on spiritual enlightenment through a change in the physiology of the body, based on transmutation of the sexual energy. For example, in that context, Alchemy

---

19. John 1:14, "The Word became flesh and made his dwelling among us. We have seen his glory, the glory of the one and only Son, who came from the Father, full of grace and truth."
20. 2 Peter 1:16-18.

in the Kabbalistic Christian Tradition would surely make one perceive or know that the Philosopher's Stone, say of the Rosicrucians, is Christ himself. The third part is the *Sacred Alphabet*, which contained the hidden meanings of the Occult Sciences, including Astrology and Real Magic.

The *First Initiate into the Mystery of the Word* concealed these three aspects of the Kabbala in the Sacred Alphabet. This secret knowledge was to be imparted only to the *Initiates*, who would have to interpret their visions, as Enoch did, and discern the true meanings of the Tradition. Symbols that directly engage the *Initiate* during that secret experience hold mystical significance that evokes the unconsciousness into a conscious condition of itself. It thus creates an awakening state of the *inspirational and intuitive knowledge* of the *Initiate*.

One needed to be fully aware of the Tradition to become an *Initiate*, and this would tell us that the Phoenician Tradition of Enoch and the Egyptian one of Thot that stemmed from and accompanied it are so much in concordance with Christianity in its utmost spirituality and sainthood, say, esoteric Christianity.

On the other hand, however, the Jewish tradition of the Kabala roots back, as we shall see later, to the time of the Chaldeans and is essentially related to the Babylonian Talmud. The Hebrew Kabala is not a written tradition but a purely oral one. It became popular at the time of the Knights Templar in the 12th and 13th century AD and is based on both the *Sepher Yetzirah*, known as the Book of Creation or Formation, and the Zohar or *Sefer-ha-Zohar*, known as the Book of Splendor or Lights.

In the Zohar, we learn that God is described as Ein-Soph, No-Thing, the endless, infinite, and the all. It stands above the First Sephiroth, called Kether, where Yahweh is crowned over the principles of Dualism. However, Yahweh is the God *Iao*, *Iaho*, or *Yaho*; the Chaldean Mystery God of creation, the *breath of life* generated from an upright *male* and an egg-shaped *female*, which are dualistic principles of the manifested nature. Ye(a)va, *Jehovah*, or *Yahweh* is, therefore, the Androgynous Supreme Divinity of the Hebrews and Jewish Kabbalists alike, being Ievo-hevah, Adam-Eve, or *Yod-Heva*, thus the Demiurge.

The Jewish Kabala teaches that God projected from Himself ten rays of light: the Sephiroth. Initially, there was a unity between God and the world, but that broke apart when evil appeared, and the goal of Jewish Kabbalists became then to restore that unity. Along with that, it represents a complete system of symbols, angels, demons, and magic, or better say, sorcery. It also includes a complex form of cosmology and the origins of humanity in the scheme of existence.

Furthermore, Jewish Kabbalists believe that the Old Testament's language contained some form of coded secrets, so they created an esoteric system of interpretation known as *gematria* by assigning a number to each of the twenty-two letters of the Hebrew Alphabet, taken initially from the Phoenician Alphabet.

No matter how one goes around it, the Jewish Kabala seems to conclusively appear as a composed element of the Chaldean Kabala, including at the same time, much of the Persian magic, or the dualist principles of good and evil in Nature and takes into account the main Pythagorean concept of restoring Unity between God and Man. The great Pythagoras believes that one must conquer the evil deed of the *Dyad* if he or she should aspire to reach unification consciously, mentally, and spiritually with the One, God, the Universal Mind—the *Great Monad*. That said, how can Unity with Ein-Soph occur while worshiping Yod-Heva? And if such union is accomplished, God cannot be perceived as a Negation or No-Thing.[21] Does it? Is it?

---

21. El Koussa, Karim, *The Phoenician Code*, 268-270.

2.

The Tradition of Enoch

Angels are supernatural beings of light similar to Archangels[1] both in nature and function, only that Archangels are considered of higher stature. In almost all mythologies and religions, Angels or like beings played important roles in the theology of nations worldwide. They were generally depicted as benevolent celestial beings who act as intermediaries between God and Mankind through their *Higher Selves*.

The Book of Enoch is based on the teachings of Angels he met and their guidance as well. Enoch mentioned two types of Angels; the Fallen Angels and the Good Angels. The Fallen ones are those who rebelled against the Most High God El and *fell* to earth, descending upon Ardis, the top of Mount Armon[2] (Hermon), to fiddle with it and its inhabitants, so to speak, simply put, corrupt it.

Knowing that perverting the course of the *Divine Plan* destined for Earth would put him at great risk, Samyaza, the leader of the Fallen Angels, extremely concerned he would personally take the fall for what they are plotting, asked for their loyalty by hinting they should swear their allegiance to him. This is directly expressed in the Enochian text, for we clearly read[3]—

> Then their leader Samyaza said to them; I fear that you may perhaps be indisposed to the performance of this enterprise; and that I alone

---

1. Archangel is higher than Angel, yet both are messengers of God, and are pronounced as *Melki* for the first and *Malak* for the second in the Phoenician-Aramaic language.

2. 1 Enoch 7:7.

3. 1 Enoch 7:3-6.

shall suffer for so grievous a crime. But they answered him and said;
We all swear; and bind ourselves by mutual execrations, that we will not
change our intention, but execute our projected undertaking.

As such, they swore all together and bound themselves by mutual impreca-
tions upon it, forming a legion of two hundred and were led by twenty leaders
who were their chiefs of Ten. We have included alterative names (in *Italic*) from
different translations and added two names that appeared in the text, not in
the list, but one of them could be the missing name, *Sariel* or *Bezaliel,* to equate
with the twenty fallen leaders. In the version we have, the number is nineteen.
Enoch listed[4]—

> These are the names of their chiefs: Samyaza (*Shemyazaz, Shemihazah*),
> who was their leader, Urakabarameel (here are two angels combined
> in one, but are not to be counted one: *Urakaba, Arakiba or Arakiel and
> Rameel*), Akibeel (*Kokabiel*), Tamiel, Ramuel (*Ramiel*), Danel (*Daniel*),
> Azkeel (*Ezeqeel, Chazaqiel*), Saraknyal (*Sarakuyal or Baraqijal, Baraqel*),
> Asael, Armers (*Armaros*), Batraal (*Batarel, Batriel*), Anane (*Ananel,
> Ananiel*), Zavebe (*Zaqiel*), Samsaveel (*Samsapeel, Shamshiel*), Ertael (*Sa-
> tarel, Satariel*), Turel (*Turiel*), Yomyael (*Jomjael, Yomiel*), Arazyal (*Azazel*).
> These were the prefects of the two hundred angels, and the remainder
> were all with them.

So these Angels, having descended to earth by their own free will, attracted
by the beauty and elegance of the daughters of men, took them wives and
begot children by them. They also taught men sorcery, the making of weapons,
cosmetics, and many other things that were absorbed by the children of men,
which led to an increase in impiety, the multiplication of fornication, and all
their ways became transgressed and corrupted.

Now, the Good Angels, having seen what happened on earth, decided to
interfere to save the human race by transferring it into a new phase. For Mt.
Hermon is consecrated from the dawn of time as the secret abode of El's
Divine Assembly of the gods, the *Elohim.* These Angels were Michael, Gabriel,
Raphael, Uriel (Auriel), and Phanuel. Most of the time, they are just the first
four of them or four of those five, but the appearance of the first three is
consistent in the Book of Enoch, and in other times they are eight, adding

---

4. 1 Enoch 7:9.

Suryal, Raguel, and Remiel. They selected or elected Enoch amongst the people of Earth to execute the Divine plan and be thus prepared for the flood God wanted to send as a way of punishment before ultimately fixing it again.[5] Phenoch would also assist the Good Angels in their celestial war against the Fallen Angels and bring them to justice by judging them and chaining them, especially their leader Samyazal, but mostly Azazyel[6], to the spiky rocks of Dudael[7], where they would abide in total darkness until Judgment Day when they will be cast into hell, consumed by fire forever. On that, he wrote[8]—

> Again the Lord said to Raphael, Bind Azazyel hand and foot; cast him into darkness; and opening the desert which is in Dudael, cast him in there. Throw upon him hurled and pointed stones, covering him with darkness; There shall he remains forever; cover his face, that he may not see light. And on the great day of judgment, let him be cast into the fire.

Now, the four Good Angels: Michael, Gabriel, Raphael, and Auriel, who had given great help to Enoch in his holy mission and worked with him on Earth, stood as the four Cardinal Angels monitoring the *workshop* of Earth. For it is *de facto*, the cosmic laboratory, divinely planned as such, for the human triune evolution. Each one of them taught Enoch great learnings.

Michael[9] taught him the whole mystery. He, in fact, *Initiated* him. He took him by his right hand, raised him up, and brought him out *to* where was every secret *of* mercy and every single mystery *of* righteousness. He showed him all the hidden things of the extremities of Heaven, all the receptacles of the stars, and the splendors of all. And he concealed his spirit in the *Heaven of Heavens*, where

---

5. 1 Enoch 10:10, "Restore the earth, which the angels have corrupted ; and announce life to it, that I may revive it.

6. 1 Enoch 10:12, "All the earth has been corrupted by the effects of the teaching (work) of Azazyel. To him therefore ascribe the whole crime.

7. Dudael is the place of imprisonment set by God El for the Fallen Angels, the *Evil Watchers*. Some say its entrance is located east of Jerusalem. It is somehow comparable to hell, the region of the dark underworld.

8. 1 Enoch 10:6-9.

9. Michael is revered by the Phoenician-Enochain Religious Tradition, in Judaism, Christianity, and Islam, and regarded an Archangel, the Supreme Commander of the Heavenly Hosts, the chief of all the Angels of God. His name derives from the Phoenician-Aramaic *Mikha'el* or *Mankha'el*, meaning, "Who is like God" or "One who is God". In Christianity, he was first seen as a healing Angel, and then over time he became the protector of the Church and the leader of God's Army against Satan and the forces of evil in a final battle both on the Physical and Spiritual planes. He is merciful and long-suffering, and identified with the pre-incarnate Christ, and recognized as the "eternal word," the "logos," the "Son of God," Jesus Christ himself.

he beheld, amid that light, a building raised with stones of ice. And amid these stones' vibrations of living fire. Enoch saw sleepless Angels (the Seraphim, Cherubim, and Ophanin) surrounding that *flaming habitation*, encompassed by rivers full of living fire on one of its extremities and guarding the throne of His glory. He saw next innumerable Angels, thousands of thousands, and myriads of myriads, surrounding that habitation. Then he beheld the Ancient of Days and fell upon his face, *while all his flesh was dissolved, and his spirit became changed*, as he blessed, glorified, and exalted. Finally, Michael showed him the *Son of Man*.[10]

Gabriel[11] taught him the use of the power of the mind over the physical world and how to interfere in the transformation of things willingly, say, *Alchemy*, to make them better under the *Grace* of El. Raphael[12] related to Enoch about the great importance of compassion toward all things. He taught him how to channel his energies to heal mankind from all illnesses, both physical and psychological.

Finally, Auriel[13] taught him *Astronomy* and *Astrology*, showing him the sun, moon, twelve gates (zodiac), the luminaries of heaven, and taught him about their progress, revolution, and regulation, according to their respective classes, powers, periods, names, places of their original progress, etc. The whole account of them was explained to him by Uriel; he who conducts them, according to every year of the world forever, until a new work shall be effected, which will be eternal.[14] He also taught him the art of masonry.

---

10. 1 Enoch 70:1-24

11. Gabriel is venerated in Phoenician-Enochain Religious Tradition, Judaism, Christianity, and Islam, and regarded an Archangel. His name derives from the Phoenician-Aramaic *Gabri'el* or *Kabbir'el*, meaning, "Powers of God" or "God is my strength". In Christianity, he is seen to have appeared to Zechariah, foretelling the birth of John the Baptist, and to the Virgin Lady Maryām, announcing to her the Great Destiny she would undertake as bearer of the Son of the Highest, the savior, *Immanuel*, meaning "El with us". Looked upon as the Angel in charge of all powers, he is often portrayed as working in concert with Michael in El's Assembly and His Army against Satan and the forces of evil.

12. Raphael is also revered in Phoenician-Enochain Religious Tradition, Judaism, Christianity, and Islam, and looked upon as an Archangel. His name derives from the Phoenician-Aramaic *Rafa'el*, meaning, "God Heals" or "Healings of God". He is described as the Angel of the spirits of the children of men, set over all the diseases and wounds, and to heal the earth which the *Fallen Angels* have defiled. He is also portrayed as working in concert with Michael and Gabriel in El's Court and in His Army against Satan, the forces of evil, and against Azazyel himself.

13. Auriel is venerated in Phoenician-Enochain Religious Tradition, Judaism, and Christianity, and regarded an Archangel as well. His name derives from the Phoenician-Aramaic *Auri'el*, meaning, "God is my Light" or "Light of God". He is identified as ruler of the sun, which is the physical reflection of the Most High, and that's why he is sometimes confused with *Phanuel*, meaning "Face of God". Angel of divine presence, Auriel presides over Dudael (hell), where Azazyel was casted. He is occasionally portrayed in the company of Michael, Gabriel and Raphael in El's Assembly, holding a papyrus scroll representing wisdom and arts.

14. 1 Enoch 71:1, and 73:1, 74:1-15, 77:1-21, 79:1-2.

And, among the very few teachings he received from all of them stands firmly the Kabbala.

The Kabbala—accepted by the first seer, *Phenoch*—is figuratively represented by the Shaft of the Shepherd that would lead true Kabbalists up in spiral ascension along dualist principles, though not engaging in them or attached to them whatsoever, toward ultimately reaching the wings of Liberty—*Wings of the Phoenix*—in the abode of the One, the Great Monad.

Now, the Enochian Tradition is divided into three parts:

* Divine Inspiration
* Emerald Tablet
* Sacred Alphabet

What is *Divine Inspiration*?

Tradition says that Angels of God—those Exalted Beings or Higher Selves he saw in visions during his *Ascension or Rising* to the Celestial realms and in the course of their *Descent* on top of Mt. Hermon, revealed to Enoch a great universal, spiritual, and occult doctrine that he reverently received and called the *Kabbala*, which means "accepting, from the verb root to accept" in the Phoenician-Hamitic tongue. The secret knowledge he was taught throughout his mystical experiences at the heart of the *Divine Inspiration* contained the *Omnific Word* that was never written but instead given in secret as Angelic whispers from *mouth to ear*. Enoch is Henoch (Phenoch), the Phoenix symbolizing the *Secret Cycle and Initiation*, standing as the first *Teacher-Initiator* of men and women, linking Humanity through an eternal concordance with the Father.

What is the *Emerald Tablet*?

The Phoenician Tradition relates to us that the *Emerald Tablet*, also known as the Sacred Tablet of the Shepherd—of Enoch-Taautus-Hermes—was found by a Phoenician priest, most certainly an *Initiate* of the Great White Fraternity, on the dead body of Enoch-Hermes, in the land of the *Kabbirim*, the ancient land of Phoenicia. It was said to have been written by Henoch himself[15] in Canaanite-Phoenician letters on a piece of emerald stone with the purest of gold.

---

15. Or by his son Methusael or by one of his faithful adepts.

One of the most important Initiatory teachings it contained at its very foundational core is the delicate process of *Alchemy*, which focused on spiritual enlightenment through a disciplinary change in the physiology of the human body and based on an ascending transmutation of the sexual vital force[16].

The location where the findings of the Sacred Tablet occurred is not well known, but suggestions have been given to four different places:

- Mt. Hermon (where Enoch received Initiation or Divine Inspiration transmitted to him by the Angels of God),
- The ancient Canaanite-Phoenician city of *Rušalim,*[17] known today as Jerusalem,
- Gebel[18], known today as Byblos, and
- Somewhere in Egypt, most probably Memphis.

Other researchers, however, suggest that the *Emerald Tablet* was found by a certain man called Apollonius of Tyana, known as one of the most famous Pythagorean Initiates. Pythagoras, undoubtedly of Phoenician origin[19], often regarded himself as one of Hermes' incarnations or manifestations. Moreover, it seems Pythagoreans believed that their Master was not only an incarnation of Hermes but like it was clearly related to us by Iamblichus—who doubted it—that *Parthenis*, meaning the virgin, had been known by Apollo, the Sun God, conceived from him and gave birth to Pythagoras.[20]

At any rate, whoever found that Tablet, he or she indeed discovered the *Wisdom of the Light*, and the light shall set Humanity free. For centuries, the Hierophants of Enoch-Hermes have solemnly whispered akin the Angels of El, the words herein, into the ears (from *mouth to ear*) of new adepts during their Initiation. It surely contains the essence of the *Enochian Wisdom* of all ages. Should we retrieve now the papyrus from the hand of the *White Magician*, we would therefore read what to meditate upon in silence (Italics are mine)—

The Emerald Tablet of Hermes
The Sacred Tablet of the Shepherd

---

16. This is explained figuratively but clearly in the Book of Enoch, which is an *Intiatic* book *par excellence*.
17. It is the "Spirit of Šalim" in Hamitic/Afro-Asiatic tongue, and over which Milki-Sedek presided as High Priest of the Most High El.
18. It is the "Sacred Land of El" in Hamitic/Afro-Asiatic language.
19. El Koussa, Karim, *Pythagoras the Mathemagician*.
20. Iamblichus, *Life of Pythagoras*, 2–4.

What I speak is True, without error, true and most certain:

1. What is below is like that which is above, and what is above is similar to that which is below, to perform the miracles of the one thing, (*the Unitas*).
2. As all things were produced by the mediation of one being, so all things arose from this one thing by adaptation.
3. Its father is the Sun; its mother is the Moon; while the Wind carried it in its bosom, the Earth nursed it.
4. Its Father is that of all perfection, dispersing throughout the whole world.
5. Its power is vital if changed into Earth.
6. Separate the Fire from the Earth, the subtle from the gross, gently and with a good deal of sagacity.
7. It ascends from Earth to Heaven and again descends to Earth and revives the strength and unites the power of things, superior and inferior (*God and Man*).
8. Thus, you will possess the light and the glory of the whole world. Therefore, all obscurity will flee from you.
9. This is the strong fortitude of all fortitudes, for it overcomes every subtle thing and penetrates every solid thing.
10. This is how the world was created . . .

Hence, all wonderful adaptations were of this manner. Therefore, I am called Thrice Great Hermes, possessing the three parts of the Philosophy of the whole world, and that which I have written is achieved through the Operations of the One.

What is the *Sacred Alphabet*?

It is a coded Initiatic work ancient as the beginning of time, believed to be the Book of Enoch-Thor, the Geblite. The first Initiate into the mystery of the *Word* concealed these three aspects of the Kabbala in the *Sacred Alphabet*, all with the hidden meanings of the Occult Sciences. The Thrice Great Hermes—the Trismegistus—is Thot the great, the great, the great, possessing the three parts of Wisdom (Sophia, PhiloSophy) of the whole world, which are to be known as *Alchemy*, *Astrology*, and *Theurgy* (Real Magic).

Each of the twenty-two letters of the Sacred Alphabet has a physical de-notation and spiritual meaning. The structure is Alchemical—it is the Alchemy of the Letters. This secret knowledge of the One Divine Nature in the Trinity was to be imparted only to the very few Initiates, who would then have to interpret their visions and discern the true meanings of the Tradition, as they devotedly follow on the path of their primary *Initiator*. Therefore, the Symbols that would engage the selected *Initiates* hold mystical significance that awakens the unconsciousness into a consciousness of itself. It creates an enkindling frame of mind of the *Initiate Inspirational and Intuitive Knowledge*.

Barka-Thor was said to have been one of the few Scribes working under Qdm[21] (Kadmus) similar to Qadym[22], who himself was initiated by Enoch-Thor, so it was related to us, orally. He was his loyal and devoted adept in the world of the Sacred Alphabet. Qdm Initiated him, not only into the exoteric part of the system that was only meant to be given to the profane but also into its esoteric dimension, which was kept safe only for the Initiates. Before he left for Europe, Qdm appointed *Barka-Thor*, meaning the "blessing of Thor," as Keeper of the Secret of the esoteric elements of the Alphabet, hidden in the Temple of Gebel—the Sanctuary of Thor-Enoch, on the coast of Phoenicia.

Barka-Thor and his descendants, generations of Phoenician elites, re-mained loyal to the Tradition of their first Teacher. All, one by one, swore an oath to keep the Secret meaning of the Alphabet hidden from the ears and the eyes of the profane. For more than three thousand years, the Secret was kept safe. Having done that and believing now that Time of Revelation(s) has finally arrived, we are going to open the sacred box and retrieve the ancient

---

21. In Greek Mythology Qdm is a Phoenician prince, known by the name Cadmus or Kadmus, was the first Greek hero, slayer of monsters before the days of Heracles (Herakles), known by the Phoenicians by the name of Melkart (Melqart) and the sun-god Ba'al, whose temple in the city of Sūr was famous; the Temple of Ba'al-Melkart. He was the son of King Agenor and Queen Telephassa of Tyre, brother of Phoenix (Phenok-Enoch of the Phoenician Kabbalistic Tradition?), Cilix, and Europa (from whom the name of the continent Europe derived) who was kidnapped by the Grecian High God Zeus, disguising as a bull, from the shores of Tyre. Legend-history says that Qdm, meaning "he who excels in grandeur and comes from the ancient east," was sent by his royal parents to seek out his sister Europa and escort her back to Tyre. However, in earliest accounts, *Qdm* and Europa were mentioned as children of Phoenix. Could Qdm be then identified as Methusael, the son of Phenoch, a generic name, or perhaps an avatar in a different era? At any rate, Kadmus is credited for the founding of many cities in Greece, most importantly Thebes, and its acropolis, originally named *Cadmeia* in his honor. Greek historians, like Herodotus (c. 485–425/414 BC), believe that it was Qdm who introduced the original Phoenician Alphabet to the Greeks who then adopted it and formed their Greek Alphabet.

22. Now Qadym is the ancient living man, better known as the Primordial Man, and recognized as Adam-Kadmon for the Kabbalists, being himself Hermes-Kadmos for the Greeks, thus Enoch himself, as we have seen before.

papyrus—rolled and tied with a golden ribbon. We will untie the bow, unfold the manuscript, and place it in front of your eyes.

With a clear mind, we'll begin to see:

CYCLE I

1. Aleph is the Father, the Creative Force, connected to the Fire element.
2. Bet(h) is the Hermaphrodite dual-nature of the created Kosmos. It is the Body or the Temple that holds the Spirit, associated with planet Saturn.
3. Gimel is the wandering in Nature, connected to planet Jupiter.
4. Dalet(h) is the Door and Path to the constellation of Taurus (the Bull).
5. He(h) is the window of Revelation and Inspiration, related to the Aries constellation (the Ram).
6. Waw (Vau) is the material gain that attracts the physical, nailing man to Earth.
7. Zayin (Zain) is glory taken by the sword, war, connected to Planet Mars.
8. Chet(h) is the Sexual Instinct binding humanity to Gemini (the Twins).
9. Tet(h) is the Serpent of Foundation. It is mud, the Organic Earth that blossoms into Life, linked to the Cancer constellation (the Crab).

CYCLE II

10. Yod(h) is the Hand connected to the Water element.
11. Kaph is the Palm of the Hand, a sensible creator under the Sun.
12. Lamed(h) is the Teaching and Learning by the power of the Scepter, under the constellation of Leo (the Lion).
13. Mem is the Water of Intuition and Intelligence ruled by the Virgo constellation (the Virgin).
14. Nun is the Fish springing out of Water, like the Child of Prophecy for the continuation of Time, manifested under Libra (the Scales).
15. S(h)amekh is the Help and Support given to escape the pointed arms of the Scorpio(n).

16. Ayin is the Eye of Providence and Source of thinking that protects humanity from the danger of Sagittarius (the Archer).
17. Pe(h) is the Mouth uttering Words that make changes under the planet Venus.
18. Sadhe (Tsade, Tsaddi) is the other side, the Dark Side, Satan. It would hit like an Arrow or capture Humanity with a Fishing hook under the power of the Capricorn.

CYCLE III

19. Qoph is the Keeping of Secrets inside the Back of the Head, under the constellation of Aquarius (the Water Bearer).
20. Resh is the Head that lives in Poorness and challenges Misery for the work of Sacrifice under planet Mercury.
21. Shin is the abode of Mystery where Secrets are kept safe and close to the Light under the constellation of Pisces (united as one).
22. Tau (Taw) is the Sign of the Cross, the Initiate, and the Elected to the Great Power, up in the sky, when the light of the Moon fades out.

Now, these twenty-two letters represent the Alphabet Sacred and Occult Doctrine, the Kabbala. They are the secret keys of the Universe and its absolute principles. If one knows how to use them by will, since they can now identify their codes, they will be able to obtain wisdom and power.

They are divided, esoterically speaking, as follows:

- Three of them represent the elements: Earth, Water, and Fire, whereas the fourth, the Air element, is considered to be the link and mover of the other elements.
- Seven of them represent the seven planets that influence Earth and its inhabitants: the Sun, the Moon, Saturn, Jupiter, Venus, Mercury, and Mars.
- The remaining twelve letters are images of the twelve signs of the Zodiac.[23]

We will find out next where *The First Initiation Temple* has been built from a more explanatory perspective.

---

23. El Koussa, Karim, *The Phoenician Code*, 270–272.

3.

The First Initiation Temple

O riginally, Enoch erected an open semi-Temple with the help of his first adepts, among them his son Methusael on top of Mt. Hermon. This semi-Temple could have been composed of a flat horizontal rock lying at the top of a broad vertical rock, forming an altar, probably the first, framed by two pillars on both sides. The vast star-illuminated sky above the Mountain stretched as a dome for the Temple. The sky was God's habitat, surrounded by Angels. The altar atop the Mountain created the proper link between Earth and Heaven, man and God, and that, through the ever-ascending and descending energies processed by the power of the two Pillars.

Esoterically, it is always good to know that the two Pillars around the Altar are represented by the two serpents around the Shaft of Hermes, the Shepherd. It is the Tree of Life. Should we explain the meaning behind the Caduceus of Hermes, recognized as Enoch-Thor or the Egyptian, Ibis-headed god—law-giver, the divider of time, and the counter of the stars, Thot-Taautus, we will instantly come to realize something of great importance. Curious and strange as it may sound, the Caduceus (its symbol revealed in the Mystic Symbols, Part II) resembles the double helix structure of the DNA! Could it be possible that the Great ancient seer had discerned it? This question remains impossible to prove, but it brings us to reflect upon the possibility.

In the ninth vision of the Sacred Alphabet (shown in the Vision of the letter and the ninth Meditation, Part II), Tet(h): the Old Serpent—which the seer saw coiled around the tree of life—is our unconscious, a reminder of who we are in fact, and who we would become. Toth or Teth[1] is the awakening of our memory, long hence latent—ever since we lost contact with our true nature. It is the Old Serpent who laid the foundation for our godhead lotus to blossom, lifting us upwards from the mud that constitutes our material, organic life, and into immortality. Like a Hierophant to a neophyte, it solemnly whispers divine words from *mouth to ear*. Our revealed DNA, our hidden memory, our cultural-genetic rhythm of Truth, long fallen short from its divine archetype.[2] The falling man or mankind, *Adam*: the red earth, mud.

While pondering on that indispensable point, and since we don't want to lose track of the *First Mountain of Initiation*, it is crucial to take careful notes on what is coming next! Most of the well-known teachers in esoterism, occult, and ancient secret knowledge that are still preserved or hidden by certain religions, secret societies, and mystery schools, highly consider Mt. Hermon's importance as being at the foundational core of all *Initiatic* circles around the world.

Among them is H.P. Blavatsky, to whom we owe a lot of that lost knowledge. In one of her most appraised books, she wrote[3] (Italics are mine)—

> May we not look for the solution to the mystery in the Masonic manual? The keystone has an esoteric meaning, which out to be, if it is not, well appreciated by High Masons. The most important subterranean building mentioned in the description of the origin of Freemasonry is the one built by Enoch. The Patriarch is led by the Deity, whom he sees in a vision, into the *nine* vaults. After that, with the assistance of his son, Methuselah, he constructs in the land of Canaan, "in the bowels of the mountain," nine apartments on the models that were shown to him in the vision. Each was roofed with an arch, and the apex of each *formed a keystone*, having inscribed on it the mirific characters. Each of the latter, furthermore, represented one of the nine names, traced in characters emblematical the attributes by which the Deity was, according to ancient Freemasonry, known to antediluvian brethren. Then Enoch constructed two deltas of the purest gold, and tracing two of the mysterious characters on each, he placed one of them in the deepest arch, and the other entrusted to Methuselah, communicating to him, at the same time, other important secrets *now lost to Freemasonry*.

---

1. Also as Seth, he is not the enemy of Osiris who is known by the same name but written sometimes as Set.

2. El Koussa, Karim, *The Phoenician Code*, 345.

3. Blavatsky, H.P, *Isis Unveiled*, vol. 2, 571–572.

She also wrote[4]—

> The Omnific Word traced by Enoch on the two deltas of purest gold, on which he engraved two of the mysterious characters . . .

This understanding is shared by most Masons in higher degrees or grades and is well known by the most knowledgeable Church fathers and Kabbalists worldwide. Should we research more on that particular point, and the Tradition Freemasonry has given to Enoch, concerning the nine vaults and the two pillars, we find it noted by many earlier Masonic western researchers, like Thomas Smith Webb in a book[5] he penned back in 1797. Recent Masonic researcher, Robert W. Sullivan, quoting Bernard E. Jones in his *Freemasons' Book of the Royal Arch*, 1957, wrote[6]—

> The legends incorporated in the English, Irish, and Scottish Rites are not the only ones by any means. The many variants cannot be given here (they belong to more certain additional degrees), but reference may be made to a vision of Enoch, father of Methuselah and author of a Biblical book, which is known in a considerable number of versions. A.E. Waite, in a paper read before the Somerset Masters' Lodge in 1921, speaks of "The Book of Enoch," said by him to be a series of visions beheld "by the Prophet when he was in the spirit . . . a prototype of Masonic Tradition . . . especially reflected in the Royal Arch. It is said that God showed Enoch nine vaults in a vision, and that, with the assistance of Methuselah, his son, he proceeded to erect in the bosom of the mountain of Canaan a secret sanctuary, on the plan of which he had beheld, being vaults beneath one another. In the ninth, or undermost, Enoch placed a triangle of purest gold, on which he had inscribed that which was presumably the heart, essence, and center of the Sacred Tradition, the True Name of God."

Such essential information, say revelations, communed to us by the founder of the Theosophical Society and Masonic authors confirm our teachings that the "mountain of Canaan" they mention in their books is no other than Mt. Hermon itself, the earthly abode of the Most High God El and his Angels. And

---

4. Blavatsky, H.P, *Isis Unveiled*, vol. 2, 371.
5. Webb, Thomas Smith, *Freemason's Monitor or Illustrations of Freemasonry*, 284–287.
6. Sullivan, Robert W., *The Royal Arch of Enoch*, XXI.

now, to keep track of what has been said in the previous chapters as well as of what would follow next with the coming chapters, and according to the ancient secret Phoenician Tradition, Mt. Hermon was known as the clandestine dwelling place of the Fallen Angels, *aka*, the Anunnaki, before they were completely expelled by Enoch and the Four Cardinal Angels, as we shall see soon. However, it was in point of fact, from the earliest beginning, known as the Mountain of the Meetings—the Divine Assembly of the Most High El and the gods, the *Elohim*, their secret abode. That being said, we believe that in the bosom of this mountain resided the secret sanctuary of the authentic Tradition of the Enochian Kabbala, which had been secretly communicated to us by the very few Lebanese-Phoenician Initiates to keep safe for the generations to come, and where the *Omnific Word* traced by Enoch on the two deltas or triangles of the purest of gold, on which he had engraved two of the mysterious characters, the True Name of God, radiating at the very heart and essence of the Sacred Tradition, is undoubtedly "E.L" or "E.L.O.H."

At any rate, the time has come to unveil it in a more revelatory way in this volume, as we did reveal parts of it in previous books.

And then Mme Blavatsky added[7]—

> And so, among these arcane secrets, now lost to their modern successors, may be found also the fact that the keystones were used in the arches only in certain portions of the temples devoted to special purposes. Another similarity presented by the architectural remains of the religious monuments of every country can be found in the identity of parts, courses, and measurements. All these buildings belong to the Age of Hermes Trismegistus, and however comparatively modern or ancient the temple may seem, their mathematical proportions are found to correspond with the Egyptian religious edifices . . .

Again, this paragraph proves nonetheless that the sanctuary built by Enoch, with the help of his son Methusael and his direct disciples, remains to present itself as the *First Initiatic Temple* ever been built in the world, and on which sacred architectural designs of keystones and arches, all religious temples around the world were constructed, for the secret knowledge of the art of masonry was transmitted to Egypt through Gebel from its source; Mt. Hermon.

---

7. Blavatsky, H.P, *Isis Unveiled*, vol. 2, 572.

There may have been temples erected in other places around the world before the era of Enoch or perhaps after it but had not been in contact with the Phenokian Tradition and were not considered *Initiatic Temples*, rather simply ordinary sanctuaries of worship.

And thus, Enoch or the Enochian Priests walked down the Mountain, carrying the Tradition with them to Gebel, which could be articulated as *Geb-el* in the Hamitic tongue, meaning, "the Sacred Land of El." There, in Gebel, Phenoch, who became known as Thor, established his doctrine and ordered the building of a model Temple on the image of the open semi-Temple one erected on top of Mt. Hermon and on that of the *hidden* one built underneath, to dedicate it to the God EL, the Most High.

In Gebel, subsequently, the few adepts of Enoch-Thor meticulously worked on the construction of that ideal Temple, secretly known as the "Great Phoenician Temple," and esoterically as the "Seven Pillared Temple," following the sacred architectural blueprints of *keystones and arches* they learned from Enoch who built the sanctuary in the bowels of the Mountain. A secret craft Phenok could have learned from the Angels of God!

The Mystery Chamber, in particular, reserved only to High Priests, included a wall painting picturing the Phoenician High Priest performing a sacred ritual— the finest ever, that of *Wine & Bread*. The cubical altar upon which the religious ceremonies were enacted had two pillars on its sides; the Left Pillar had a motif showing an ear of *Wheat* (the Bread) with a bright golden stone shining over its top, whereas a glowing purple stone on top of the Right Pillar having a pattern that reveals the *Vine* (the Wine). The four surrounding walls were ornamented with shapes and numbers, and the ceiling was engraved with the Zodiac constellations, most importantly, the Taurus Constellation, which was very sacred to Phoenicians and Egyptians, as well as the seven Heavenly Bodies.

It is vital to remind the reader that another open semi-Temple structure of two Pillars was mentioned by the 10th century BC Canaanite-Phoenician Historian and Priest Sanchoniaton of Birot (Beirut, today). The text shows that Sanchuniathon, translated by 1st-century Phoenician historian and writer Philo of Byblos (c. 64–140 AD), related the existence of perhaps the first quasi-Temple to be erected in the city of Sūr (Tyre). Its two Pillars could have been the *first or second Initiatic* symbols of worship ever mentioned in the history of the world.

Sanchuniathon wrote through the words of Philo and mentioned in an account preserved to us by the first Christian Church historian, exegete, polemicist, and bishop, Eusebius[8] of Caesarea (c. 260/263 to 339/340 AD), that after furious rains and winds had occurred upon the city of Sūr, trees were caught by fire and the village burned. Ousous took a tree and sailed[9]. He consecrated two Pillars to *Fire* and *Wind* (or *Rains*) and worshiped them as physical representations of natural powers he could not control. The festivals or rituals continued to be practiced by the generations that followed[10].

If this narration proved to be historically accurate, then it is very logical to believe that the two Pillars were, in fact, erected on the island of Sūr. It is imperative to note that in the old days, Sūr was divided into two parts, an inland, and an island, before they were joined into one during the conquest of Alexander the Great and his siege of the city, sometime around 332 BC, while during his campaigns against the Persians.

However, a similar story of the two Pillars was also related to us by the Romano-Jewish historian Flavius Josephus (c. 37–100 AD). He gave an account of these Pillars in the first book of his Antiquities[11]. He ascribes them to the children of Seth, the father of Enoch as we shall see in a bit, and wrote that after knowing the world will be destroyed by the force of fire and quantity of water, they made two Pillars in the land of Siriad—the one of brick, the other of stone, and inscribed their discoveries on them both for the future generations after them.

Now Josephus could have undoubtedly known of Sanchuniathon's narrative from the work of his contemporary, Philo of Byblos, and copied it, especially the information referring to an earthly catastrophe, and the twin Pillars of *Fire* and *Water*, which were of *Fire* and *Wind* (or *Rains*) by the Phoenician historian. That being said, the Land of Siriad mentioned by Josephus would be the land and island of Sūr!

This is by no means a contradiction to the Masonic Tradition of Enoch or Phenoch building the Two Pillars after seeing his mystical visions from the top of Mt. Hermon that overlooks the great city of Sūr, and that of Hiram Abiff, the Sūrian Architect of the *alleged* temple of Solomon on Mt. Moriah in Jerusalem. However, such a temple for that biblical person did not exist, for the Temple we believe was built there was accomplished before the date given to Solomon by the Biblical tradition and went back to sometime during the days of the Phoenician King-Priest Melki-Sedek of the Most High God El. It

---

8. Eusebius, *Praeparatio Evangelica*, Book 1, chapter 10.
9. He was probably the first who embarked on the sea to erect his Pillars in the Surian Island.
10. El Koussa, Karim, *Jesus the Phoenician*, 234.
11. Josephus, Flavius, *The Antiquities of the Jews*, Book 1, chapter 2, paragraph 3.

was constructed to venerate Shalim[12] in his city Urshalim, Rūšalim (Jerusalem, today). It has been "renovated" by Hiram Abiff on the image of the famous Temple of Ba'al-Melkart in Sūr, which he had just built for his King, Hiram.

Should we have a look now at Freemasonic Tradition, we may indeed find that there are two sets of Pillars; the most known one represents *Jachin* and *Boaz*, the two brass right and left pillars standing at the porch of the *alleged* Solomon's Temple, and the other set not so much known by ordinary people, are the Pillars of Enoch. These Pillars are not part of Blue Lodge Masonry but are essentially important in texts and lessons of Higher Degrees/Grades, mainly the "Royal Arch of Enoch" we mentioned in the first chapter.

In referring to few books on the origin of Freemasonry, we may have undoubtedly come to the vital understanding that the most important (underground) temple mentioned in the description of the Craft's origin is the *Initiatic* Temple of Enoch. Therefore, with all the esoteric knowledge we have gathered from the ancient Great White Fraternity Phoenician Tradition and, combining it to Theosophical, Freemasonic, Religious, etc., information and account, we may sum the narration up as follows—

> Enoch, who walked with God and the Angels whom he saw in visions in Heaven and on Earth, had learned of the coming deluge (the flood) by which God intended to end Humanity because they have sinned with the *Fallen Angels* and then start all over again. Enoch, wishing to preserve for mankind the knowledge and the secrets he have learned from the *Good Angels*, he, with the assistance of his son, Methusael, constructs in the Land of Canaan[13], "in the bowels of the Mountain"[14] *nine vaults* situated perpendicularly beneath each other on the model he saw in the prophetic vision. Each was roofed with an Arch, and the apex of each formed a keystone, having inscribed on it the mirific characters. Each vault represented one of the nine names or attributes by which God was known to him, Enoch, the *First Initiate*. Then Enoch constructed two deltas[15] of the purest gold[16], tracing two of the

---

12. Shalim, Šalim, was regarded as the god of dusk and one of the Elohim.

13. We believe that construction of Initiatic Temples continued all through the Land of Canaan, in Gebel, Sūr, Ba'albek, Saydoun, Mt. Carmel, and Rūšalim, etc.

14. It is Mt. Hermon as we have explained, but some believe that the divine secrets Enoch wanted to preserve for mankind were on Mt. Moriah, or the Great Pyramid of Egypt as some have suggested according to yet another Enochian Phoenician tradition.

15. It could be a triangle instead of a delta, like the Pythagorean Tetraktys, the Sacred Decade.

16. It is a white porphyry stone in one version of the story.

mysterious characters on each[17], he placed one of them in the deepest Arch, the other, also inscribed with strange words Enoch had gained from the Angels, he entrusted to his son Methusaël to keep, communicating to him at the same time, other important Secrets now lost to the world.

Of course, the story does not end here, but it continues by imparting to us that the Nine Vaults were then sealed by a door of stone[18]. Upon the spot (*from above, head of the Mountain*) Enoch erected Two indestructible Pillars or columns, one of metal[19], so that it might not sink in *Water*, containing the history of creation, all pre-deluge wisdom, and knowledge[20]; the other of marble, so that it might never catch *Fire* and burn, and contained mathematical wisdom to some, while to most, coded Enochian Inscriptions that indicates the existence of a great knowledge concealed in the arches underground, and where the priceless subterranean treasure vault—containing the golden delta—was located, a short distance away (*in below, heart of the Mountain*).

In Freemasonry, the narration ends with Enoch retiring to Mt. Moriah in Ur-Šalim, where he was lifted to heaven. In time, some Freemasons say that the *alleged* King Solomon uncovered the hidden nine vaults while constructing his legendary temple and learned of their divine secrets. Moreover, in Freemasonic literature, and contrary to our Tradition, one of the Pillars was destroyed! The earlier Masonic western researcher we mentioned before, Thomas Smith Webb, wrote[21] (Italics are mine)—

> The marble pillar (*of Fire*) of Enoch fell in the general destruction; but, by divine permission, the pillar of brass (*of Water*) withstood the water, by which means the ancient state of the liberal arts, and particularly masonry, has been handed down to us.

While pondering on that in complete silence, we should take note of the following revelations. Therefore, we believe that the *Two Pillars* survived the

---

17. It is certainly the ineffable name of God, "E.L," "E.L.O.H," or the Lost Word of a Master Mason!

18. It was placed under the flat horizontal rock on top a wide vertical rock forming the altar of the open semi-Temple, framed by a Pillar on each side, and that which we've described at the opening of this chapter.

19. It is laterus, brass, or brick.

20. It is the knowledge of the arts and sciences—from which the seven liberal arts, sciences and principles of masonry come from.

21. Webb, Thomas Smith, *Freemason's Monitor or Illustrations of Freemasonry*, 287.

flood, surely and safely conclude that the Masonic Tradition was taken from Sanchuniathon's account on them. However, from where exactly the idea of the *Nine Vaults*, hidden in the bowels of the Mountain, came, and what they represented is unknown to Freemasonry, unless they refer to the *Nine Levels* of mystical Initiation contained in the esoteric teachings of the authentic Enochian Hermetic Kabbala, presented and described very well by Pythagoras (himself, an incarnation of Hermes) in his "Sacred Decade," as the picture of the Tetraktys shows.

At any rate, this *Temple of Initiation*, the model of the "Seven Pillared Temple," built by the Enochian Priests in Gebel, was later copied by the Canaanite-Amorites under the leadership of Milki-Sedek or Melchizedek[22] for the Temple of Šalim in Rūšalim (and later by the leadership of Adoni-Sedek)—or by the Hyksôs, a Canaanite tribe, according to the Egyptian Historian Manetho—on Mt. Moriah, the Mountain of the Amorites in Urušalim way before the Hebrews/Jews entered into real history, and where he presided as King and High Priest of El. Another copy of yet an amazing beauty was made later in Tyre by Hiram Abiff to Baal-Mekart for his King Hiram of Tyre, both adepts of the Great White Fraternity, as we have seen in Chapter 1. It is possible that Hiram Abiff was requested by Adoni-Sedek[23] to "beautify" the already existing Temple on Mt. Moriah even more or built yet a new one there on the ruins of the ancient one, similar to the beautiful one he previously built in Tyre!

The *Temple of Initiation*[24], known as the "Seven Pillared Temple," had two Pillars, standing majestically outside, flanking the entrance door made of cedarwood, and leading to the anteroom. Another two Pillars, smaller in size than the initial ones, stood at each side of a small altar, where incense was burned, and that was in the main hall, the *Saint*, just before the inner stairs, leading up to the door of the third section. And there, inside the *Saint of Saints*, another two Pillars, smaller than the previous ones, stood at either side of what looked like a Great Altar. The seventh Pillar appears to be standing just behind the Great Altar and looks like a statue of the God El. There probably existed two Sphinxes-Cherubim in the *Holy of Holies* as per the Archeological findings made

---

22. Most probably Late Bronze Age.

23. Adoni-Sedek was one of the followers of Milki-Sedek, to be more precise, he was of Milki-Sedek's Priestly Order.

24. More on that in the final chapter. We will then provide some additional albeit introductory information on how the Temple of Initiation was actually built and maybe on how it worked through *Initiation*.

by the ninetieth-century French historian Ernest Renan at Oum-Al-Awamid in ancient Tyre and recorded in one of his most reputed books[25].

It is also imperative to remind you that the famous Temple of Ba'al-Melkart and his twin Pillars, of which we have some tangible historical references, were recorded by the famous Greek historian Herodotus who confirmed having seen the whole Temple at Sūr. He mentioned the two Pillars, the one of pure gold and the other of an emerald stone of such size as to shine by night[26].

To conclude this section, the *Temple of Initiation* is not at all the *alleged* temple of Solomon that Freemasonry considers in their rites, whether historically or even symbolically. Solomon and his temple did not exist! History and Archeology do not support such Biblical claims. Truth has been long tarnished by the Babylonian Brotherhood, purposely and deceitfully altering the name from the *Temple of* Šalim to the *temple of* Šlomo, thus Solomon.

A moment of meditation on that is required herein. We will continue next with the *Transmitting of the Tradition to Egypt, then around the world . . .*

---

25. Renan, Ernest, *Mission De Phénicie*, 704.
26. Herodotus, *The Histories*, Book II, paragraph 44, 94.

4.

Transmitting the Tradition to Egypt and the World

From the ancient port of Gebel, Enoch, known as Thor therein, his son or/and some of his adepts, sailed to the *Land of Ham* and introduced the Enochian Tradition to Egyptian priests in Memphis and Giza, where the Pyramids were built. The Canaanite-Phoenician Enoch-Thor became known under the name of Taautus-Thot in the Egyptian Religion. The Pyramid denoted nothing more than a grandiose symbol of the *Temple of Initiation*, built in Gebel, or equated with the *nine vaults*—underground *Initiatic* Temple—hidden in the bowels of Mt. Hermon, and was dedicated by the Egyptians to their divine messenger, Thot-Taautus.

In a theological work accredited to the 1st century AD Phoenician historian and writer Philo of Byblos (c. 64–140 AD) in an account preserved to us by the first Christian Church historian, exegete, polemicist, and bishop, Eusebius of Caesarea (c. 260/63–339/40 AD) in his *Praeparatio Evangelica*[1] (Preparation for the Gospel—a work consisting of fifteen books) and attributed to a most ancient Canaanite-Phoenician historian and author, Sanchuniathon in his *Theology of the Phoenicians*, translated and interpreted by Philo, Taautus is mentioned as the son of Misor, brother of Suduc. In fact, what has been conveyed in the work of Sanchuniathon proves the familial ties between Canaan-Phoenicia and Egypt (Misor), which we have been thoroughly talking about. The name Suduc, potentially from the Phoenician root *ṣ-d-q*, cited by Philo as the father

---

1. Eusebius, *Praeparatio Evangelica*, Book 1, Chapter 10.

of the Cabeiri[2], was given its Greek meaning as *dikaion*, which is translated into "righteousness, justice, just, or the just one." Suduc, Saduq, Sydyk, Sydek, or Sedek, is, therefore, one of the deities mentioned in the Canaanite/Phoenician pantheon, most probably not as the son of El like Shalim, Adon, Ba'al, and Yāw (Yam), but rather in the form of Tzedek, being one of his attributes or epithets; *Righteousness*, thus our Priest of the Most High El, Milki-Sedek (King of Righteousness or my King is Righteous).

And in time, the Great White Fraternity was officially founded around 1500 BC, or even a few hundred years earlier, as we have seen before. However, Enoch is theoretically recorded to have lived sometimes around 3000 to 4000 BC, but perhaps before the flood, which happened years before 4000 BC[3], and which mainly hit the region of Mesopotamia (ancient Sumer) and parts of Persia. That said, and therefore, theoretically speaking, the Fraternity finds its foundational roots with Phenoch.

According to the Book of Enoch, the flood happened because the people sinned with the *Fallen Angels* and were corrupted by them, and that is at the core of the Tradition of the Great White Fraternity, which also teaches that the authentic teachings of the *Good Angels* of El to Enoch had also been corrupted by the Chaldean-Babylonians. In fact, it is not a coincidence to learn that Gilgamesh made a spiritual journey to the *"Mount of the Cedar, the home of the Immortals,"* in search of immortality by receiving *Initiation* into the authentic Enochian Tradition.[4] We will explore more onto that later and expose the differences between the Phenokians and the Babylonian Brotherhood who sought to kill the divine at the Tower of Babel!

Now, the Great White Fraternity survived as an ancient religious community that sought with anchored faith the resurrection of the self to its higher level and believed in the immortality of the spirit. With Monotheism at the foundational core of its theological concept, it began to function as an esoteric

---

2. They are known as the "inventors of ship," among many other things. They are the Kabbirim; Great Man and Women, Sons and Daughters of Anak, Enoch.

3. Some occultists, esoteric researchers, archeoastronomists, and authors would like to suggest an anterior period, the previous flood that happened sometimes around 12000 BC, and that which would automatically take the Enochian Tradition back to that era in time. That remains, however, a possibility, farfetched as it may seem, but we are not certain of it, as yet, due to the lack of concrete evidence that support such a claim and would thus require us to add *Atlantis* (though many believe it's mythical) to the scene. Hence, we better stick to the era few years prior to 4000 BC, since it copes well with our belief about why the flood occurred in Mesopotamia and parts of Persia, the original territories of the Babylonian Brotherhood.

4. Gilgamesh, *Epic of Gilgamesh*, The Fifth Tablet. Of the fight with Humbaba.

secret society in Phoenicia and was then immediately adopted by Egyptian Priests.

There existed a wonderful religious and spiritual connection between both ancient Egypt and Phoenicia. As Memphis stood for the religious twin city of Gebel (Byblos), so did *Akhetaton* (Horizon of Aton) to *Krm-el* (Mt. Carmel: Vine of El). For example, the death of Osiris and his resurrection is the Egyptian version of the death and resurrection of the Geblite Adon (Adonis), and the Phoenician's belief in the One Most High God "Al-Elyon" was leveled as the corner stone of the Temple of Akhenaton in Egypt, who preached the belief in the One God, Aton[5].

Among prominent and earliest Great White Fraternity Initiates worth mentioning and remembering always were the Canaanite-Phoenician High Priest/ King Melki-Sedek of Rūšalim (Spirit of Šalim, the god of dusk), Kings Ahiram of Gebel and Hiram of Sur (also known as Ahiram), as well as both Egyptian Pharaohs Thutmose III (Initiate or born of Thot), Akhenaton (It pleases Aton) and his lawful adept Osarsiph (or Hosarsiph).

So, after being primarily established in Canaan and Egypt, the Enochian Tradition journeyed across the globe. The Divine Messenger Enoch-Taautus was mostly known under different names, in various regions on Earth, and at different times. Here are some of the most important generic known names attributed to him in person, his direct adepts (or Mystery School) who transmitted his Tradition:

- Mithra for the Hindus and the Persians;
- Enki/Ea/Oannes in Mesopotamia;
- Nabū/Nebo in the Babylonian mythology;
- Quetzalcóatl for the Mexican Aztecs;
- Thor in the Scandinavian tradition;
- Hermes-Kadmos for the Greeks, or Inachus in Grecian mythology;
- Mercury for the Romans;
- Adam-Kadmon for the Kabbalists;
- Edris for the Arabs and Muslims;
- Enoch for the Druzes.

Sometimes, the *Father of Religions and Spiritual Laws* was also regarded as the god of Wisdom, Science, and the Occult Teachings. His Sacred or Initiatic

---

5. It is most probable that the Egyptian name *Aton* has derived from the Phoenician *Adon*.

Tradition appeared somehow similar everywhere, with perhaps minor changes, before it got corrupted first in one of the regions of the Earth before spreading fast, as division began to take hold in other parts of Earth, leading to the very foundation of the Babylonian Brotherhood and its widening schism from the Great White Fraternity, as we shall see!

It was with the Chaldean savants and magi later on that the authentic Tradition took a different turn, a completely deviated path from its original conception on Mt. Hermon. They began to practice the Kabala, which was based on the esoteric meanings of the Sacred Alphabet, incorporating one of the most ancient languages on Earth, to invoke the spirits of the dead and the anima of the *Evil Watchers*, either in the written form of talismans or in the oral form of incantations. This led to sorcery and bloody rituals, dark ceremonies already transmitted to men by Azazyel.

It was there in the ancient Babylonian territory that the *Fallen Angels*, so to speak, were extensively engaged with humanity and their affairs, leading them astray, to wars, errors, and sins, and filling the earth with blood and unrighteousness. These were the fallen Anunnaki,[6] and these were the ones mentioned in the Book of Enoch, the ones to be judged by Enoch who walked with El and was given extensive support from the four Cardinal *Good Angels* who form the Kosmic Cross in the following order: Michael, standing in the East and representing Air, Gabriel stood in the South and represented Fire, Raphael standing in the West and representing Water, and Auriel stood in the North and represented Earth. We may see more about that later in the book.

What happened in ancient Babylon surely constituted the great deviation from the original Phoenician/Egyptian source of the Enochian Sacred Tradition. That led to the formation of the Chaldean-Babylonian-Judaic Kabala, which we came later to know and understand as the mystical Jewish tradition of the Kabala.

However, not only the Book of Enoch showed great corruption to mankind caused by the evil watchers, but also the Book of Revelation, supposedly

---

6. We have enough reasons to believe that the *Fallen Angels* who appeared in the ancient Sumerian, Akkadian, Assyrian and Babylonian legends and mythologies, and were known by the name of *Anunnaki* (from *An*, the sky god and Ki, the earth goddess, forming by that chthonic kind of deities, which literally means "subterranean," thus describing deities, spirits, or angels of the underworld—those who from the sky fell) were actually the *Evil Watchers* that first descended on Mt. Armon (Hermon) as informed in the Book of Enoch. After that both their leaders Samyaza and Azayel were thrown into Dudael (Hell) by the *Good Angels*, they fled the region of Phoenicia and decided to re-appear in ancient Mesopotamia, where they enslaved the population there and conditioned them to their evil powers. They were led by "Enlil" who we believe is no other than "Ananel," one of the twenty leaders of the *Fallen Angels* cited by Enoch.

written by John, that unveiled huge deviation done in Babylon. It reminds us of the "Great Harlot of Babylon, Destruction of Babylon, Judgment of the Beast, the Devil and the False Prophet, End of the Old Jerusalem, Rising of the New Jerusalem on a New Earth under a New Heaven where God and Humanity dwell together after the curse has ended, and where both the river and the 'tree of life'—the Spirit of Christ—appear for the healing of the nations." A very Kabbalistic work indeed as the work of Enoch.

Throughout history, many religious sects and secret societies, whether in the East or the West, adopted the Kabala in their ceremonies of *Initiation*, most certainly under the influence of the Chaldean, or its later version—the Hebrew Kabala. On the other hand, however, others around the world underwent *Initiation* into the secrets of the authentic Kabbala of Phoenicia and Egypt, and very few Orders today still hold on to the secrets of that Tradition. That said, these very few Orders that stem directly from the Great White Fraternity or indirectly through worldwide missionaries shall revolve in time around a more magnificent reality; a resurrection of all the true faithful *Initiates* of Enoch-Hermes—the *First Instructor and Savior of Humanity*—a son of God who triumphantly announced, "Oh men, live soberly . . . Win your immortality; I will lead you on to salvation."

Throughout Human history, they appeared as great men and women of fame and spiritual beauty, mastering both the outer (exoteric) and the inner (esoteric) worlds. These selected people have lived in different countries worldwide and were sheltered in selected places, receiving their *Initiations* inside "Mystery Chambers" that transmitted the same Secret. Other than *Temples of Initiation* in Phoenicia and Egypt and their respective Chambers as the ones of Gebel and Memphis consecrated by Thor-Thot the Thrice Great, himself, so to speak; his descendants organized and secretly built Enochian *Initiatic* Sanctuaries around the world in specific and well-chosen places in countries they have reached like Greece, Iraq, Palestine, India, Tibet, Japan, Germany, France, the United Kingdom, Spain, Italy, Mexico, and the New World, Americas—for the same purpose of *Initiation*. All these Hierophants, Keepers of Chambers, Scribes, Priests, Priestesses, etc., who emerged in those and a few other countries, followed the same Tradition as that of Canaan-Phoenicia and Egypt; and tried hard to keep the Secret hidden from the eyes of the vulgar.

There is plenty of evidence that Phoenician seafarers roamed the entire globe in the ancient past, built Temples, cities, etc., and transmitted knowledge! There is no place here to tackle that aspect in its entirety, and we may keep this subject for another volume. However, we couldn't leave the following behind. In his well-accredited book, 20th-century Canadian-born author, lecturer, astrologer, and mystic, Manly P. Hall wrote[7]—

> Robert Brown, 32nd degree, is of the opinion that the British priests secured their information from Tyrian and Phoenician navigators who, thousands of years before the Christian Era, established colonies in Britain and Gaul while searching for tin.

Information like this about the cultural and religious Phoenician influence on the Western world has been well documented and was known by many great authors all across the globe, like the 19th century British Lieutenant Colonel, Fellow of Royal Anthropological Institute, Professor, amateur archaeologist, explorer, and author, L.A. Waddell, who extensively presented them in his distinguished work, *The Phoenician Origin of Britons, Scots, & Anglo-Saxons.*

At any rate, it seems nowadays that all around the world, the *Initiates* of that special Order count very few since the Order itself is not working. Still, in each Mystery Chamber, the transmitting of the Tradition to new adepts is done from *mouth to ear*. However, it is important to know that very few were the religions and secret societies in direct affiliation with the Great White Fraternity and/or indirect relation through international Phenokian preachers. Here are the most important of them all:

- The Hermetists (like the Church of the Hermetic Sciences);
- The Pythagoreans;
- The Therapeuts of the Egyptian desert;
- The Asayas—with their ascetic Nazarene branch of Mt. Carmel and Galilee that which included Jesus Christ, John the Baptist, and Mary Magdalene;
- The Christians, with all their confessions and especially those who believe that the Father of Jesus Christ portrayed in the New Testament, could not, or rather was not the Jewish God of the Old Testament;
- Several non-dualist Christian Gnostics (like Marcionism);
- Several Alchemists of the Hermetic Tradition (like Paracelsus);

---

7. Hall, Manly P., *The Secret Teachings of All Ages*, 44.

- Several Theosophists (of H.P. Blavatsky);
- Several Anthroposophists (of Rudolph Steiner)—who believe that Christianity is a unique spiritual system for the evolution of humanity and that—without Christ—humanity might well bring about its own destruction;
- Some Poor Knights of Christ (Knights Templar who don't follow Rashi of Troyes), but secretly follow the Enochian-Hermetic Tradition, and consider Christ the Temple of which they are his Knights;
- Some of the Sufis (like Rumi, Al-Hallaj, etc . . .);
- Some of the Druzes (of Lebanon and other places);
- Some of the Freemasons who secretly adopt the Temple of Šalim in their rites and consider that the 3rd Master Degree represents the Resurrection of the Master Christ on the 3rd Day and others who follow ancient Egyptian rites. These Freemasons know for sure that the *real* Temple of Shalim built by Melki-Sedek and renovated by Hiram Abiff at the time of Adoni-Sedek has been replaced by the *symbolic and mythical* temple of Solomon by the Judeo-Christian culture. They also know that Melki-Sedek, Adoni-Sedek, and Jesus Christ are of the same Order of Priesthood—that of *Righteousness*;
- Several Rosicrucians who seek to accomplish the Great Work by identifying Christ as the Philosopher's Stone.

Many Keepers, Initiates, and Priests of similar authentic Orders worldwide watchfully shielded the Mysteries from the ignorant commoners. Unfortunately though, and despite all this wariness, the shape of the true *Word* has been stolen, and eventually got corrupted, say, deviated by the Chaldean-Judaic system and the many secret societies that followed it, and which are known secretly and collectively by the highly *demoniacally symbolic* name of the Babylonian Brotherhood. The true *Word*, however, is not lost!

Therefore, our mission in this life and in the many others that may follow, and as true *forgotten* sleeping adepts of the ancient and accepted Great White Fraternity was, is, and remains to recuperate the Authentic Enochian Tradition, as well as spreading the everlasting Light of the Most High God El, and revealing the Secrets of the Holy Grail—keeping it forever protected from being ever stolen again, thence manipulated.

In that respect, it would be as important as necessary to reflect herein upon the following enlightening words mentioned in yet another great work by Manly P. Hall. He beautifully wrote[8]—

> Every truly intelligent man and woman who is working to spread light in the world is *christ*-ened, or *Light*-ened, by the actual labor which he or she is seeking to perform. The fact that light (intelligence) partakes of the natures of both God and the earth is proved by the names given to the personifications of this light, for at one time they are called the "Sons of Men" and at another time the "Sons of God."

With this in mind, it is very inspiring to mention here and now that *Alchemy* in the most Ancient Authentic Kabbalistic Tradition would surely consider the transmutation of the Philosopher's Stone as described by the Rosicrucians to be Christ himself—the Christ Spirit, so to speak. And that reminds some of us of the Ritual of the 18th degree of the Rose-Croix in Scottish Rite, Southern Jurisdiction[9]—

> Most Wise. — What hour is it?
> Respectful K.S. Warden. — It is the first hour of the day, the time when the veil of the temple was rent asunder when darkness and consternation were spread over the earth — when the light was darkened — when the implements of Masonry were broken — when the flaming star disappeared — when the cubic stone was broken — when the "word" was lost.

But to us, Phenokians, Keepers of the Word of the Great White Fraternity, we shall always repeat: the shape of the true *Word* that has been stolen and falsified is already *found*. As for now, and at this stage, a few moments of meditation are required before we proceed with the next chapter that deals with *The Sacerdotal Line to Jesus Christ*.

---

8. Hall, Manly P., *Melchizedek and the Mystery of Fire*, 12.
9. Blavatsky, H.P, *Isis Unveiled*, vol. 2, 348.

5.

The Sacerdotal Line to Jesus Christ

In the 1st Book of Enoch[1], we read the following words, ". . . Enoch is the son of Jared, the son of Malaleel, the son of Canaan, the son of Enos, the son of Seth, the son of Adam. This is the commencement of the word of wisdom to be declared and told to the people of the earth . . ."

This is also in total agreement with chapters in the Old Testament[2]. Yet, even those chapters are a bit confusing to most readers, especially what concerns the similarities of the names included, we understand that with Enos the father of Cainan, "men began to call upon the name of the Lord,"[3] because Enoch "walked with God: and he was not; for God took him."[4]

And what is most significant in the New Testament concerning Enoch is that the Apostle Luke relates him to Jesus in his genealogical list. Luke[5] starts with Jesus, "as was supposed," son of Joseph, son of Heli or Eli, son of Matthat, and ends with Adam, son of God, passing by Abraham, Cainan, son of Arphaxad, Enoch, and Kenan, father of Mahalalel and son of Enosh. This genealogy is so important for us at the time being and throughout the process of identifying the Sacerdotal Line from our mysterious prophet Enoch to our Christian savior Jesus Christ. I have elaborated extensively on that specific

---

1. 1 Enoch 37:1-2.
2. Genesis 4 & 5.
3. Genesis 4:26.
4. Genesis 5:24.
5. Luke 3:23-38.

genealogy and the one listed by Matthew in the Introduction of my previous work, Jesus the Phoenician[6].

It is quite relevant for us to understand that **Cainan** is a variant of **Kenan**'s name in the generations of the first man, Adam, included in the lists of antediluvian human patriarchs, and who were most definitely not Hebrew as the Torah wants us to believe. The Hebrew element was not yet in physical existence anyway, in the plan of history! Many Archeologists, Historians, and Anthropologists, even Israelis and Judeo-Christians, were, and are not able to correctly define, discover, and/or scientifically prove any Hebrew/Jewish element whatsoever in nowadays Israel itself. All excavations done there are only revealing, and extensively, as we speak, the Canaanite-Phoenician element, which debunk the Biblical narration. Therefore, Biblical scholars have been in total confusion ever since science, say, any credible anthropological, historical, theological, archeological, and sometimes geographical data were introduced in the study of the Bible.

Proceeding with that in mind, we find that Enoch's direct disciple or *Initiate* (or son) was **Canaan**, Cainan, or Kenan, son of Enosh (Enos), or vice versa, Enoch being the son and Canaan, the father. Whatever is the case, and whoever fathered who, the relation between Jesus to Canaan or Kena'an[7] and Enoch or Phenok[8] is unmistakably evident in Luke and supported by the Book of Enoch, as we shall see.

In the 2nd Book of Enoch[9], there is a very important section entitled *The Exaltation of Melchizedek*, which outlines the Sacerdotal succession of Milki-Sedek as the direct inheritor of Enoch's secrets. Indeed! Among the Enochian Priests who operated in Canaan-Phoenicia was Milki-Sedek[10], the High Priest of Šalim, after whose "Order" Jesus was portrayed in the New Testament itself by Paul as High Priest forever, "Thou art a priest forever after the Order[11] of Melki-Sedek,"[12] and portrayed by John as well as the "word became flesh,"

---

6. El Koussa, Karim, *Jesus the Phoenician*, pages 7 to 10.

7. He is the father of the Canaanites from a *Physical* perspective.

8. He is the father of the Phoenicians from a *Spiritual* perspective.

9. 2 Enoch 69 to 73.

10. In 2 Enoch 71, Melchizedeck is said to have been born of a virgin by the name of Sopanim or Sofonim (Nir's wife!) who became pregnant in her old age, having been sterile.

11. The Order of Melki-Sedek is a Priestly Order founded by the High Priest himself to do the work of God the Most High El on Earth, and this Order is clearly identified in the New Testament as the Order Jesus adhered to.

12. Hebrews 5:6.

thus, the incarnation of the Father El[13], being himself the Temple that will be destroyed and built again in three days through the supernatural, miraculous feat of Resurrection.

In remembrance of one of the most exalted rituals of *Initiation*, Enoch, the High Priest, performed upon the altar inside the *Sanctum Sanctorum* of Mt. Hermon, the most sacred ritual of all time, that of *Wine & Bread*. The purple stone on the Right Pillar stood for the Wine (*Spirit*), while the golden stone on the Left Pillar was meant to symbolize the Bread (*Body*). These are the true meanings of the two *inner* Pillars as per the *Ancient and Primitive Phoenician Rite* that we will legitimately introduce and perform in the Great White Fraternity— Phenok Council, destined, say scheduled to be fully revived in the upcoming future.[14] Thereafter, Melki-Sedek practiced the same Rite at the Temple of Šalim in Jerusalem! Wheat and Vine . . . Bread and Wine! The link would not escape the wit of the non-dualist Gnostic thinkers that Seekers of Truth and Lovers of Light are in reality. So it happened that *Yāwshua Meshiha*, Jesus Christ himself, performed the same Rite at the Last Supper! Therefore, *Beth-Lahem*[15], which means "House of Bread" and Mt. Carmel, *krm-El*, meaning "Vine of El," thoroughly complete the scene of the Alchemical Initiation, and its Divine Incarnated symbolism!

In the most famous letter of Paul to the Hebrews, we read[16]—

> Therefore, if perfection were through the Levitical priesthood (for under it the people received the law), what further need [was there] that another priest should rise according to the order of Melchizedek, and not be called according to the order of Aaron?

This is a straightforward declaration from Paul of one spiritual priesthood that did not link Jesus to Aaron[17] but rather to Milki-Sedek and straight back to Enoch, whom we believe have seen with his *inner eye* the Son of Man in one of

---

13. Jesus Christ was called *Immanuel* in the New Testament, which is a Phoenician-Aramaic word composed of two words, *Immanu* and *El*, and meaning "El (is) with us."

14. We may however provide in the final chapter of this book some additional but introductory information on how the *Ancient and Primitive Phoenician Rite* is worked inside the *Temple of Initiation*.

15. *Bet-Lahem* or Bethlehem, the original place of the birth of Jesus is a grotto situated at the northeastern foot of Mt. Carmel—a mountain full of caves and used for many various purposes from meditations to prayers, even as havens, by the adepts of the Galilean and Carmelite Essenes, better termed as the Asayas. Check for the historical and geographical evidence for this place in our previous work, *Jesus the Phoenician*.

16. Hebrews 7:11.

17. Aaron was the brother of Moses as per the Old Testament.

his visions accompanying the Ancient of Days[18], as we have seen before and described again in *1 Enoch*. One of the Angels—most probably Michael—who was with him and who showed him all the secrets concerning this Son of Man answered his inquiry, saying[19]—

> This is the Son of man, to whom righteousness belongs; with whom righteousness has dwelt; and who will reveal all the treasures of that which is concealed: for the Lord of Spirits has chosen him; and his portion has surpassed all before the Lord of spirits in everlasting uprightness.

This coincides very well with John's beginning[20]—

> In the beginning, was the Word, and the Word was with God, and the Word was God. He was with God in the beginning. Through him, all things were made; without him, nothing was made that has been made. In him was life, and that life was the light of all mankind. The light shines in the darkness, and the darkness has not overcome it.

And also in John's book of Revelation[21]—

> He that hath an ear, let him hear what the Spirit saith unto the churches; To him that overcometh will I give to eat of the hidden manna, and will give him a white stone, and in the stone a new name written, which no man knoweth saving he that receiveth it.

Undoubtedly, the God of John is the same Ancient of Days mentioned by Enoch, and the very same one, the Most High, worshiped by Milki-Sedek. He is thence no other than El-Elyon, the Father of Yāwshu(a)[22], for we read in Matthew[23]—

> Behold, the virgin shall be with child and shall bring forth a son. They shall call his name Immanu-el, which means God El with us.

---

18. He is the Most High God, El-Elyon.
19. 1 Enoch 46:1-2.
20. John 1:1-5.
21. Revelation 2:17.
22. The name Jesus as spelled in Phoenician-Aramaic.
23. Matthew 1:23.

The *New Testament* and *1 Enoch* have so much in common, regarding the Righteous One[24], the Elect One[25], the Son of Man[26], and the knowledge of divine and cosmological secrets, like Angels, the Sun, the Moon, the stars, the end of days[27], and the coming of the Kingdom of God for the final judgment by the glorified Son[28], which is interesting to note here as follows[29]—

> I will bring them into the splendid light of those who love my holy name: and I will place each of them on a throne of glory . . . Righteous is the Judgment of God; For to the faithful shall he give faith in the habitations of uprightness. They shall see those, who having been born in darkness unto darkness shall be cast, while the righteous shall be at rest.

This is clearer, of course, in Matthew[30]—

> And Jesus said unto them, Verily I say unto you, That ye which have followed me, in the regeneration when the Son of Man shall sit in the throne of his glory, ye also shall sit upon twelve thrones, judging the twelve tribes of Israel.

In conclusion, the Priestly line from Enoch to Jesus through Milki-Sedek is strongly proven, with the *Phoenician Initiation Rite* at the very core of it. In reality, the death of Jesus mirrors the death of ADON, one of the Elohim, a son of "El," who fought against the wild boar and died of his injuries and reflects the death of the legendary Phoenix, killed or consumed by the burning fire. Jesus, who was crucified by the forces of Evil, and died of his injuries, resurrected after three days, mirroring both the resurrection of ADON[31] in the spring (month of April) and that of the Phoenix from his ashes, three days after. The Resurrection shook the foundations of the natural world, for it was an extension of it—a supernatural and spiritual power. "Now the Son of Man has been glorified, and God has been glorified in him," wrote John[32].

---

24. Luke 23:47.
25. Matthew 24:31.
26. Mark 10:45.
27. John's *Revelation*.
28. Luke 22:18, 29:30.
29. 1 Enoch 105:26-27.
30. Matthew 19:28.
31. Or Ba'al, the Sun god par excellence.
32. John 13:31.

That said and knowing that this book is not meant to go into additional details explaining the differences between Judaism and Christianity and how Christ is not to be connected to Judaism in any way or manner as we have thoroughly explained in *Jesus the Phoenician*, it is worth to add a few notes herein.

As early as the beginning of the 1st and 2nd century AD and onward, early Church Fathers and biblical exegetes started to display the different mind sets between Jews and Christians—a matter that classical and traditional thinking consider a separation between the two since they thought that Christianity emerges from Judaism, something that we have debased on many occasions. Indeed, the creation of the New Testament has been based on a different divine alliance than that of the Old Testament, which only shows a sole alliance between Yahweh and the "Chosen People" of Israel through the person of Moses, whose true identity will be exposed in Part III of this work as well. The New Testament, on the other hand, substituted that *tribal expired alliance* with a *Universal New Alliance* that has been interlinked between the Most High and Jesus Christ as his *Son*, addressing it to all world nations alike, including even some of the Jews who believed in Christ and became known as Judeo-Christians.

Logically speaking, if Jesus were Jew, there would be no need for a new alliance anyway, and the Christian community would not then entirely center its religious movement and faith on Jesus Christ as Son of God and Savior while abolishing altogether the Law of Moses, which is the basic tenet of the Old Testament religious foundation itself. And there happened to appear two ways afterward, two religious and social realities; "Israel and the Synagogue on one side, and (Jesus) Christ and the Church on the other side."[33]

And thence, on the Mystery of God, Christian thinkers of that early period during the emergence of that *new human community* at the heart of a *New Divine Alliance* began "using more and more concepts and methods of philosophical analysis borrowed from Pagan culture. They haven't denied their religious faith but estimated that all that, in ancient culture, attested to the *passing* of man towards a transcendent Being could, rightly, be recovered by Christianity."[34]

We undoubtedly believe that such philosophical notion describing the relation of Man, the Microcosm and God, the Macrocosm at the heart of the ancient pagan culture, completely resides inside the *Prisca Theologia*, the "Primordial Theology" of the Hermetic esoteric Tradition, *hence*, the Phenokian

---

33. Lenoir, Frédéric, et, Tardan-Masquelier, Ysé (Sous la Direction), *Encyclopédie Des Religions*, Tome 1, 377.

34. Ibid., 399.

Initiatic Tradition. Some of the learned early Fathers of the Church spoke of that *prisca theologia* connection. It consisted of a combination of manuscripts that completely proved the truth of this wisdom of all ages. These Manuscripts of fifteen discourses, known as *Corpus Hermeticum*, were attributed to Hermes the three times great, the Trismegistos, the First Teacher, divine messenger, and *Initiate*.

Now, the first three degrees of the Craft or Blue Lodge Masonry are composed of the *Entered Apprentice Degree*, the *Fellow Craft Degree*, and the *Master Mason Degree*—consecrated to Hiram Abiff, the Master Architect. In the Phoenician *Initiatic* language, Hiram could well mean the *Enlightened One or Divine Messenger and Teacher*, just like the meaning of the word Enoch we saw earlier as *Teacher-Initiator*, or it could derive from the word *Khur-Um*, which means "lifted up to life."

The legend of the Phoenician Architect, Hiram Abiff—and his assassination by three evil brothers inside a temple—was first incorporated into the Freemasonic rituals by the English Grand Lodge. The ritual bestowed the names: Jubela, Jubelo, and Jubelum on the killers of Hiram Abiff, known collectively as the *Juwes*[35]! Sometimes, Hiram Abiff is shown as an allegorical Jesus Christ, killed, so to speak, by Judas, Caiaphas, and Pilate. However, as mentioned in Matthew[36], "when Pilate saw that nothing was being gained, but that a disturbance had started instead, he took water and washed his hands before the multitude, saying, 'I am innocent of the blood of this righteous person. You see to it. All the people answered, 'May his blood be on us, and on our children!'" Henceforth . . . Annas—the father-in-law of Caiaphas—should be the third assassin, not Pilate; for Judas, Caiaphas, and Annas were the three Jewish men (*Juwes*) that masterminded his arrest as clearly stated in the New Testament. That historical incident was what led to his Crucifixion by the Romans and his Resurrection three days after.

It is worth noting here that during a discussion with modern American Templar and Master Mason, Timothy Hogan[37], concerning the Freemasonic symbolism of that dramatic ritualistic scene, which of course does not fall into any historical context in relation to Hiram's masonic work in the land of Canaan-Phoenicia, nor does it reflect a direct relation with our interpretation

---

35. Robinson, John, *Born in Blood—the lost secrets of Freemasonry*, 220.

36. Matthew 27:24-25.

37. Timothy Hogan is a lecturer and author of many books on Templarism and Masonry, perhaps one of the very few erudite who often states that western esoteric traditions and mystery schools are rooted in the ancient traditions of Phoenicia and Egypt.

of the historical Jesus. At any rate, he was happy to share his interpretation and understanding, explaining it as follows—

> In the ritual drama of Freemasonry, there are three ruffians who kill the central figure of Hiram. They do so because they are jealous of what he knows, and what they think he has, and they feel entitled to it without having actually done the work that he had to earn it. They thought that they could attack him and get it from him, not realizing that it doesn't work like that. In the end, they sealed their own fate by thinking so deceptively. If you feel entitled to something that you personally have not worked for, then you may be acting as a ruffian . . . The worst part of the allegory, is that Hiram thought these ruffians were his brothers. Remember that true brothers will do everything to lift each other up rather than knock each other down. Mastery involves surviving the deception and still moving on to lift up others . . .

The secret knowledge of Freemasonry reveals with precise explanation that in the third degree, the Fellow Mason would undertake a rite of *Resurrection*, better say *Raising*, to use a Masonic term[38] into a Master Mason, thus, perfectly mirroring the Resurrection of Jesus Christ on the third day. "For if we have been planted together in the likeness of his death, we shall also be in the likeness of his resurrection," St. Paul had declared in his Epistle to the Romans[39]. Therefore, in that line of understanding, if the legendary temple of Solomon has not been completed in Freemasonry, it was simply because Jesus Christ himself is the Temple of God in its Completion.

Didn't he say, in John[40], that if they destroy this Temple, *Him*, he will raise it up—*his body*—in three days?

Yes, he did . . .

To finalize this chapter before we move on to explaining in the next one who were the Babylonian Brotherhood, let us make a fast theological link between Phoenicians and Christ. The reason why it is a quick written link herein remains that this book is not planned for such an endeavor, and should you want to venture more in-depth into that strong, undeniable connection, you can always do so by referring to my previous book, Jesus the Phoenician.

---

38. Wilmshurst, W.L., *The Meaning of Masonry*, 143.
39. Romans, 6:5.
40. John 2:19.

In Judaism, the concept of their god Yahweh having begotten a child, say, a son, is totally rejected. Yahweh had only prophets, as the Old Testament narrates and as all the Jewish tradition has been teaching for centuries. An important question then lingers still in our minds! From where thence did early Christians and writers of the Gospel got the idea that Jesus was the son of God? What God? Certainly, this is not in accord with Jewish culture *per se*, but rather it is in total concordance with Phoenician and Egyptian Traditions, thus the teachings of the Great White Fraternity.

Not only that, but also the Christian trinity of Father, Son, and Holy Spirit is coming from the triune nature of the divine principles presented by Phoenician Priests as such; El, Astarte, and ADON (or Ba'al), El being the Father, ADON the son, and Astarte the Mother, or Holy Spirit. This coincides very well with the Egyptian Osiris, Horus, and Isis.

In addition, and what is most strikingly interesting is the idea that this Most High God El has sent his only begotten Son to be sacrificed for the salvation of the community. This has been done with ADON as we already know and explained and, with Ledud, as per Eusebius, in his most famous work, *Preparation of the Gospel*. Eusebius claims to have quoted both Porphyry of Sūr/Tyre[41] and Philo of Gebel/Byblos[42] on accounts originally written by Sanchuniathon of Berytus/Beirut[43] who obtained records on Phoenician History and Tradition from a certain Hierombalus[44] who was a priest of the god *Ieuo* or *Yāw*, not the Hebrew Yahweh[45], as we shall see later on in Part III.

It is also reported, however, that Sanchuniathon based a few parts of his work on Religion, Cosmology, etc., on some secret collections written by the priests of Ammon[46], and discovered in the shrines—a collection of Sacred Tradition decoded from mystical inscriptions found on *Pillars* standing in Phoenician Temples, mostly, *Temples of Initiation*—ancient lore that revealed the truth and was later covered up by allegories, myths, and symbols. Very *Initiatic*, Masonic indeed! For, we have previously related that the Masonic tradition has been greatly influenced by the Phoenician Tradition and *received* the idea of the twin Pillars from both Sanchuniathon and Enoch, but unfortunately, it got

---

41. He was a Phoenician philosopher, c. 234–304/5 AD.

42. He was a Phoenician historian and author, 1st century AD.

43. He was a Phoenician historian and priest, 10th century BC.

44. He was most probably Hiram'ba'al or Hiram, King of Tyre, who built the temple of Ba'al Melkart in Sūr with the expertise of our famous Architect, Hiram Abif.

45. El Koussa, Karim, *Jesus the Phoenician*, 231–232.

46. There is no doubt that there has been a great connection between Phoenicia and Egypt, as we have been stating in this book, however, we believe the connection was mostly founded with the Priests of Aton!

mixed up between two ancient Traditions at odds with each other for a long period; the Great White Fraternity and the Babylonian Brotherhood!

At any rate, what concerns us now here is the following quote from Eusebius on El sending his son to be sacrificed. We should note that Eusebius is not completely trusted in matters concerning both Phoenicians and Egyptians. However, he kept for us some important information he received from texts related to us initially by Phoenician historians and authors—information he could not deny or ignore. Anyway, he wrote[47] (Italics are mine)—

> It was a custom of the ancients in great crises of danger for the rulers of a city or nation, in order to avert the common ruin, to give up the most beloved of their children for sacrifice as a ransom to the avenging daemons; and those who were thus given up were sacrificed with mystic rites. Kronos then, whom the Phoenicians call Elus (*El, Elyon, or Eloh*), who was king of the country and subsequently, after his decease, was deified as the star Saturn[48], had by a nymph of the country named Anobret[49] an only begotten son, whom they on this account called Iedud[50], the only begotten being still so called among the Phoenicians; and when very great dangers from war had beset the country, he arrayed his son in royal apparel, and prepared an altar, and sacrificed him.

That being said, this testimony by itself reveals the great resemblance between the Phoenician theological concept of sacrificing the son of El for the sake of the nation and the Christian one of *Immanu-el* (Jesus Christ) being sent by God to sacrifice himself on the altar of Humanity. And, to quote from *Jesus the Phoenician*, page 188—

> As for human sacrifices, the nobler and the more honorable the better—children in particular, the eldest sons or the most pure of them, offered by their parents to Moloch as in Carthage—they were consumed by fire in order to pacify the wrath of the deity! However, all

---

47. Eusebius, *Praeparatio Evangelica*, Book 1, chapters 9 & 10.

48. It should be interpreted as Kronos/time because Saturn was not at all sacred to the Phoenicians and could not hence be related to El.

49. It is a bit confusing, because El's escort was Ashirai, Anat, or Astarte.

50. It is indeed a strange name, for El's sons were known as Šalim, Yāw, ADON, Ba'al, and to a certain extent Mot and Hadad, unless it was meant to write Hadad instead of Iedud!

that we have of that terrifying practice has been proven, historically and archaeologically, to be nothing but a deliberate propaganda fabricated by jealous people such as the Romans in the course of the Punic wars against the Great Hannibal, and the Hebrews, as cited in the Old Testament (2Kings 21:1-11), against the Canaanite/Phoenicians (Amorites) who were shown to be one of the biggest enemies of Biblical Israel.

We will certainly not linger on that nonsense another instant, for we believe, like any other reasonable mind, that the Canaanite/Phoenicians, with their sophisticated and innovative religious system and spiritual aspiration, were not at all barbaric. Instead, they were a people of great faith in El, God the Most High, and their salvation as a nation happened through the sacrifice of his Son presented as Adon, who himself was but a preamble of the sacrifice of Christ for Humanity as a whole. Yet, they both conquered death and gloriously resurrected.

As for now, let us please take a few minutes in deep thoughts and meditate on that particular point in preparation for the next chapter; *The Babylonian Brotherhood.*

6.

The Babylonian Brotherhood

When we read the title of this chapter, The Babylonian Brotherhood, we instantly think of something dark when we compare it with the name and resonance The Great White Fraternity may have on us. This is true because everything dark and evil started in that region of the world. We will certainly explain every possible side of it so that it won't confuse the Seeker of Truth and Lover of Light that we all are.

We have already mentioned in Chapter 4, the section that dealt with *Transmitting of the Tradition to Egypt, then around the world*, that it was with the Chaldean savants and magi that the Authentic Tradition of the Great White Fraternity took a very different turn, and what happened there in Babylon and Ur of the Chaldeans was surely a great deviation from the original Phoenician-Egyptian source. This had later on led to what we know as Judaism and the Jewish Kabala.

The Chaldean-Babylonians seemed to have manipulated the Authentic Kabbala received by Enoch on Mt. Hermon and used to invoke spirits, demons, etc., either in the written form of talisman or in the oral form of incantation, accompanied with the practice of sorcery and bloody dark rituals. So it was there in Babylon that the *Fallen Angels* whom they invoked, so to speak, got engaged with human affairs, enslaving them, and leading them to wars and sins, filling the earth with blood and unrighteousness. These were the winged Anunnaki[1], and we believe these were the ones mentioned in the Book of Enoch

---

1. This is the name some would like to call them for they are described as giants, winged gods and are found only in ancient cuneiform texts written by the Sumerians—ancient Mesopotamia, as we have seen earlier. These *Anunnaki* are somehow credited for teaching humanity many sciences from astronomy to weapons, and this has been destroyed as a consequence of a flood that hit parts of Iraq and Iran sometimes around 4,000 to 5,000 BC.

to be judged by him, Enoch, who walked with El. To do that, he was given great support from the four Cardinal Angels who formed the Kosmic Cross: Michael, Gabriel, Raphael, and Auriel.[2]

Not only is this revealed in the Kabbalistic Book of Enoch, but it is also exposed in the Kabbalistic Book of Revelation written by John. It reminds us of the "Great Harlot of Babylon, Destruction of Babylon, Judgment of the Beast, the Devil and the False Prophet, End of the Old Jerusalem, Rising of the New Jerusalem on a New Earth under a New Heaven where God and Humanity dwell once again together after the curse has ended, and where both the river and the "tree of life"—the Spirit of Christ—appear for the healing of the nations."

Therefore, it is not by coincidence that John related the end of the Old Jewish Jerusalem with the destruction of Babylon that had preceded it. Thus, his Revelation would be understood through the correct historical accounts of the people[3] to whom Christ and Christianity have been tied so erroneously. It is conceived from the early beginnings that the Church and the Synagogue do not match. And under this light, we, therefore, understand him (John) saying in his Revelation[4]—

> Behold, I will make those of the synagogue of Satan who say that they are Jews and are not, but lie—behold, I will make them come and bow down before your feet, and they will learn that I have loved you.

Having said that, and since we have now come to realize and decrypt the hidden link of that subterranean dark background origin of The Babylonian Brotherhood, and its daemonic rituals of blood, it had nevertheless, not taken form, we believe, as a fully organized Brotherhood, until the time of the Persian King, Cyrus II, sometime around the 6th century BC. Should we desire to comprehend the historical background of The Babylonian Brotherhood, we foremost need to understand the concealed connection between the *Aebirou-al-Nahara* (the Hebrews) and the Persians.

---

2. We have seen before that these Good Angels helped Enoch to cast the *Fallen Angels* out of Phoenicia to re-appear in Sumer under the name of Anunnaki, and were led by "Enlil," who we believe was no other than "Ananel," one of the twenty leaders of the *Fallen Angels* mentioned by Enoch. These were the *Evil Watchers* who conditioned ancient Mesopotamians (Sumerians, Akkadians, Assyrians and Babylonians) to their evil powers.

3. The people here means ancient Mesopotamians, in exact terms and timeline, therefore; the Chaldean-Babylonian origin of the *Aebirou-al-Nahara* of the Jewish Jerusalem.

4. Revelation 3:9.

Therefore, we shall briefly present our interpretation of the Jewish biblical text and clearly explain their entwined cultural history with the Persians. However, I have already tackled that interesting and revelatory point in previous works, but I thought it is quite necessary to relate it herein for my new readers.

It is traditionally believed that Abraham, the genetic father of the Hebrew people, originated from the city of Ur of the Chaldeans in Babylon, and this piece of information is no secret at all, but found in the Old Testament itself in the Book of Genesis and the work of the Scribe Nehemiah[5]. The striking similarities in both books are crucially important regarding the *religious and geopolitical* promise made by the Hebrew God to Abraham and his descendants.

In Genesis, we read[6]—

> And Terah took his son Abram and his grandson Lot, the son of Haran, and his daughter-in-law Sarai, his son Abram's wife, and they went out with them from Ur of the Chaldeans to go to the land of Canaan; and they came to Haran and dwelt there.

We read in Genesis[7]—

> And God said to Abraham: 'As for you, you shall keep My covenant, you and your descendants after you throughout their generations.'

Here it is in Genesis[8]—

> Now the LORD had said to Abram: Get out of your country, From your family And from your father's house, To a land that I will show you. I will make you a great nation; I will bless you And make your name great; And you shall be a blessing. I will bless those who bless you, And I will curse him who curses you; And in you, all the families of the earth shall be blessed. So Abram departed as the LORD had spoken to him, and Lot went with him. And Abram [was] seventy-five years old when he departed from Haran. Then Abram took Sarai, his

---

5. There are enough evidence and based on the biblical timeline that prove Nehemiah was definitely not a Jewish scribe, but rather Persian, as we shall see in a bit. There is an interesting plot here, we mean, a plot very well interposed in the text of the Old Testament.

6. Genesis 11:31.

7. Genesis 17:9.

8. Genesis 12:1-7; 17:1-8.

wife and Lot, his brother's son, and all their possessions that they had gathered, and the people whom they had acquired in Haran, and they departed to go to the land of Canaan. So they came to the land of Canaan. Abram passed through the land to the place of Shechem, as far as the terebinth tree of Moreh. *And the Canaanites [were] then in the land.* Then the LORD appeared to Abram and said, To your descendants, I will give this land. And there he built an altar to the LORD, who had appeared to him.

And also in Nehemiah[9]—

You [are] the LORD God, Who chose Abram, And brought him out of Ur of the Chaldeans, And gave him the name Abraham; You found his heart faithful before You, And made a covenant with him To give the land of the Canaanites, the Hittites, the Amorites, the Perizzites, the Jebusites, and the Girgashites—To give [it] to his descendants. You have performed Your words, For You [are] righteous.

So, according to the Biblical narration, Abraham was called Abram first, but when the Hebrew God then chose him to keep the Covenant and enter the Land of Canaan, Yahweh changed his name into Abraham[10] and seemed to have changed the name of his wife[11] too, probably for the same reason of giving them new names and new identities in a new land—the Promised Land, their God, wanted to offer them! Whatever the case is, or the hidden meaning was, if there were one behind that story, Abraham or Abram remains still a Babylonian native, and the above quotes from the Old Testament prove our point that he was undoubtedly Babylonian, *transferred*, so to speak, by the Jewish God to another land.

Yet, was he, Abraham, the Aramean wanderer mentioned in the Old Testament? Is there any possibility they are the same person? Historical records show that the Chaldeans, although a Semitic group of people, were distinguished from the Aramean stock of humanity. Something to think about indeed!

At any rate, should we read carefully, we would certainly find the original place from which Abraham departed and the destination he had in mind, as the Old Testament shows to have been inspired and directed by the Hebrew God.

9. Nehemiah 9:7-8.
10. Genesis 17:5.
11. Genesis 17:15.

There is undoubtedly the notion of a conquering mentality in the biblical text. If we may say, as always has been the case for all conquerors throughout history, a stealing mentality. The text shows that the Hebrew God chose a group of people actually belonging to another land to rob the adjacent lands and occupy the Promised Land—Canaan. It is no secret. Everybody read it in the pages of what is called the Holy Bible. But this is not what it seems!

And the Book of Genesis continues elaborating on that particular point, saying that while Abraham was in the Land of Canaan, the Hebrew God appeared to him[12]—

> On the same day, the LORD made a covenant with Abram, saying: To your descendants, I have given this land, from the river of Egypt to the great river, the River Euphrates . . .

The selection of these particular territories herein shown and were decided to be given to Abraham by his God through occupation, are mentioned in many other different places in the Old Testament[13] and are in reality the same territories occupied by the Persians at the time of Cyrus II—who reigned from c. 559-530 BC—over that part of the ancient world.

If you are familiar with the Old Testament narration, you may immediately realize a difference of almost 1500 years between the date Abraham was said to have lived and Cyrus II, who appeared in the 6th century BC. Yes, the differences are obvious, thus dating Abraham back to around 2000 years BC is one of the Persians' biggest machinations. We will come to that in the current chapter. Thus, it would be a serious error to believe that Abraham existed around two thousand years BC as the Old Testament wants us to think. Not only that, but it becomes evident to most free-minded academics and Seekers of Truth that the preceding claims of the Old Testament are pretty obsolete. Great uncertainties have been fairly uttered not only regarding the authenticity of the Patriarchs cited in the Book of Genesis, but also, very intelligently questioning the historicity of the kings David and Solomon and personages like Moses, Joshua, and the Judges, too.

Indeed! So . . . was then the Old Testament's promise of the Hebrew God, *de facto*, that of Cyrus II? That is what we are going to find out.

---

12. Genesis 15:18.
13. Deuteronomy 1:7; 11:24; Joshua 1:4; 2 Kings 24:7.

In reality, the city of Ur is mentioned several times in the Old Testament as Ur of the Chaldeans and as the birthplace of the First Hebrew Patriarch, Abraham. The 2000 years BC proposed as the date of his birth would be nothing but pure invention, and there are many reasons he could only be a false historical figure. Why? The claim that Abraham, his wife, children, and descendants, are said to have "crossed the river" to the Promised Land of Canaan, to settle and take it as their new land, surely not a homeland, could not have happened in 2000 years BC because credible historical facts state that the Chaldeans settled in Iraq sometime around 800 BC—maybe a bit before, but not that long before—and were based in Babylon sometime between the 7th and 6th century BC.

Therefore, in a simple calculation, there is a difference of about a minimum of 1200 years. And that is in direct concordance with the latter period. The famous edict—issued by the Persian Emperor, Cyrus II (known as the Great), in the 6th century BC—is a valid historical fact; an edict in which he gave the promise to a few chosen children, say, Babylonian families and people of a new *homeland* in the Land of Canaan. Hence, the Old Testament's famous promise of Yahweh to his people was in truth that of Cyrus! No matter what else we might think of, the city of Ur stands as the primary point of foundation for the biblical Hebrews, yet, only at the time of Cyrus II. It is back then and there that things started happening for them.

This is a proven fact, for we find a notable connotation for this event in history, in the Old Testament itself. We thus read in Ezra[14]—

> The Lord stirred up the spirit of Cyrus King of Persia, that he made a proclamation throughout all his kingdom, and put it also in writing . . . Thus saith Cyrus King of Persia, the Lord God of heaven hath given me all the kingdoms of the earth; and he hath charged me to build him a house at Jerusalem, which is in Judah.

And in Isaiah[15]—

> Thus saith the Lord to his anointed, to Cyrus, whose right hand I have holden, to subdue nations before me.

---

14. Ezra 1:1-2.
15. Isaiah 45:1.

The above two quotations were written as if in homage to Cyrus and his power to take ultimate possession of all the kingdoms of the earth and subdue all nations. They are extremely important and similar in many ways—especially in terms of the psychological frame of a military doctrine brewing inside a conquering mind—to what was previously mentioned in both Genesis and Nehemiah concerning the so-called "Promised Land" Yahweh, the Hebrew God, offered so generously to Abraham, and the power he gave him to conquer additional territories, mainly from the River Euphrates to the river of Egypt, and subdue their nations.

In a way, this may appear bizarre and perhaps shocking to the majority of readers, especially Christian and Judeo-Christian scholars who probably haven't paid attention to that specific point. There is no word of homage or respect to any *Gentile* gods, priests, kings, kingdoms, or even to any group of people belonging to any nation—the goyim—by the Hebrews in the Old Testament, except for Cyrus II. It would be thus too much of a coincidence to find that the *Aebirou-al-Nahara*, at the time, who had much too often considered themselves the only Chosen People, had indeed written that their Lord God stirred up the spirit of a Goy, *say* a Persian, to build him a temple in Jerusalem, and even more, anointing him to become a sort of a Messiah, a kind of savior! Why? One may wonder . . .

Persians were not *Goyim* in the Hebrews' eyes for the simple fact that it was the Persians who created the Hebrews! It may not be neglected that the two scribes of the Old Testament, Nehemiah, and Ezra (or Esdras), were, in fact, Persians and eminent members of the Babylonian Brotherhood. The real and actual, not mythical and falsified, history of the Jewish people starts with them[16]. Additionally, the connection is not only based on the historical level alone but definitely expands to the religious level as well. Renan, the French historian we cited earlier, states[17], "The prophetic tone of many of the teachings of Iran had much analogy with certain compositions of Hosea and Isaiah." He then adds[18], "The whole book of Esther breathes a great attachment to this dynasty." Renan undoubtedly indicated that this dynasty were the Achemenidae[19], under which he then clearly declared, "Israel reposed."

---

16. We have clearly elaborated on that point and gave plenty of examples and showed many evidences even from the Old Testament itself in both my books *Jesus the Phoenician* and *The Phoenician Code*.

17. Renan, Ernest, *Vie de Jésus*, 143.

18. Ibid., 143 & (fn.7).

19. The Achaemenid Persian Empire (c. 550–330 BC), from the Old Persian word, *Parsā*, the name of the ruling dynasty, Haxāmanišiya, also known as the First Persian (Iranian) Empire in Western Asia, founded by Cyrus the Great (c. 559–529 BC) who overthrew the Median confederation. It ended with Darius III (c. 336–330 BC) in around 330 BC.

Please bear in mind again that this book and previous works that had tackled this delicate yet interesting subject are and were not meant to completely narrate the true hidden genesis of the Hebrew people, as much as we know such work would require a whole volume. We needed, however, to mention certain facts concerning their origin and foundation as essentially being the progenies of the Babylonian Brotherhood and its religious ideologies, a fact that truly helps enlighten the way ahead of us to recognize the many various and great important differences with the Great White Fraternity and its religious beliefs, founded mainly on Monotheism.

At the time of the Persian Empire's expansion, the adjacent city of Babylon fell into the hands of the Persian King Cyrus II, sometime around the year 539 BC, and became, therefore, a province of the Great Persian Empire. Like the Babylonians and Assyrians before them, the Persians seemed to have exercised a systematic relocation program—for their subjugated populace—from one occupied land to another. This particular program was greatly endorsed by an all-encompassing political and religious propaganda. And, in that concern, the 20th-century British historian and theologian, Thomas L. Thompson, so eloquently explains in his work[20]—

> They (in reference to the resettlement policies) had a very complicated impact on the development of ethnic and national identities within the empire. They also played a decisive role in the growth of ideas about monotheism and about saving 'messiahs.' The metaphors of the restoration of Israel's God in Jerusalem, the rebuilding of the temple, and the return of a repentant remnant from 'exile'—all these images find their origin in such policies. All of these concepts play a vital role in the creation of a 'new Israel,' a new 'people of God' centered in Jerusalem.

Thus, understanding the basics of the resettlement policy herein practiced by the Persians, we come to conclude that after several years of controlling Babylon, Cyrus II and some Chaldean priests could have established the Babylonian Brotherhood, almost one year after the fall of Babylon transpired. Cyrus issued his famous edict in 538 BC, which consisted of ordering the transfer of a group of people—composed of Chaldean priests and families belonging to the Brotherhood—from Babylon to the Promised Land. We have thence observed that this transfer was not a resettling plan, but instead, a settling program.

---

20. Thompson, Thomas L., *The Mythic Past*, 190–191.

That said, the promise made by Cyrus II had a hidden agenda of some sort. It was a historical declaration, all in the hope that it would strengthen their authorities, political, religious, and economic, which stated that the Persian Empire's power should not be comprised by any geographical boundary. The Persians reached the southern part of the land of Canaan-Phoenicia, including Jerusalem, and controlled it some few years after being in command of Babylon. Later on—in 525 BC, and under Cambyses II, the son and successor of Cyrus II—the Persians attacked Egypt and destroyed most of its religious monuments. In time, the Persians controlled most of western Asia.

The character who seems to have been the first to lead the people—known as the *Aebirou-al-Nahara*, the Hebrews who "crossed the river" in constant waves from Babylon toward the Land of Canaan—was called Zoro-Babel, most probably, an eminent member of the Babylonian Brotherhood. That began with him[21] under the patronage of Cyrus II the Great, and it occurred when they had just thought of building a temple in Jerusalem, as we have seen before when *the Lord stirred up the spirit of Cyrus and charged him to build him a house in Judah*. Once again, Renan had a say about that matter when he declared, as openly as he knew at the time (Italics are mine)[22]—

> The victory of Cyrus seemed at one time to realize all that had been hoped. The grave disciples of the Avesta and the adorers of Jehovah believed themselves *brothers*.

From that perspective, we would then like to note that Zoro-Babel (or Zerubbabel) was not the Hebrew leader who brought the alleged ancient Jews out of their exile and into Jerusalem and was not the Prince of Judea of Davidic lineage, as the Scribes of the Old Testament wanted the whole world to believe. Truth be said, the name Zoro-Babel is purely a Babylonian or Assyro-Babylonian name, written as such, *Zeru Babel*, and it surely means, "Seed or Son of Babel (Babylon)." By birth, he was Babylonian before the Hebrews (or the Jews) existed as an ethnic historical group.

Henceforth, on Zorobabel and the Persian-Hebrew religious connection, we have many authors lining up like Renan who tend to prove it and thoroughly support it. H.P. Blavatsky was clear enough to state in her book[23]—

---

21. Or with his uncle Sheshbazzar or Shenazzar, as we have explained in *Jesus the Phoenician*, 165.
22. Renan, Ernest, *Vie de Jésus*, 143.
23. Blavatsky, H.P., *Isis Unveiled*, vol. 2, 441.

It was Darius Hystaspes (Darius I, the Great) who was the first to establish a Persian colony in Judaea; Zoro-Babel was perhaps the leader. The name Zoro-babel means 'the seed or son of Babylon'—as Zoro-aster (Zoroaster), is the seed, son, or prince of Ishtar. The new colonists were doubtless Judaei.

She next added—

When the Asmonean (Hasmonean) period began, the chief supporters of the Law were called Asideans or Kasdim[24] (Chaldeans), and afterward Pharisees or Pharsi (Pârsîs). This indicates that Persian colonies were established in Judaea and ruled the country; while all the people that are mentioned in the books of Genesis and Joshua lived there as a commonalty.

Another important passage worth mentioning is from the 19th-century American author, Albert Pike, the Sovereign Grand Commander of the Supreme Council 33° of the Scottish Rite, and author of *Morals and Dogma of the Ancient and Accepted Scottish Rite of Freemasonry*, an interesting work that was meant only for the brothers within the Craft, but then became public. Pike declared that the dominant religious system among the Hebrews/Jews was indeed that of the Pharisees (or Pharoschim). He wrote[25]—

Whether their name (the Pharisees) was derived from that of the Parsees, or followers of Zoroaster, or from some other source, it is certain that they had borrowed much of their doctrine from the Persians. Like them, they claimed to have the exclusive and mysterious knowledge unknown to the mass. Like them, they taught that a constant war was waged between the empire of Good and that of Evil. Like them, they attributed the sin and fall of man to the demons and their chief; and like them, they admitted a special protection of the righteous by inferior beings, agents of Jehovah. All their doctrines on these subjects were at bottom those of the Holy Books.

---

24. They are the Hasidim, or Hasideans (Hasidæans or Assideans).
25. Pike, Albert, *Morals and Dogma of the Ancient and Accepted Scottish Rite of Freemasonry*, 259.

Blavatsky adds[26]—

> The Jews, coming from the Persian country, brought with them the
> doctrine of two principles. They could not bring the Avesta, for it
> was not written. But they—we mean the Asideans (Chasîdîm) and
> Pharsi—invested Ormazd with the secret name of YHWH, and Ahri-
> man with the name of the gods of the land, Satan of the Hittites, and
> Diabolos, or rather Diobolos, of the Greeks.

In that line of thinking and in the concern of academically identifying the
historical ethnicity of the Hebrews (or Jews) as per the narration of the biblical
text, nothing confirms it as true, and this is supported in the work of many
professional historians and archeologists like Thompson, who explained that
very well in his book[27]—

> Related terms show up in Sumerian, Assyro-Babylonian, and Egyptian
> texts in the forms of *Hapiru* and *Apiru*. These terms refer to individu-
> als and groups who were not accepted within the accepted political
> structures of patronage alliances and loyalties that governed society.
> These 'Hebrews' were both literally and figuratively 'outlaws,' not ter-
> ribly unlike such legendary characters in story as the David of I-II
> Samuel or the Abraham of Genesis 12 and 14, where they are called
> 'Hebrews.'

Further explanatory notes concerning that issue were related by 20th-
century Israeli archaeologist, professor emeritus at Tel Aviv University, Israel
Finkelstein, and American archeologist and historian Neil Asher Silberman,
authors of *The Bible Unearthed*. They wrote[28]—

> In the past, scholars have suggested that the word *Apiru* (and its alter-
> native forms, *Hapiru* and *Habiru*) had a direct linguistic connection to
> the word *Ibri*, or Hebrew, and that therefore the Apiru in the Egyptian
> sources were the early Israelites. Today we know that this association
> is not so simple. The widespread use of the term over many centuries

---

26. Blavatsky, H.P., *Isis Unveiled*, vol. 2, 501.
27. Thompson, Thomas L., *The Mythic Past*, 79.
28. Finkelstein Israel, Silberman Neil Asher, *The Bible Unearthed*, 103.

and throughout the entire Near East suggests that it had a socioeconomic meaning rather than signifying a specific ethnic group.

Thompson had suggested[29] earlier in his book herein footnoted that, "The lack of a reliable historical context for the Bible[30] has been a great hindrance to modern Biblical studies." We so much agree this is true since Biblical scholars were looking for historical and archeological proof as per the narration of the Old Testament itself and have utterly neglected the "Persian Case" that we are disclosing *once again* here in this work. Hence, with no historical and/or archaeological verification whatsoever offered regarding the kingdom of Biblical Israel and the temple, the issue would not, therefore, be a resettlement program for rebuilding a temple and the restoration of ancient Israel, but rather a settlement plan and the creation of the *biblical* State of Israel accompanied with building a temple for it, crediting it as such by a divine religious power of some sort.

Most respected Biblical historians, such as Thomas L. Thompson, Philip Davies, Niels Peter Lemche, Israel Finkelstein, Neil Asher Silberman, Keith Whitlam, etc., share, to a certain extent, similar exciting explanations. They tend to believe that, for some ideological and political reason, the whole Biblical narration of the history of Ancient Israel could be nothing more than the intricate operation of a skillful clandestine group of priests living in Jerusalem at some *post-exilic* time. We would add that this secret group of priests was actually: The Babylonian Brotherhood.

Let us not linger too much on this breathtaking truth now and again, yet we urge you, Brothers, Sisters, and dear readers to give it a profound thought. At any rate, and by now, we should have comprehended the essential differences of the national character/culture and religious-esoteric systems obviously existing between the Great White Fraternity, represented back then by both the Egyptians and the Canaanite/Phoenicians, the indigenous people of the Land of Canaan, and the Babylonian Brotherhood, played then by the Chaldean-Babylonians, the Hebrews, and ideologically supported by the Persians—the Achaemenid Empire (c. 550–330 BC)—who *conquered* the Promised Land and *created* Biblical Israel for their expansionary pleasures that suit their political and economic agendas.

Moreover, throughout history, many religious sects and secret societies, whether flourishing in the East or the West, have followed the Babylonian

---

29. Thompson, Thomas L., *The Mythic Past*, 4.
30. He most surely meant the *Old Testament*.

Brotherhood, adopting, for example, the Chaldean-Babylonian-Judaic religious system and their Kabala in their ceremonies of Initiation.[31] Hence, we are going to expose herein some of the most important religions and secret societies that followed and *still follow* the Babylonian Brotherhood:

- The Chaldean-Hebrews (Hasidim-Pârsîs);
- The Jews (Judaism surged from Babylon to serve, in fact, the purposes of the ruling Persians back in time! Judaism is thus Persian propaganda! Note, for example, the word *Pharisees* that describes the Rabbinical powers within Judaism, which is the Religious sacerdotal body of the Jews, is, in fact, a derivation from the word *Pharsi, Pârsîs* or *Parsees*—the Persians, or followers of Zoroaster (*Zoro-Aster*: seed, son, or prince of Ishtar). However, there are many Jews today who don't believe in the narration of the Old Testament, and perhaps some may consider themselves Elohists, not in the Biblical term and timeline of the narrative, but throughout their historical and cultural connections with the Phoenicians in Canaan, after they were initially deported from Ur and Babylon by Cyrus II;
- The Mandaeans;
- Several dualist Gnostics;
- The Priory of Zion;
- Several Alchemists of the dualist principles;
- Some Knights Templar, followers of Rashi of Troyes who initiated the search for the alleged Arch of the Covenant and promoted the existence of the temple of Solomon, considering it the source for their politico-religio-economic power;
- Some of the Freemasons who adopt the temple of Solomon in their rites and exalt the Babylonian Brotherhood in some of their appendant bodies, like the seventh degree, the Royal Arch of Jerusalem;
- The Illuminati;
- The Jehovah Witnesses;
- And a few others, of course, like the Elders of Zion or Zionists.

One may surely need to ponder these facts for some time now before we move into the Kabbalistic Visions, personally experienced through the

---

31. However, very few underwent *Initiation* into the secrets of the authentic Kabala of Phoenicia and Egypt and we have listed some of the most important in Chapter 4.

knowledge of the Enochian Tradition and the letters of the *Sacred Alphabet* that would alchemically take us into its mysterious world of colors, sounds, and sacred revelations.

So, in preparation for that, let us breathe in Unity and Truth and exhale out duality and illusions . . .

~ PART II ~

7.

The Sacred Alphabet

The 1st Level

1.

ALEPH

*It is the Father, the Creative Force,
connected to the Fire element*

At the beginning, there was the void, and the void was like a big thick black cloud stretching out in all directions towards *Infinity*. However, behind that void, there was something our human physical senses could not discern. The intensity of His mysterious presence overpowered our minds through the Holy Spirit.

He must be the *Force*, hidden and concealed beyond the manifested void. He is the Creator, the Primordial Harmony, the Unbecoming, the Unborn, and the Unformed! He is the *Source*.

Then God, the Source, ordered: "Let there be light!"

The *Shining Light* then proceeded forth from that Central Fire and diffused through the immense darkness. This Intelligent, self-sustaining, and self-moved Divine Spirit is unique. Without being divided or even manifested, it is eternal and unchangeable.

God, the Central Fire, the *One*, is indeed the "Unity Point" that contained Infinity. He is the Absolute Creator and the *Father* that circulated through the circumference of existence, yet to come.

Father-Light . . . What a power of Love!

~ ~ ~

Lying on the floor, a soggy sensation crawled on the skin of my hands. I opened my eyes and barely recognized my surroundings. It was like staring at the Sun and then at another object.

I rubbed my eyes and opened them again. The torches on the walls operated still. My eyes focused on their lights and followed their beams through the mysterious Chamber to halt at the unknown forms and shapes sprawled all over the floor around me.

I gazed around, still in confusion, and saw an Altar, paintings on the walls, the Celestial ceiling, and mosaics on the floor. Awareness prevailed. Then, almost at the same time, when I shifted to stand up, I felt tired and heavy, somehow. I looked as flattened as I felt. I wondered why.

"What a strange dream!" I exclaimed, muttering under my breath, and my voice reverberated back to me.

I woke up!

2.
BET(H)

It is the Hermaphrodite dual-nature of the created Kosmos.
It is the Body, or the Temple that holds the Spirit,
associated with planet Saturn

"Be it!" God ordered. "Let me be . . . physical."

The voice echoed everywhere, and instantly, sounds and harmony beckoned the Cosmic Energy and Matter out of chaos and void.

Creation . . .

Creation of indivisible essence and divisible substance resulted from the union of Eternal Male and Female. Life odyssey began, following an order of broken Divine origin! Far distant galaxies and stars beamed one after the other in the dark blue sky. God seemed to have held Time captive in His hands.

A holy moonlit night turned into day when the Sun appeared from the bosom of Light, the Most High. The Sun appeared as a Son of God, standing like a Master in the center of its solar system, radiating energy in all directions toward, and throughout, the circumference. In that circle, *planets* followed an order of consistency, as they seemed to have breathed in the Sun's heat, looping around it like disciples in an act of worship.

Earth moved fast, rotating around itself and the center—the Sun. Billions of years must have passed to transform it, bit by bit. Volcanoes, floods, and temperature changes seemed to have cooled its atmosphere. Then, Earth lost its virginity and was ready. The birth labor ceased, so to speak. Life was to appear anytime now, somewhere in its womb.

The brush of the Great Artist painted the Horizon with an orange-red color. Uncanny grayish-blue clouds hovered above the sea. Yet, the Sun had already seeped through and drew its own reflection in golden lines upon the surface of the water. Through the mist, those luminous lines appeared like trodden paths, at a time when life beat in the abyss of the ocean, to evolve in *silence*, in cold and darkness. Life took its first steps on those paths towards lands, where trees and vegetation welcomed the children of the water with open arms. They lived and multiplied, and, in time, some of them soared into the air.

Born into blind matter under the force of Saturn, we appeared, though embodying God's energy! Then, the curtain dropped, and the many different masks we wore seemed so heavy, concealing our true nature from our own sight, so we felt. This meeting between the mysterious and invisible in us and the obvious, our visible bodies, seemed to have impeded our awakening from the realm of a deep sleep! We somehow entered a circle—the *Circle of Necessity* and turned inside a wheel—the *Wheel of Life*, where the surrender to the dual forces of this world took place.

Darkness and Light, Blindness and Awareness, were manifesting quickly on Earth and enfolding us, perhaps the whole existence as well. *We breathed in Life and breathed out Death.*

Then, the sound of sea gulls gliding in the air created a musical harmony in our minds and spirits, awakening me to the present. These kinds of interchange between sea gulls and me were very much perceptible to my senses, to our senses, I guess. They made us aware that life communicated in so many different ways. It was as if all Earth creatures followed the same coherent laws, simply by their connection to God's energy diffused through all existence.

The Sun, shimmering on the even surface of the sea, declared a day of early spring. On that beautiful sandy beach, we, men and women, strutted one after another, creating an unbroken chain of Nature's most beautiful creatures. Women's bodies shone vibrantly, like bamboo recently painted. *From where did they come up with such a marvelous color of skin?* I marveled, like all men. They jumped in the water and swam like gracious dolphins, these peaceful creatures of the sea.

They dove in and out, gliding on the surface, their bodies sprinkled by water and swathed with light. Gorgeous, almost magnetic, they caressed their hairs and moved their heads backward, staring at the sky above. Their eyes glittered splendidly like stars amid the void of night. They appeared like goddesses of the sea. They were mermaids . . . They were Astartes! The Sun strongly reached down to them and all over their skins for the heat to blaze their bodies and elevate their desires to its light.

I tried to shun my eyes away in an attempt to escape the delightful vision ahead of me, surrounding me from all sides. Then a thought came rushing into my head and I felt I had to switch from that state of mind, which vivid imagination gripped me, and unwillingly. So I thought! Who would not, in front of such a mesmeric revelation?

I couldn't!

3.
GIMEL

It is the wandering in Nature,
connected to planet Jupiter

Grey *Kafieh* swathed my head. The heat of the Sun blistered the bare parts of my face. My body sweated profusely under my beige caftan while my sandal dragged me along the way . . . to nowhere. I spotted no mountains, neither around me nor in the far distance. A few small hills caught my eyes here and there. I was tired, alone somewhere in the desert through which I traveled like pilgrims and wandered like prophets.

With no destination whatsoever in my mind and no map in my hand, I lost perception of the four directions, for the Sun was in the middle of the sky. I glimpsed over my shoulder and detected the trail of my footprints marking their different sizes on the soft sand. I wondered!

My past has been recorded since my first steps along the path. I reasoned as I perceived my beginning hazily. My visual sense betrayed me. I beheld the sudden fact and confirmed my deficiency. A foggy beginning, the one I had, and no idea of the end.

Was it near or far? Was it an illusion or plainly undefined? I simply did not know!

Same arid region everywhere I traipsed. Time elapsed slowly, dull as an empty Space. Dunes, sand, and scorching sun.

The bareness that overwhelmed me with anxiety veered soon to despair. My march, on that desolate tract, became slower, heavier, hopeless. I wanted to act brave and infused hope in my heart, my *sole companion* of fate at this instant, but words dried in my mouth. The moment I reached the peak of my gloom, hope reinstated in the form of Human and animal traces; remnants of a caravan that has previously camped on the hill. Footprints marked the path of their departure, and with a renewed energy, I stalked their course. Whatever the identity of these travelers and whatever the destination I pursued on their footprints, I heartened at realizing that I was not alone any longer.

The Sun rolled down into the Horizon, donning an orange-red attire. Temperature lowered in degrees, and early sensations of cold crawled on my skin. From almost nowhere, the wind blew in a swift and wafted the sand around me in a creepy hiss that altered, at full tilt, into an angry whistle through the wilderness.

The view dimmed dramatically, and I felt lost in that turbulence. I covered my eyes in the fold of my arms and turned around myself in protection but found no direction safe enough from the furious thrashing of the sand. I whirled uncontrollably, unbalanced by a greater power that risked swallowing me any time soon.

Chaos prevailed, and Nature fooled me.

Was it an eternity that elapsed, or minutes? I thought. When the storm ceased, I mislaid all sense of time. The footsteps along the path disappeared. Confusion inhabited my soul as I gathered around one spot, somewhere in the center, the center of nowhere! Again, I lost orientation. Night descended on me like the shadow of an ominous ghost.

In the wilderness of the Sahara, illusions initiated their peculiar tricks on my mind. I began hearing voices all around me. Elves, Jinnis, Angels, or Demons . . . I was not sure, not doubting if they even existed, or perhaps they were but fantasies triggered by my imagination!

Fear of the unknown extorts hazy thoughts, images, and sounds hidden deep in the souls of Human Beings. I thought and trembled deep down my heart, pumping at a higher speed, hard, like a thunderstorm.

In a trance-like state, I chased the sounds of voices to stop abruptly at the sight of the vale below. *An oasis! Life!* My mind screamed, and my heart jumped inside the frail body of mine, swept by the weariful journey.

A fire camp under palm trees revealed the presence of men seeking heat in this cold desert night. At their side, camels knelt on the sand, relaxing. *So, these were the travelers which path I have just tagged along!* I wondered to myself.

The strange voices held nothing supernatural then! Nature had indeed distorted their echoes to reach my exhausted mind in eerie sounds. I almost tumbled on the soft sand as I dashed toward the oasis. Water was what I sought first and the most to stench my thirst, and I could see human forms looming over a well.

Yet, at nearing these strangers, I slowed down in caution. For a moment, I doubted my eyes as no one from them budged at my approach.

Were they real? I asked myself.

"Hello . . ." I said in a perturbed kind of voice.

Silence! Emptiness!

"Shalam," they then answered in what sounded like a low, surprised tone. A few seconds later, they all turned their heads in my direction. It was strange, that expression in their eyes, so cold, so vague, as if from the past. Without a saluting word or even a convivial gesture of welcome, they reverted their attention to the campfire and their conversation.

The language was unfathomable; a weird dialect of some ancient tongue. *Could it be a mixture of Afro-Asiatic, Canaanite, Egyptian, and Arabic!?* I wondered while heading first to the well. Having satisfied my thirst and washed the sand off my face, I joined them prudently and sat at the same campfire. The red and blue flames flickered and diffused gentle warmth to my face. The blazing timbers cracked much too often to my peace of mind.

It was hard to communicate with words, but we found a way through gestures. Despite the unfamiliar setting, a sense of belonging comforted me, somehow!

An old man, probably the elder amongst them, decided to give me his attention finally. He turned to me a face burned by the Sun and wrinkled by age. He gazed at me with deep brown eyes. These eyes, which seemed to have seen a lot, weighed me for a moment before he uttered in a profound tone, "I will tell you the story of the crying Spirits."

Startled, I gawked at him, mysteriously comprehending the language he talked. Fascinated, I waited anxiously for him to impart to me what he had to say. I felt inexplicable tranquility and peace of mind.

"It all started when Earth fell from Heaven!" The old man pointed his finger up to the sky and nodded. "The Sky wept in silence, for it had lost one child. It tried to get it back, but the Baby Earth floated away, wandering in the long and wide distance of space. At that time, Earth was naked, lonely, and feeling cold, but the Spirit of Fire gave it warmth. This fire, which we are burning now, is a ritual we perform to keep the heat alive on the soil of Earth when the Sun is at rest."

Kindliness embraced me as I stared at the burning fire in appreciation of its compassionate offering of itself.

"The Spirit of Water cried so much that it fell to Earth from the sky above. The water in this oasis is nothing but a few drops of tears. We drink from it to survive," he added. "Here, have some from this cup!" he stretched his long generous hand towards me.

I wanted to tell him that I just drank from the well, but he insisted with focused eyes. Therefore, I drank again with delight from that water in recognition of the love it comprised. With only one potion, and I vanquished my thirsty soul. Its taste much more soothing and refreshing than the water I drank from the well.

"The Spirit of Sand," he continued, "resides in the stars that adorn the Celestial Kingdom. They are shiny dots in the dark-blue sky, writing our fate akin to the grains of sand marking our footsteps along the path of life. And the trees . . . Oh, they are the link, the cords that join Earth with Heaven. They are the *Trees of Life*. Their fruits are the food that makes us differentiate good from evil. The dust of the sky fell on Earth and became the seeds that grew up as trees." He sighed deeply. "Behold that truth . . . and remember it at all times," he concluded with eloquence.

Immediately after that, I felt the strong presence of the spirits of nature within me. The scorpions and serpents that crawled nearby could not harm me, for the spirits of the Sahara inhabited them too. And the night took me by its cover.

I woke up early the next morning only to realize they were already gone and so proceeded with my journey alone again, traveling across the distances. I headed North. The sea extended in front of my eyes, calmly, reflecting the Sun light through little white spots dispersed on the surface.

The shore that I reached resembled considerably the ancient city of Gebel that I know very much. Temples and great monuments stood impressively under the glorious Sun. A few artisans worked with impressive energy on a splendid Sarcophagus of white limestone. I came closer to admire a beautiful engraving of a King on his sphinx throne welcoming seven people into his Royal hall. At the rim, one of the artisans finished an inscription in Phoenician letters.

The sunlight became too bright all of a sudden, sparkling one letter, *Daleth*, the 4th of the Phoenician Alphabet, into my eyes.

With a fast-spinning movement, it absorbed me!

4.
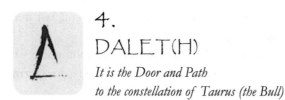

DALET(H)

*It is the Door and Path
to the constellation of Taurus (the Bull)*

Dawn surged on me. The awkward path I walked stretched ahead of me toward a rocky mountain. The farther I walked, the narrower the path became. The Sun rose from behind the mountain, preceding me above.

It was hot, and the Mountain was high, yet lightness lifted me to the top. I felt free like a bird. An amazing sensation of flying dwelt in my soul. The screech of an Eagle, or a Phoenix, I could not tell, echoed in the valley below. My eyes searched in the sky and found him gliding freely in his pace, his sharp eyes on me. He was living proof of *freedom* I longed for, a reminder, a conscious awakening that seemed to be unreachable as long as I sustained my physical form. I was only human!

I could have stayed for ages there, enjoying the exaltation of those rare moments and the purity of the air at that high altitude. However, the powerful call of the exploration road impelled me to proceed. I followed my instincts, there, wherever the spirit of the Alphabet leads me. Soon, I found myself descending the other side of the mountain. Halfway through, I encountered a natural spring of water, so abundant that it cascaded down on the vertically hanging rocks and toward the valley below to form the most beautiful waterfall ever.

I lingered in admiration and contemplation until a light flashed strongly on my eyes. I tried to detect the source and noted something like a mirror on the far distance, reflecting the Sun toward me. The mirror sparkled again. Puzzled, I decided to hunt it down. Hiking down such a steep mountain meant to pull back my body against the power of gravitation that could pull me to the abyss . . . at every step along the way.

I moved cautiously. I then trekked through a long narrow path, shoving, as I moved, the tree branches that stooped from both sides. The muddy ground restrained my advance, and my feet were sinking to the ankles. But I persisted, more determined than ever, braced by the sense of adventure toward the unknown.

Or was it the spirit of the Alphabet? I wondered.

Hours later, when the road seemed endless, and the day gradually turned into night, dusk tinting nature with more splendors, I shoved away the last tree branches and came to a standstill.

There, in front of my eyes, stood in all its magnificence, a monument of two Purple and Golden pillars. A large stone *connected them* from the top to form a *perfect square.*

What was it? I marveled at the sight of it.

It's a Door . . . I reasoned.

A weird kind of sound echoed inside me and, glimpsing at the surroundings, I knew, from the expression of awareness on my astounded face, that I have rather received an inner message than a sound.

I breathed in!

5.
HEH

It is the window of Revelation and Inspiration,
related to the Aries constellation (the Ram)

Herald bizarre voices met me from the very first steps I made into the unknown. Powerful energy filled me as I started to inhale a different kind of air.
It was unfamiliar, almost peculiar, the feeling that inhabited me once I crossed
the threshold. Mysterious textures tinted the unusual forms and shapes of the
surrounding existence.

I was in a different world and dimension, so I thought, and there was
something rather unclear in that wide space stretching all around me. Voices
echoed everywhere, and an aroma like the one never smelled before seemed to
have entered my nostrils, almost elevating my senses.

Quite understandably, the concealed nature of this world puzzled me to
the very last neurons circulating in my brain.

Was it hostile or peaceful? Demonic, or angelic? I ignored its nature.

Yet, despite the strong hesitation that has been building up in my mind, I
pursued the path with will and determination, wanting to know; an awkward,
dull and delusional path at first. Then, it soon changed into something else,
something straight, alive and real, I suppose, for the nearby running river enticed the very fabric of my imagination that fast became openly receptive to the
odd vibrations in the air I thus breathed.

"The wilderness of the Egyptian desert?" I mumbled under my healthy
breathing, deep inside my awakening realm.

A time holy books and correct history had registered in the collective memories of nations!

I continued my journey into unknown voices and veiled revelations of
hidden messages, traipsing on the cracks of long-time dried soil. Suddenly, at
a crossroad, to the right, a light kindled from a tree, a Cedar or Acacia, I could
not tell then, but it blazed before a young man. I stopped to watch and listen in
fascination, or was it in disbelief!

His name resonated vaguely but sounded like it was meant to announce
him as a certain Thot-Taautus sailing from the land of the Phoenix, where he
was known as Enoch-Thor. Then the sweet voice whispered into my ears with
such delight at the sight of the *Angel of Peace*, coming to me in the body of a

Ram, taking a stand still under the tree, as it introduced itself, saying softly, "I am the way".

I, therefore, embraced the vision!

6.
VAU

It is the material gain and the attraction of the physical, nailing man to Earth

Venturing again through a labyrinth of another world, more eccentric this time and full of unexpected meanings and encounters, an imperfect square-like shape caught me hardly, switching back and forth into an imperfect triangle-like shape. Harsh creaking and crunching sounds echoed in my ears from the very first moment I entered that unknown world, that geometrical imperfection. Powerful energy filled me as it vibrated from Earth and pulled me strongly with a remarkable power of *magnetism*, from which I felt I could not escape, at least for now!

Then I began to inhale the air that surrounds me with great difficulty. It was disturbing, almost overloading the feeling that haunted my being. Undoubtedly, I was unwillingly engrossed into a dissimilar dimension, in a world I thought I saw before, but there was something shadowy in the wide space unfolding ahead of me and around me. Peculiar sounds echoed everywhere, and a smell never sensed before painfully entered my nostrils, almost suffocating me.

Not so understandably, the hidden nature of this world dumbfounded me to the very last neurons running chaotically inside my brain.

Was it hostile, demonic? I was not sure, but the nature of its mysterious textures and colors transformed the natural forms and shapes of the surrounding existence.

I came to a sudden halt, thinking, calculating before I decided to pursue the path with strong hesitation again, an awkward, dull, and delusional path that didn't change this time like in the previous vision, for there was no river running nearby to entice my imaginative and perceptive faculties for the reception of the vibrational air, but rather a dry, burning atmosphere.

"The wilderness of the Egyptian desert! Again?" I doubted it as I muttered under my smothering breath, trying to survive the traction.

A time religious books and fake history had registered in the collective memories of nations!

I continued my journey into the world of concealed revelations, traipsing on the cracks of long-time dried soil. At a crossroad, the same one, but to the left this time, a fire kindled from a bush before an old man. I stopped to watch and listen in uncertainty!

His name was Moses, so it groaned forcefully in my ears, and the bush introduced itself, "I am what I am."

I stood in disbelief, rather doubts!

Consequently, and in a more chaotic manifestation of the invisible, I found myself treading through a simulated virtual yet substantial pattern of space— an imperfect square-triangle. Inside this shape, people congregated in unruly movements, trading, negotiating, making deals, and breaking them; sort of a marketplace. Some expressed satisfaction, others greediness. Selling and buying represented the two faces of the same coin, and everybody there tossed the coins and increased possession. The blind force of money dominated them.

"We have the best oxen in the field," a trader announced loudly. "We have the best sheep too!"

"Come on! Get closer and change your money here!" Somebody shouted from his corner to my left. "We can lend you money if you want. And, we'll keep your interest secure," he added with a mischievous grin.

"We'll give you an eighteen days credit," another man at the next booth offered at the top of his raucous voice. "If we reach a deal, we'll give you six more days to pay back your debt, with just a bit higher interest rate."

"Don't worry," his partner assured stridently. "All that we care for is really your comfort."

More people gathered and directly engaged in that insatiable system of traders' and customers' devious needs, expressing voracious thirsts and im-moderate hungers for more and more gain. Incited by the amount of generated profits, I stood in line for my turn, longing for my profitable deal. Greed that seemed to stream in their veins and the selfishness that controlled their minds have invaded me.

Coins piled up on the palms of the dealers while their eyes rolled left and right with an impish gleam, attentive to grab all opportunities and keep control of the generating process. Skillful, shrewd, they never lost to their customers, presiding on the monetary reign. I tempted to engage, but in vain, in that battle of profit and power. Overwhelmed by greediness, that instinct of survival and control that prevailed in humanity, I struggled for more, thus more power to grant me immunity against extinction. Fear played me!

Yet I failed!

I moved on to the next booth where a richly attired trader has begun selling his jewelry. A young, pretty woman stopped to negotiate a deal, selling her offer with seductive sensuality. Her tricks failed to achieve for the jeweler proved to be a shrewd trader. He succeeded in convincing her of the great importance of the precious necklace she wanted. At hearing it belonged to an ancient Hebrew Queen, whom she physically resembled, the young woman did not hesitate and, with joyful excitement, fell in the trap of the vicious mind of the dishonest trader. She bought the necklace, willingly manipulated by her *ego* to possess it no matter what.

"We sell doves . . . we sell doves . . . ," an old, skinny man called out from behind a booth jammed with birdcages.

A few meters to his left, a colorful crowd stood at a bakery booth. Amidst the mass appeared a thin woman, almost gaunt. She stretched out her hand for a piece of bread. The baker turned his eyes away, disdaining her, and busied himself in attending to others. She was very poor, her clothes worn out. For how long could he neglect her, standing in front of his face like a pitiful ghost? Her eyes lifeless, she remained immobile like a statue, her hand begging for a pity that would not come.

Later, when all the clients were gone, he had no choice but to give her some attention, "No more bread . . . we're closed for today!" His dry tone rebuffed her in glacial conceit.

Her response came unexpectedly. She sprinted at once toward him, snatched him a piece of bread, and ran away, leaving the marks of her nails bleeding in the hands of the outraged baker.

Suddenly, a man, the *Son of Man*, draped all in white, stepped firmly into that imperfect shape. With a fascinating authority, he shoved out, from the Temple, all those traders of oxen, sheep, and doves. Marching angrily by the fiscal dealers, he hurled their counters to the floor with a strange lightness.

His voice intonated, "It is written: *My house shall be called a house of prayer*, but you have made it a den of robbers! You've made it imperfect!"

Then, he turned and stared at me, smiled and said, "The true battle for survival in this world is not material, not for, or by, the money, but by prayers, compassion, love, and peace; a spiritual victory, my brother." He paused for a thought. "The road is awkward and long, but don't be afraid," he added. "Truth shall always prevail."

The sweet tone of his voice reverberated still in my ears for a long time after he disappeared.

I smiled in hope!

7.
ZAYIN

*It is glory taken by the sword, war,
connected to Planet Mars*

Zazae'il . . . Zaza'el . . . A name roared again and repeatedly from the small
Mount Hellion standing ahead. A black bird flew over it; most probably a crow,
for Phoenixes and Eagles only flew over High Mountains. In his flight, the
black crow directed me to the top of Mt. Hellion.

The air I breathed was different there, both cheering and tempting. I sensed
its power in my head and body. In my veins, it mingled with my blood to boost
me with incredible energy. My eyes browsed all around and opened to worlds
beyond. Somewhere within that space, the crow screeched louder and louder.
The distances ahead stretched beyond my field of vision. The cities, which
nestled in the wide plains below, hypnotized me.

I felt like a King in search of his Queen, tempted by kingdoms that would
lead my mind astray, and the wind blew hard on my face, forcing me to close
my hungry eyes. Then immediately, a voice, powerful as the sound of a *trumpet,*
emerged from nowhere else but from my fragile soul. It whispered right onto
my ears, "Your wishes, made here on top of Hellion, can be accomplished
down there within the walls of those cities. These kingdoms will be yours if you
listen to me. I am Azazel, and I tell you, behold the glory among the livings."

"Oh! But how can I have that glory?" I automatically questioned the voice.
"How can I become a King, and I am only an ordinary man?" I asked, though
with excitement, speaking to that inner voice with such eagerness.

"The key to the city gates is within the power of your sword. The taste of
victory is as sweet as honey," the voice decreed with a seductive tone.

"Uh, but . . . holding the sword against these people! They are not my
enemies!"

"Of course! You don't have to have enemies to be victorious, but since you
strongly desire to be a King now, that would be the fastest way, my dear fellow,"
the voice argued all too softly, all too mesmerizingly.

"I, therefore, think I need an army!" I put forward, wondering with some
growing determination.

"Then, follow me . . . March to it . . . Glory is waiting!"

We beheld each other, and, without hesitation, I conformed to the imperative call of the voice as I scampered down the steep mountain of Hellion in a swiftness that felt mysteriously easy and light. My heartbeats matched my thrill of conquest. Draped in animal skin and fur and crowned with a horned helmet, I galloped down toward these cities like a fearsome warrior. I carried my sword. For this lethal war to power, I adhered to the black flag of crossed bones underneath the skull of death.

More and more warriors joined me, suddenly and unexpectedly, from all sides, carrying old-time weapons like swords, knives, spears, axes, and shields forged from the metals of the earth made known to them by Azazel. Clothed in suits of breastplates, bows, and arrows on their backs, they appeared like demons who just crawled out from under the rocks. The mad gallop of my horse, pounding the ground, must have awakened them to tag along. No more than a few miles away from the city gates, we roared like ferocious animals and thrashed our horses forward.

Drums of war hit harder and faster, enticing our evil instincts for killing and destroying. In no time, the city gates took fire and then shattered to the floor in pieces. We raided the city with terrific force. With no mercy whatsoever, we vandalized, burned, and slaughtered whatever stood in our way. We destroyed houses and razed them to ashes. We stabbed people of all ages or beheaded them. There was no difference, for we were not able to focus on the gravity of our animosity. The blood in our veins pumped in tremendous fierceness, our hearts banged at the rhythm of the drums, and our twisted minds relished in our bravery; cold and immune from any human feelings.

Eventually, our savage raid conquered the first city, but greed conquered us as well! My covetous eyes searched beyond the city walls to comply with *glory* that craved for more. And more was on the way, as I summoned my army, those demons who heard my raging voice and the pounding gallop of my horse. We then resumed our invasion through the gates of other cities, demolishing habitations, temples and exterminating lives.

However, each time we raided a new city, we encountered more challenges and stronger resistance from the citizens, alerted by the fast-spreading news of the imminent danger. Yet, we won a battle after another, creating more enemies along that path. A war I'm winning in the name of the *awaiting glory!*

Time ceased.

The heat of my cold-blooded heart cooled down. It was a conditioned desire to assess reposefully the aftermaths of the hitherto victory I claimed.

My demons waited for their indemnity. The first thing I felt right to accomplish was declaring myself King over those desperate people who survived and then seeking a Queen to acclaim for my powers.

The ceremony began with the blow of trumpets and the loud beats of the drums. Around me stood some of my demons, and next to me sat the Queen I gained on a throne I made for her mounting pleasure and ambitions after I ornamented myself with a golden crown and enthroned myself on a golden seat, staring down at the expressionless faces of the subdued people at my feet.

Somehow, my eyes met the pure sadness in theirs, suddenly reminding me of the destruction I have caused them and the bloodshed I have inflicted upon them. The whole extent of my acts dawned upon me unexpectedly. Tears ran down my cheeks to stop at once by my mastering will to impede that soft part of my human nature. Glory justified the means!

Still, I rule . . . and to increase my power over the people and their minds, I decided I need a religious doctrine, and henceforth, I ordained priests and elected a high priest to serve the deity I now believe in, that bass voice I heard ringing out on Mt. Hellion, coming from inside me—Zazae'il.

Time passed so fast.

Then came a time when I secretly convened with my high priest and asked him how the temple we were to build looked like. He took me to a secret place and invited me inside what he called the *holy of holies*. He told me about a mystery that would yet increase even more my power of control. I accepted his generous offer, for sure. The time arrived when I headed toward an altar he had previously geared up in his secret lodge. He opened an imperfect cubical metal box and, instantly, a geometrical shape materialized in front of my fervid eyes.

"Repeat after me . . . the name of Cheth," the high priest demanded.

I did, and in consequence, *Cheth* shone strongly into my eyes before it shifted my vision toward something else, perhaps something more dominative than what has been given so far, as he had promised.

I smiled in greed!

8.
CHET (H)

It is the Sexual Instinct,
binding humanity to Gemini (the Twins)

Chanting joyfully, a bizarre air floated inside the imperfect cube-like shape that I entered. My steps led me farther ahead to a mass of hundreds of people. I stopped to watch their weird outfits and wondered at once at the trapped expression of their faces as they passed me by. Turning to myself, I startled at my attire, similarly odd!

The women were beautiful, almost sensual, with all that coloring tinctures applied on their faces and hairs. Adorned with bracelets and all kinds of costly stones ornaments, their foreheads showed a strange symbol of an upward triangle. Their eyes blazed like the auburn rays of Sunset contrasted by antimony or mascara, that cosmetic substance used for darkening, lengthening, curling, coloring, thickening, and defining the eyelashes that beautify their eyelids altogether. The men looked strong, perhaps *warriors*, on their foreheads an inverted triangle. From afar, echoes of drumbeats reached to us all gathered there inside that imperfect geometrical shape.

I followed the sound, tumbled down here and there, unaware of my forthcoming destination, yet, conscious of the path framing me and impeding me to return. Barefooted, with peculiar necklaces around their neck, people hummed discordantly as they strolled through that awkward, dull, delusional, and imperfect cubical path.

The line of worshipers extended to the foot of the small Mount Hellion at the steps of an entrance to a temple. It was a small monument constructed with massive flat stones and surrounded by torches that illuminated its walls. The entrance stairs were a bit wide and protected from both sides by two statues, one of a man to the right and another of a woman to the left—the Twins, naked!

"We must build a temple like this one, only bigger this time!" announced the high priest.

Slowly and rhythmically, the drumbeats got through to their very bones.

The ceremony is about to begin. I thought. Suddenly, a strong sound reverberated. People fell to their knees at once, bent forward to the ground, and their hands stretched out in submission. The drums stopped. They could not fathom the meaning of that unfolding scene or the source of that strange sound. Yet, driven by a toxic impulse, they prostrated themselves more and more in homage to a deity they ignored.

As for me, I don't kneel to anyone! My mind exalted. *I am the King of this Kingdom! I only heard the voice that brought me here.* I tried to comfort myself.

At any rate, the system absorbed them, integrating them in its ways and means. It seemed that kneeling and touching the ground was a sacred gesture of the body. It was a way to thank the gods for their imminent generosity. A few moments later, I turned my head and looked up toward the peak of that small mountain above the temple. A statue that was never there before suddenly emerged, showing the twins in embrace, standing under the dark-blue starry sky.

"Celebrate! Oh, people of the city. Celebrate! The gods have listened to the prayers of our King and Queen!" The high priest's authoritative voice summoned from inside the temple and filled my heart and the one of my Queen with joy.

Unexpectedly, an extraordinary shift of events occurred, as I found myself back to my Kingdom escorted by my Queen, golden thrones and crowns, observing the people down from the terrace of my castle. Total control!

They opened up their arms, raised their hands toward the twins, and shook them in a gesture of adoration, swinging their bodies right and left on the musical rhythm that vibrated all around. Both hypnotic and energetic, it combined the alert beating of the drums and the mesmerizing lowest sound of the trumpet. Drums and trumpets were two essential musical instruments used in the culture of some ancient people, and especially in ceremonial kind of ecstatic feats of the bodies. The religious atmosphere, however, soon changed into a crazy dance and intake of drinks. It was indeed a bizarre permutation in the course of things.

Then, they began to share their happiness and express their deepest gratitude for a grace that they would receive from the dualistic nature of the deities they believed in. Moments later, drinking and dancing became punchy. Soon, their ecstatic behavior developed into a state of euphoria and trance as musical rhythms amplified.

Hypnotized by the music, drunk from the excess of wine, and weary from their frantic dancing, they succumbed to the weaknesses invading their minds, spirits, and bodies. Every thought, spiritual elation, and even every *atom* trembled in front of an enchanted desire to lose control. Both women and men beseeched each other, their eyes blazed in a reddish hue, their bodies exhuming sensual magnetism that soon took control. The power of basic instinct heaved them progressively into complete nudity.

From the terrace of my castle, we, I and my Queen relished in the erotic scenes, captivated to the point of forsaking our own rising needs.

Below, men inhaled the hot womanly aroma and rousingly identified their rising and arousing smell of sex. Then, manly hands fondled female breasts, triggering the male perceptive convulsions, and they committed adultery and fornication. Moans of pleasure rose in crescendo to load the atmosphere with heavy vibrations that persisted long after the general climax. Yet, the aftermath did not bring along the satiety their bodies sought. Anarchy prevailed, as basic human instincts edged a primitive, visceral state known to the animal realm. The mass below regained the sexual pulsations that soon rejuvenated their bodies and unleashed them into continual obscene orgies . . .

The world turned and whirled, almost perceptible to me. They fell like feathers to the ground, powerless and forsaken, and on the way to lose contact with their senses. They finally did, dropping down as if paralyzed. A sound, a last moaning of the statue—the twins in embrace—faded and vanished. Their eyes, ajar toward the sky, absorbed the last twinkle of the stars above.

My own special sensual moments with my Queen began in the silence of time that prevailed.

The high priest was right.

Now I rule . . . endlessly!

9.
TET(H)

It is the Serpent of Foundation.
It is the mud; the Organic Earth that blossoms into Life,
linked to the Cancer constellation (the Crab)

The far distance cleared up before my naked eyes to lead me to what looked like a "Circle of Trees." Evergreen grass appeared behind the trees I approached. As I made my first steps into the circumference, the air changed, and oxygen increased. The sound of my feet stomping on the grass cracked within the radius and expanded through the entire Circle. I followed the path to the center, as I noticed that I was not a King! That this was not my kingdom.

Another smaller "circle of trees" emerged ahead. The moment I entered, I gasped at the Old Serpent entwined around an old grey tree in the middle of the circle. The Old Serpent must have felt the vibration of my silent fear for its eyes, yellow and hard, pierced mine and held me in its enchantment. The Eyes showed times, and the look persisted, cautious and in wait as if they rarely met visitors in that Circle.

With steady yet careful steps, I approached farther ahead towards her. Our eyes communicated on a high level of vibrating heat and imponderable light. The Serpent rattled . . .

She might be the mythical, biblical Serpent of the Garden of Eden that would lead me into another temptation—the Devil! I thought. *But the Devil does not exist outside my fragile soul!* I reasoned out for I have seen the previous three visions and somehow felt that I had been now awakened by the changing air and the new oxygen the "Circle of Trees" have finally created for me to breathe and healthily.

The Old Serpent hissed, surprised me with a nod of her head as she welcomed my approach. Encouraged, I drew closer and closer, gathering all too slowly around her, and, captured by her magic charm that held my stares, I waited, just waited for something to happen.

"I'm the Old Serpent of Wisdom and Immortality," a guttural tone of voice came from within her throat, a controversial fusion of velvety yet confident intonations.

Bewildered by her capability to speak, I stuttered as I introduced myself, "I am . . . a traveler . . . on this mysterious . . . path of life."

"I see," she then said, "but how did you get here? Did anybody show you the way to the Circle of Trees?" her voice echoed.

I looked inside me, confused, very confused. In truth, I had no idea how I ended up there. I tried to remember, but suddenly there remained nothing in my memory to remember—total emptiness as if my memory of the previous three visions has been deleted from my system. Somehow, I felt I was born anew with a new fresh memory, ready to record my actions along the path that follows.

"It's not really a problem," the Old Serpent said. "I know how, anyway. There is but one way only . . . the way of the Cancer, also known as the Crab Constellation. I can easily tell by scrutinizing your void mind. It disclosed the way that led you to me, I, the only *Guardian of the Tree of Life.*" The strange words reverberated in my ears like the sound of a waterfall cascading down into my heart.

Naturally, I wanted to know more. I needed more explanation.

"Oh, wise serpent, what shall I do? I am confused, totally lost. What shall I know to continue the Journey?" I pleaded with commendable courage.

The Old Serpent crawled up along the thickly wrinkled Tree and ogled me down. A vault of deep-blue sky beamed over me and framed the enchanted Circle.

"Fellow brother, you should know, deep inside yourself, the Good from Evil!" The Serpent spoke in a sigh and continued, "I tell you, here is the fruit of the Tree of Life. You can eat it and rejoice in its divine taste or spit it out to the muddy ground if you find it infected with worms or poisonous smell and taste. You should bear in mind all along the journey, a sense of *will* that keeps you vigilant, and a sense of perseverance that allows you to find *faith* in the Kingdom of Heaven." She took a very long breath that sounded like an eternity.

"I've been around for years . . . , centuries . . . , millenniums . . . , teaching the same principles, over and over again, to all those who have walked inside the Circle. Heed out . . . ," her hypnotizing voice paused for a while, then uttered in exultation, "Very few have entered the Circle, and much fewer of those had succeeded in triumphing over the temptations and illusions of the phenomenal world. Very few, yes I know, have reigned the right Kingdom and sat on the right throne, the seat of knowledge, and worn the crown of immortality."

The words navigated forcefully through the air to penetrate my soul and knock on my doors of intuitive and inspirational energies. In her timeless sagacity, the Old Serpent have detected a *True Seeker* of wisdom in me, read my enthusiasm and perseverance, and felt my strong *will* and *faith* in belonging and becoming what I really am. *But am I what she thinks I am?* I wondered in the stillness of my mind.

"Wake up from your deep sleep . . . oh, little god; don't be a traveler, but rather a pilgrim on this mysterious path of life, and behold the *ascension* has begun!"

A sweet melodious sound of a flute reverberated around the Circle following that announcement. I gathered even closer like a neophyte around a Hierophant in an *Initiatic* Temple. Inspired, I revealed in my true nature—*divine nature*.

The Old Serpent possessed powerful breathing, swift moves, impressive power of maneuvering, and a weird body modulation; all based on her substance of Fire.

"Watch out, man of Earth! Do not waste the Fire, the Spiritual Energy that resides inside you, on fake kingdoms of greed for money, glory by the power of the sword, and sexual energy—those instinctive un-evolved desires haunting your frail body, and which there arose much godlessness. Instead, I tell you, elevate the Fire, bit by bit, through the double helix, the seven elliptic spiral levels along your spine, starting at the base and ending up at the top. Open those doors of perception, one by one, and behold at last the crown of the *Godhead!*" she inhaled deeply and then exhaled noisily.

Her capabilities to read my mind astonished me, as did the acknowledgment of my admiration toward her breath of Fire. Yet, those words intrigued me. I may win the battle over the greed for money and power, but it was not at all easy for my *Adamic* earthly body to refrain from sexual delights, as I had suddenly remembered and came to recognize that I had been given my body to enjoy . . . life!

"Enjoy it!" The guttural velvety voice suddenly exclaimed. "You are actually *free* to do whatever you want, but, since you have entered the "Circle of Trees," you must then abide by its rules. Oh, my child, know that the Demiurge is already crowned. Yes! Heshe governs as a deity in the lower regions of the self and strives to defy and thwart the plans of the Godhead. *HeShe* brings shame to the Higher Self and curses the name of the Most High."

"I," the Old Serpent rattled, "was looked upon as divine, by the great Enoch-Thor-Taautus-Thot-Hermes, the first Kabbir, because of my healing powers and my words of wisdom. I say, you decide what to do, but bear in mind that I have defeated time. I am *Agathodaemon*, the Good Spirit, standing at the center of the Circle. I move the world!" The Old Serpent uttered her final words.

Hypnotized by those powerful golden eyes and thrilled by those deep words entering my entire being, I recognized in her substance of Fire and Wisdom, the *Ancient Guardian* of the "Tree of Life." Under it lay the organic basis of Earthly life. With it were safely kept the foundations of Knowledge, and above it, flapped freely the wings of Eternity.

The Old Serpent tightened her body around the tree's trunk and branches and squeezed hard for her old, worn-out coat to tear away. A new bright skin appeared to make her look younger and more vivid. It was a clear testimony that life never began, nor would it end beating in the heart of the Serpent that has defeated time again . . . as she had stated. She would certainly get older by time and, till then, would remain at the center of the *Circle of Trees*, waiting for some neophytes to come along to blow divine whispers in their ears and for a new cycle to begin.

Mine has just begun!

10.
YOD(H)

It is the Hand,
connected to the Water element

Yellow leaves fell plentifully, in front of my eyes, from a line of trees at the edge of a majestic mountain. It was a little bit chilly. I gazed at the mountain and admired its strength. The bountiful trees enhanced its natural beauty. Somehow, something in the air I breathed alerted me that my destination would not end there where my eyes reached. I turned around to look at the few grey clouds that hovered in a slow movement and then changed, bit by bit, into some sort of abstract images. I realized that some kind of a natural half-amphitheater framed me. I made a few steps forward until I reached the edge of the line of trees.

I looked downward. There was not much depth in what my eyes perceived, but rather a small valley, reposing peacefully underneath. With not much effort, as if carried by a smooth gravity, I drifted down the walkway to my right. No more than a few meters onward, my feet touched a flat surface. My walk became steady, but the way seemed long. The air was different, the ambiance over the valley a bit mysterious. Something hidden lurked in wait. I felt it. The peculiar forms of rocks, and the weird vegetation above the grey-white soil, reinforced my sensation.

I pondered on the unfamiliar selection of the non-organic and organic species, which nature has produced around this place. The aroma filling the air entered my nostrils smoothly, and alerted my mind to a pure presence of an *Angelic* order. It smelled like burnt incense in sacred places—incense burnt for the Divine; that unseen power which resided behind the *manifested* world of forms. Moments of silence and stillness passed like a memory of mystic awakening of my triune nature.

The twittering of birds, the flying of butterflies, and the echoing of breath in my depths reminded me of the long path. With a peaceful mind, a sense of elation in my spirit, and a serene tranquility in my heart, I resumed my walk with a subtle smile on my face. Strangely, I never felt tired, and sensed nearing my goal.

Time . . . time was running so fast, like shadows of human forms, moving actively under the Sun. And it transpired when I finally saw a group of people dressed all in white, walking in a procession and reciting some unknown hymns, in exquisite harmony. I followed them as they led the way. My walk behind them did not break their linear configuration, nor did it distort their apotheosis rhythm. For a minute or two, I thought they were aliens to this world. A few seconds later, I began to think that I have met them at an invisible intersection of both worlds—theirs, the beyond, and mine!

Could they be an order of Angels, which have just stumbled down to Earth, or simply jumped at will? Could their mission be to show me the way, back or forth, yet, safely to the shore of true life? Would they lead me to the point of no return and the determined point of confirmation? Those were the thoughts that tingled the depth of my mind.

Then, a few steps ahead, I ceased caring about their identity and intention, for a great feeling of peace and wonder besieged me when we arrived at the ridge of a picturesque lake. It was there when they turned and gazed into my eyes. Their faces glowed with striking transparency that it became almost hard to discern their facial features.

Up in the sky, white clouds glided smoothly toward me, from above the majestic mountain. With delicate gestures of the hands, the people in white invited me to enter the lake. In a spontaneous reflex, I stepped back.

"Don't be afraid . . . and do not hesitate. This is the *Lake of Remembrance*. Water is an element of love and compassion!" A serene watery voice resonated in that wilderness, but I didn't know from where it came. Maybe it didn't come from any one of them. Perhaps it came from a higher sphere. They then reverted to the lake and entered the water with great devotion. My eyes followed them, only to lose contact with them a few seconds later.

Maybe, they were Angels, after all! I marveled at the idea.

After a second thought, I went into the water. I did not want to disappear like them but rather to emerge back clean, both physically and spiritually. It was a wish, a strong desire to remember my spiritual essence, in an eternal moment which I have always longed to affirm!

Immerged to the waist in the water, I opened my eyes and raised my hands to the sky in a religious act. Released from bonds and restraints, I floated up to the surface. Up in the sky, a white cloud, among many, changed its shape progressively into what looked like an open hand, and unexpectedly, poured rain over my head.

A sound was then heard coming from the heavens above it, uttering strange words that I kept remembering for so long. That same serene watery voice I heard before says again, "I am Rapha'el, the Healing Angel of the Ancient of Days, I surely testified on your behalf before our Father El, and asked for divine intervention upon your soul. Granted, I tell you now, liberate yourself, human!"

I closed my eyes as I kept repeating his name over and over again, totally rejoiced yet, perplexed. *An Angel just came to me?* I asked myself.

I then smiled in freedom!

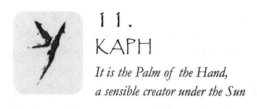

11.
KAPH

It is the Palm of the Hand,
a sensible creator under the Sun

Keeping my smile intact, I opened my eyes, and through that whirlwind of light, I heeded the silhouette of a Human Being in front of me. In a defensive reflex, I stepped back awkwardly. Fast enough, he grabbed my hand firmly in his and hauled me back to him, impeding my fall into the void behind me. I could not retrieve my hand from the warm and friendly touch of his. Swathed in a long white robe, purple mantle across his shoulders, head concealed by a hood, his countenance almost dazzled me, as did the sensation of great mystery enfolding him.

"Fear not! I'm the Guardian of the Sacred Alphabet," he introduced himself in a magisterial tone that left no doubt in me of his magnificence. All too slowly, he released my hand.

I grew thoughtful and pulled myself together. He took the hood off his head, and his face glittered in front of my eyes, commending them for witnessing an amazing halo.

A long moment of silence followed as I gawked at him in awe. His eyes, pure as crystal, were deeply set, revealing a gaze, keen as fire.

"I've been watching you ever since the first vision of the first letter of the Alphabet, but somehow I knew you'd be among the very few who would continue the journey," he stated firmly and quietly.

"Some people may be too busy for this journey. Others may feel just frightened to engross in it," I felt the need to defend the human race and excuse their general retreat from the world of mysteries. "They may think they would disturb the dormant spirits of the Ancients by invoking the letters of their hidden names. They may also think the spirits would cause them pain or death!"

"But you . . . you didn't think the way they did. That is why you came back to your original self and invoked the name of the first sacred Letter. Isn't that true?" The question needed not an answer, as it appeared to me that he knew all too well. I simply nodded.

"Well, honestly, I had my doubts for a certain period. I did speculate that the Alphabet may cause pain or death should I disturb its occult realm, but since these are only speculations based on unfounded superstitions, I then rejected the idea completely. Something strange, however, actuated my mind and guided me back. That's true," I then confessed with a rare humbleness.

My mind tried hard to recall the essential thing that *paved the way for me* deep inside my very soul. I could not remember. Perhaps the water in the *Lake of Remembrance* washed away everything, but that was contradictorily confusing. The moment I intended to ask him about it, he preceded me with a tranquil penetrating voice, "It was the spirit of Enoch-Thor, the inventor of the Alphabet, that has summoned you to be present in his realm."

An extraordinary radiance deepened the corner of his eyes. It made me tremble, not from fear, of course, but in astonishment. *Who am I anyway, that the spirit of Thot, the Master of the Alphabet, would be pleased to receive as a neophyte!* I wondered. *Who am I that the Healing Angel Rapha'el would testify on my behalf before our Father El and ask for divine intervention upon my soul!* I mulled over the various possibilities.

Who am I?

With a delicate gesture of his right hand, he invited me to walk with him through an enchanting display of nature's most beautiful sceneries. Farther ahead, he abandoned his leisurely pace, and his walk became more decisive as if he intended to subdue the Earth element under his feet. For the lightness in which he traipsed resulted not from the soft wind blowing on our faces but rather from the serenity that exalted his being. The profound silence that accompanied us across the fields helped me reflect deeply on the nobility of his character.

To my amazement, we approached the *Lake of Remembrance,* and I came to recall almost everything, bit by bit, the previous vision and the strange disappearance of the people in white in that same body of water. Standing at the edge of the lake, I wondered why the Guardian had brought me back there. At once, images of their glowing faces flashed with striking transparency in my inner mind and shook me in dread as I began to discern their facial features. Something that was almost impossible to do when I first met them on that invisible intersection of our two worlds.

"You presumed the people in white disappeared just like that, but they did not. They are the *Spirit(s) of Water,* and the lake always regenerates their memory for the newcomers!" His voice, fast as the speed of light, vibrated in ripples on the surface of the lake.

"The Sun!" He raised the palm of his hand to the sky and appeared to hold with it the shining disc, so to speak. "Remember that, my brother, every time you feel the spirit of Taautus-Hermes summoning you, come to me. I'll always be waiting for you. From now on, use the name *Kadmus* as your password to cross the hidden bridge linking both our worlds."

"Kadmus! Oh, I've heard of that Kabbir. He was a very distinguished person from the remote past. He brought the Alphabet to Greece and changed its rhythm forever. Do you know him?" I asked in excitement.

He loomed over, his face bright as the sun he hid with his majestic height, his stares piercing my eyes with a smart flicker, and the words came so close to my ears, so warm to my heart.

"I am Kadmus!"

His voice vibrated like the blissful sound of an ancient bell.

And I heard it well!

12.

LAMED(H)

*It is the Teaching and Learning by the power of the Scepter,
under the constellation of Leo*

Legendary Kadmus was real indeed, standing there with all his glory, the way I recalled him from the previous vision; same long white tunic draping his tall height, and same purple mantle across his shoulders. This time, he held a wooden Scepter in his hand and watched me approaching him cautiously, a peaceful smile on his face.

Our eyes met with the transparency known only to knowledgeable mates, and we shook hands in a brotherly manner.

With no words needed to be said, he turned and led the way through the fields of olive trees, beset by the quivering silver blue of the ether. The man was impressive, even in his silence. His overall attitude proclaimed a personality of great determination and profound knowledge.

We paused at a Cedar tree perched on the top of a high hill. The Guardian struck his Scepter on the ground. He pointed his finger at the wide sky, as if searching a map, then halted at the *Constellation of the Lion*. He turned to stare into my eyes and nodded. With no words still but the silent communication of our minds, we sat to rest at the feet of the Cedar, under the shadowing branches. I watched him; his eyes beamed with a new great light to reflect the memory of a glorious moment that seemed to have crossed his mind.

"God created the Universe with the great power of Love," he began his tutoring. "Life started on Earth after being first planned in the mind of the *Father*; however, the Demiurge broke the divine chain between the Father and the Children. Different animal species strolled through the Earth, and the most intelligent among them all evolved into Humanity. Inhabited by the *spirit group*, a blind primary power, men and women walked the path together, forming with their children the early structure of human tribes.

"They looked up in a vertical direction and saw the majesty of the sky. Then, they looked down in a horizontal direction and beheld life here on Earth. *What's that?* They first wondered. Life and death preoccupied their minds, days and nights. They refused to surrender to death, for they have loved life. Nature, however, frightened them the most. They erected monoliths, gave godly names to the powers they worshiped, and asked for Salvation!" He paused for a breath and added, "they ask still."

His words challenged my thirst for more knowledge as I could not swerve my attention away from him. A shadow slithered behind him and dimmed the sunlight for a few seconds.

Was it a memory of dark hours crossing his mind? I could not tell.

As a window to the past, the crystal ball or was it the eye of the Phoenix, at the head of the Scepter, that projected into my scope of vision recurring images of the History of Man, a long history that seemed to have passed by all life's occurrences one may think of, by those difficult to imagine, or/and by others even hard to perceive. Two serpents wrapped the crystal eye in a spiral form, their heads up toward the sky.

Again, silence prevailed, and for the *third time*, since I first met him holding that wooden Scepter in his hand. This time, he came to mentor me. A very important lesson I must heartedly appreciate for the time being.

Silence!

Kadmus appeared plunged into a deep meditation himself. As for me, I let my hands laze in the cool shadow of the Cedar tree.

And waited . . . impatiently!

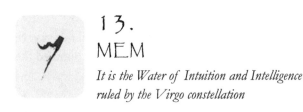

13.
MEM

It is the Water of Intuition and Intelligence
ruled by the Virgo constellation

Moving down my eyes, I proceeded in between infinite lines of trees, probably one large Oak forest. I was alone, yet unafraid since Kadmus had shown me the way, the way to *Virgo*. I stopped instantly. The Moon light seeped through branches and yellowish-green leaves to beam upon the circle of worshippers. They appeared like shadows of forgotten ancestors haunting my memory.

I then resumed my steady walk towards the path that bridged over the river water. A mysterious silhouette appeared to me on the other side. Shafts of moonlight bathed the symmetrical female form in an aura of splendor. A soft breeze wafted her long white robe, not enough to nudge the blue hood that concealed her face.

From my side of the bridge, two sturdy men in short trousers and sandals played some exotic beats on big tambours touching the ground. *Could it be some sort of a ritual ceremony of an ancient female cult?* I wondered.

When the music stopped seconds later, she uncovered her face and talked in such a serene voice that would elevate human souls, "Welcome all around here, to the *Kadosh River*, the Sacred River of life. I'm Anat-Astarte, the Mother-Goddess of Love." After proclaiming herself in such a superior style, a great vibrating light encircled her being, revealing a beautiful faultless face.

Believers bowed their heads in awe and veneration. They then murmured some strange undetected dialect of words while they knelt and prayed. Bald men and black-draped women wept; women beat their chests with their fists, lamenting the death of Adon, the sacred Lover of the goddess they now beheld. His blood flowed fast down the River and reddened the colorless water.

At some point along the running River, an extraordinary phenomenon occurred. Every drop of blood assembled and blended with the other elements of nature to bloom into a scarlet anemone, the *Naaman* flower. The magical powers of the goddess, forced by her divine Love to her Lover, worked on resurrecting the dead god into a new shape, that of a flower, which fragrance entered our realms at once.

"I'm the *Virgin Lady*. I pour Peace over your heads and multiply Love in your hearts. Fear not death, for the tears of Love had finally vanquished. The god has been resurrected, and a new life has begun."

Within the mist that embraced her while uttering these words, she disappeared. She was gone, leaving behind her hopes in the bosom of the fields. Men, one after the other, approached the Riverbank, picked up a flower, and offered them to their beloved women who took off their black tunics and threw them unto the River. *They appeared wanting to fall naked in the arms of men.*

"Stop!" The serene voice from the mist authoritatively vibrated all around. The silhouette of the Virgin Lady reappeared, somehow unclear to most, yet of similar features. She might have something to add before she disappears totally. "Can't you just wait?" She admonished the believers. "I'm sending you my child, my only son, to save you. God, your *Father,* has asked me to perform that miracle. I do on his commands, and you . . . you should follow his son's path. In a few moments, he'll be with you."

The full moon edged the horizon and radiated its last rays on the water surface. The River pursued its course under the bridge but on a lower sound this time! The yellowish-green leaves swung softly back and forth at the game of a cool breeze of autumn. The musical rustle that ensued strongly echoed in my ears. I bet it echoed in everyone's ears that night.

A wolf howled from up a hill, repeatedly. His cry resonated almost everywhere, in all directions. Little by little, the moon faded away behind him and into the darkness of space. I turned to leave when indistinct voices reached me and halted my move with their peculiarity. They sounded like cryptic words, a language that seemed to be secluded in the past, or maybe in the future! How should I know?

But then again, they might be the voices of those who were by the *Kadosh River*, the believers in a new life! *Something must have happened tonight!* I thought as the wind whooshed so strong that it broke the daunting silence. Then, a breeze tapped me gently on the face. I turned my head and caught the unexpected sight of Kadmus standing at my side with a loving smile on his face.

"You had a trip into divine space!" He declared.

"The Lady I saw on the other side of the River was so pure and holy. Her words were so sweet, seeping smoothly into my ears. I never felt much of a spiritual presence like this before," I spoke with warmth and faith.

"Your feelings are so true, I think. She is the Mother-Goddess Anat, Astarte, Isis, Ishtar, Giaia, and who appeared in almost all religions on Earth.

Humans have attributed many other names to her, as well. She pours Love into the trembled hearts. She did so to Adon, Osiris, Bel, Zeus, and many others who were her Lovers. Thus, she became the bearer of the child—*the chosen child!*" The Guardian explained considerately.

Within that entire mystical ambiance, I heard the long whispers of the Intellect, creating in me a sense of wonder about the divine child to be born. And I mystically came to understand the very differences of intimate human relations. Women and Men can join in for Sexual intercourse only for the pleasures of the flesh. In contrast, they can also join in divine union, akin Love for the creation of life, and not any other life, but a conscious life forged inside the womb, a warm aquatic ambiance, like the *Lake of Remembrance!*

"Do you believe in her?" He curiously asked.

"I believe in Love, and in the child, she pours into the trembling hearts."

There was silence in the time that followed, which made me see things differently. It somehow opened my mind to the meaning of conscious life, the kind of cosmic life we should all embrace coming out from the *Divine Matrix.*

The new revelation of Kadmus has smoothed every atom in my body, upraised every thought in my mind, and intensified every bit of energy circulating in my spirit. The Lady, say, the Queen of Heaven, seemed to have created in me an impression of considerable strength.

I might have the chance to meet and see her son, the chosen child! I thought.

"Look, my brother," Kadmus said. "In life, there are two kinds of men birthed by the Matrix. There are those and are the majority, who live an ordinary life as *sons of men*, and there are those born specifically from the divine part of the Matrix to become *Sons of God.* Let me show you."

The Guardian rose his Scepter up toward the sky, moved it all around, and created a certain shape in the air. He seemed to have written a letter . . . *Nun,* the 14th one of the Sacred Phoenician Alphabet. Its magnetic light rapidly took me through a voyage into the Heart of Mysteries.

I dived in joy!

14.
NUN

It is the Fish springing out of the Water,
like the Child of Prophecy for the continuation of Time, manifested under
Libra

Night surrounded me fully akin to a delightful dream of a better world—a world where fear, anxiety, and suffering waned from the memory of Humanity. Above, from the deep blue celestial heaven, *Grace* has been considered, and thenceforth whispered sparklingly amidst the Kosmic stars and throughout the world.

Behind and beyond the visible, there in the mind of God, a hidden thought of *Love* shone like fire. Fast as the speed of light, it traveled across the *Divine Matrix* in the sublime vibration of a *word*. A new rhythm of divine harmony transfused into the realm of time and space, carrying with it a special white ray of light, issued first from the very first Light—a comet!

I stood alone there watching, but somehow, I felt that every human being on each and every corner around the globe has seen it too, and waited now, with an ineffable joy. They probably made a wish and solemnly prayed, filled with hopes that their hearts could finally find ultimate *Peace*.

From the sphere of consciousness, divine sparks were called out of the Universal Mind with a particular mission; one holy mission to fulfill. They have already chosen the path by which they would travel down to Earth, the *Sphere of Generation*, and the vehicles in which they take form after a series of incarnations.

Across the celestial dome, a divine melody—the *Music of the Spheres* played wide, and the Libra constellation *tuned in* to the emitting vibration. A very few white rays, or shooting stars, followed the first comet, one by one, descending from the heavenly sky to the world below.

It was nearly dawn. Fields of Cedar and Oak trees stretched broad and ample all around. The falling leaves scattered above the circumference of life. Others, very few, were moved by the Spirited wind, like twinkling rays towards the center. A prism effect seemed to decompose the Central Sun into various colors, sending forth beams of *divine truth* into the minds of prophetic Children to be born. Flowers blossomed in the hearts of all fields and projected outward a mystical and sacred aroma into the air, an aroma that imbued my restless heart and awakened my mind.

With a free spirit, I felt rejoiced.

Children of air opened up their wings and flew across the sky, singing preludes to their *chants of Liberation*. Initiates, Masters, and Magicians were the very few among men who heard the heavenly melody. They traveled along the path that led them to the *Great Meeting*. They, who had the ability to see, not only with their physical eyes but also with their inner eyes of visions, appeared at the threshold of the holy place and performed their greeting rituals. Inside the cave, or in a warm corner of a hut, or even under a tree, a cry of joy and pain tore the night. Children with the *fish sign* were born.

It was the beginning of a new era.

A circular aura of unconditional *Love* enveloped the place of nativity, and perfect triangular lines of *Peace* diffused above the cubical shape of existence. Mother Earth softly murmured into the air, spreading and reaching the ears of its inhabitants, announcing the birth of the *Children of Prophecies*. Those infants smiled in silence and continued to shine with beauty, the only form of the spiritual that one could perceive and endure, even with the physical senses. An extraordinary impulse, modeled as such in the mind of God, after an intentional desire to create excellence in the bosom of nature.

Resetting deeply into myself, I meditated silently. When hence I opened my eyes a few seconds later, I saw Kadmus standing next to me. He was smiling, a warm smile, which I have never seen drawn before on his face.

"In Hindu tradition," he began, "we learn that Mahadeva, God of Light, seeped into the bosom of *Devaki*, the virgin who gave birth to Krishna, a savior! In Buddhism, the Archangel symbolized by a white elephant appeared to *Maya* and announced to her that she would give birth to Siddharta, the Buddha. And she did!

"The Pythagorean tradition," he added, "showed us a clear picture that *Parthenis*, meaning "the virgin," had been known by Apollo, the Sun God, conceived from him and gave birth to Pythagoras, the Mathemagician and Philosopher! Moreover, Christianity is based on a similar idea, the immaculate conception of the virgin lady *Maryam* (Mary). She was conceived from the Holy Spirit after the announcement by the Angel Gabriel and gave birth to Jesus, the Christ!" the Guardian finished with the same warm smile on his face.

His revelation, though beautiful as it sounds, created a certain confusion in my inner mind. The similarities and concordances spoken of by Kadmus were undoubtedly and strikingly remarkable.

Could it be the same story, repeating itself, again and again, despite the differences of these cultures separated by great distances! I marveled in the silence of time and space vastly enveloping me. Then I took a long deep breath, struggling to absorb that revelation since I've been born and raised a Christian.

But what other than Truth are we all searching for in life? Surely, we neither want to live in illusions, nor to believe in myths, do we? Do I? I asked myself. *Speaking of myths, Greek mythology, for example, related that Zeus, the Most High God, inseminated Gaia, the Earth, and made life beat in her bosom!* I thought while glancing out of the corner of my eye at Kadmus, standing serenely next to me and appearing as if he already knows.

I started to rule out the notion of coincidence. I deliberated on the correlation between the different cultures in their story of their savior's miraculous birth. However, it could be a diffusion from one basic source, one Primary Tradition, to another, then another, and so forth. *Alternatively, could it be sort of a common interpretation of collective unconsciousness?* I thought again, all by myself, not willing to shake Kadmus' long calm moments. That was a difficult question to answer indeed.

The mystery remained still!

At any rate, it was not at all that easy to lift the veil off the face of Isis and see what was there behind that transparent and yet mysterious divine look of the Goddess that would easily burn your desire for more quests.

Amidst the misty light diffused from the Scepter of Kadmus, *Shamekh*, the 15th child of the Sacred Language, embarked my spirit aboard the ship of life.

I sailed in time!

15.

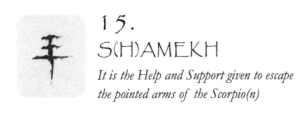

S(H)AMEKH

*It is the Help and Support given to escape
the pointed arms of the Scorpio(n)*

Sailing across the ocean of continuous flow, the ship took many people of different nations and cultures onboard. On their faces appeared expressions of expectation, though no one understood what the other said or what they were waiting for. They all talked in unknown languages; chaos controlled all their feelings and thoughts.

Out of nowhere, a storm blew swiftly from all directions, lifting aggressive long-pointed waves against the ship. The cause could relate to the unmeasured coordination of the alignments of the Scorpio constellation! The wooden structure of the ship resisted the crazy and furious strikes. In moments of fear like that one, people usually tend to unite to cope with the crisis in an uplifting way. Therefore, we managed to understand the needs for our survival.

After being adrift, hither and thither by changing winds, the current steered us along the way to safe shore. Before us, a new dawn gave way to the morning Sun. We stepped down, one by one, and walked on that beautiful golden sandy beach. Kadmus was nearby. We headed toward the impeccable locations where the *Divine Will* has chosen to be implanted.

In its invisible, hidden abode of *Numbers*, the *Source*, the Divine Will had earlier, at the beginning of Creation, organized an assembly of *Angels*, or better call them the *Good Watchers, Impulses* of the Divine Mind, and assigned them to handle the tools in the workshop of Earth. They have modeled the Earth's creatures to abide by the universal law of evolution, not only as being progenies of an eternal divine generation but also through a process of natural selection!

Along that line of *Good Angels*, Powers, visible and invisible, better known as *Evil Watchers*, the *Fallen Angels*, who have co-directed the manufacturing of the human species, conjured corrupt actions at some point during their rebellious deeds against the Divine Will, and followed unregulated formulas along with the scheme of existence. Under these mischievous, yet not completely controlled malicious defects of both matter (body) and spirit (energy), these Powers, or Laws, crowned by the Demiurge, fumbled the stability of the Human race and allowed iniquity and animosity to surface among men.

By that, Humanity repeatedly fell into disdain, waging bloody wars against each other. Temples rose, not to venerate God, but Celestial Luminaries, Idols, Imaginary Deities with Human feelings, if any. Anger, jealousy, ambitions to control the world, and political appetites, also became subjects of veneration for those jealous imbecile spirits of a nation.

"The Children of Prophesies are growing rapidly," Kadmus declared with a calm voice that resonated in my ears as he walked by me. "They are the divine *flames* that will lead the Human Spiritual Fire up to Heaven, allowing the heat of Love to bloom in the hearts of people and radiate all around across the spheres of existence."

I looked at him with a mix of hope and despair, for I came from the present and have felt the coldness in the majority of human hearts, cold as ice. He, who belonged to the past, saw through my eyes sore pictures of the human present social condition. He, though, managed a smile.

"Love is like Truth. They both work slowly, very slowly. A few minds, very few, comprehend the divine tongue, but in time, Love and Truth will peacefully conquer over the human hearts and appease their cold feelings. My advice to you, my brother, is to be patient, very patient. Try always to look at things in a positive and promising way. No matter how hard the fact is in your present time, never lose faith. Believe that it is not but temporary, for we always have the future ahead. Don't we?"

He looked at me. His glowing eyes projected a great radiance into my eyes as if scanning them, heating my insides and burning the bad images that lingered still in my memory. From the very depth of my heart, I wished these painful human memories of declination would someday become extinct and forever gone.

As we sauntered through the stretching fields in easy steps, Earth embraced us with a mystical sense of perpetual vigor; birds twittered on the trees and spread their music around. The sky, tinted in azure blue, formed a circle over our heads. Then, a soft whiteness—like that of a fog—enveloped the Heaven above. Underneath the domain of the spheres, in the wide range of our visions, serenely divine laughter reached our ears like the sweet, tender tones of the lyre. It increased in harmonious succession as we drew closer. On a whim, the source of laughter became intelligible to me. It became clear. *The Children of Prophesies!* I thought. Soft and pure, like Angels or Sons of God, they played with nature and whispered in its ears highly exalted words of arrangements.

"Their feet are the corner stones of the new world," the Guardian announced in a lofty tone. "Stones upon which will rise the Pillars of Justice and Mercy—those of God. These pillars will hold up the Celestial vault during its reign over Earth. Concordantly, their divine breath will jingle solemn melodies of Love and Peace to support Earth in its equilibrium and sustain its orbit around Heaven."

"Harmony . . . *Harmony of the Spheres* will then be fashioned and established," the Guardian continued his prophecy. "It will keep its symmetry throughout the generating and ascending spiral elliptical cycles toward the *Eternal Kingdom.* Above all, I shall finally add, there presides a single and perfect wisdom, our *Father who art in Heaven.*"

Silence filled the vast multi-directional wilderness around us for a few moments. Then innocent laughter, whispers, and words reverberated again in the far distance ahead, breaking through my pending moments in that long wild existence!

Was the universal concept of Virgin Ladies, which existed in many different cultures and religions, a pure dogma? Was the universal concept of a divine savior an ancient mythological literary style added to the biographies of these Children who were later labeled and worshiped, as Sons of God? Could their stories be taken literally as a historical fact? I reflected on it for some moments and still thinking about the origin of them all!

I believed these very few great and holy men delivered an important message of Love, Peace, and Compassion, each in their own manner. They also taught a discipline, a *way* as important as the message itself. However, the miracles and paranormal forces, beautifully included in their narratives, had no considerable effects on my *morals* anyway but made me speculate on the *mysterious*, on their holiness, and their godhood *becoming* state.

Suddenly, something strange vividly caught my eyes. I saw children of men and Children of God playing together, laughing and running throughout the fields. They were all very beautiful, maybe because a child is only a child! Amazingly, they laughed every time they fell to the ground. Whether injured or feeling minor pain, they seemed unaffected. It did not matter, for they would swiftly leap to their feet and resume their game with much more excitement and joy than before. Winning or losing seemed not to be of great importance to them. They just wanted to have fun. Tireless and with great innocence, they magically passed by time, causing tremendous manipulation to its instants.

How did they get over time and space? How could they have a zero notion of fear, play without hate, and laugh every time they fell? They made me wonder.

An urge to join them overwhelmed me for a minute or so, but I was a man; a man who would disturb their delightful life by imposing the rules of men upon them. To transform children into men who might eventually find joy in the suffering of others and blindly relinquish to time and greed for money, power, and dominion would be the worst of deeds ever. To steel away their innocence that keeps them running freely would be a real crime against divinity itself and would impede their evolution from *children of men* to *Children of God*!

Let the children play together. I reasoned out.

Then, a beautiful scene unfurled clearly before my eyes . . . perhaps coming from the good stock of my memory, and at the same time, came the disciples unto *baby* Jesus, asking, "who was the greatest in the Kingdom of heaven?" Jesus called a little child unto him, set him in the midst of them, and proclaimed, "*Verily, I say unto you, except ye be converted, and become as little children, ye shall not enter the kingdom of heaven.*" His tender voice echoed mystically and continued, "*Let the children come to me because for them is given the kingdom of heaven! Take heed that ye despise not one of these little ones; for I say unto you, that in heaven their angels do always behold the face of my Father which is in heaven.*"

Beautiful and true! Without knowing why I moved spontaneously away, for I was not yet ready to become a *child*, but the Guardian was there, standing before me, smiling. He took his Scepter and sketched a shape in the sand. It looked like a golden medal around the wheel of time and space.

It's the letter *Ayin*, the 16th of the Sacred Alphabet, that conveyed my vision with great light throughout Heaven.

I soared in elliptical motion like a wheel within a wheel!

16.

AYIN

*It is the Eye of Providence and the Source of thinking that
protects humanity from the danger of Sagittarius*

Along the distance I therefore crossed, I sensed a strange presence in wait.
Yet, to reach it, numerous directions expanded. All rivers led toward the ocean,
and the ocean was wide and deep. Strangely though, nature selected. Its selec-
tions, however, were both predestined and randomly free. *How does that happen?*
I wondered. It became evident that the *Force* presided over all existence; the
Source from which everything came and which the way back was shown to all.

I took the natural flow of things, same as my ally on that journey, and allowed my heart to open to the murmurs of the elements—elements of nature.
Naturally, I refused to be distracted by unfamiliar thoughts that would break my
tranquil motion along the current I willingly submitted myself to.

With *Earth* looping under my feet, *Fire* burning my insides, *Air* pumping in
my lungs, and *Water* drizzling on my head, I opened my eyes to an odd object.
It stood erect ahead of me in the middle of a vast field, behind yellowish-green
bushes. Whether it was hostile or friendly, I could not tell at the moment.

However, something unknown and invisible enlightened my consciousness
to its mysterious and divine nature. I approached a little further and heeded a
great Pyramid, so delicate and inspiring. Perfectly measured in its geometrical structure, it sent forth positive vibrations to all visible directions. I stood
abashed like an ape before a monolith.

Moments later, I turned around and observed it from all sides. I touched
its smooth surface for seconds and then moved few steps back. Within all
that labyrinth of thoughts and behaviors, perplexity besieged me for a while.
Planted in the ground, yet appearing hovering a few inches above, the Pyramid
confused me deeply.

It was *intelligent*, I sensed. Then, something mysterious unleashed. The
Pyramid switched and evolved its shape into an *Ethereal*-like appearance. My
instinct of survival jerked me backward, my heel hit a stone, and my body
lurched to the left and dropped to the ground. I froze for a while in that position, beset by a complete numbness—all my attempts to budge failed pitifully.

An instant later, I came to realize that the Pyramid has soundlessly accelerated the speed of its vibrations as it entered into a new phase where all its atoms initiated an *intelligent* circulation. A great electro-magnetic light of three different colors; red, blue, and yellow, was diffused all around me. I failed to move again, crashed down by a semi-visible overwhelming presence that, still unfathomed, took full control of my being.

Yet, despite all, I felt no fear in me whatsoever, and at any moment during that extraordinary encounter. The moment I perceived that fact, sudden energy circulated at the speed of light inside me, inciting me to take action. As I stretched my right hand toward the shape in an attempt to communicate, a magnetic Force pulled me up off the ground. I stood still on my feet.

With confidence and belief in the liberty of my movement, I approached the eerily Pyramid once again and inserted my hand in its middle point. Slowly, the transparent field, oscillating all along the four sides of the Pyramid, enveloped my hand. I felt its atoms intermingling with mine at a higher resonance as I entered inside, in smooth yet strong assimilation.

I floated in an incredible rush inside colorful energy that encircled me with an indissoluble, indescribable, and incandescent light. It thus transferred me inside another pyramid, beyond another, and yet another. In turn, the successive pyramids conveyed audible frequencies while projecting red, blue, and gold colors simultaneously. They somehow appeared in the shape of rotating orbs inside my mind, carrying Light into my darkest realms. This looping flight seemed endless.

A splendid sensation of *Peace* overpowered my fragile atomic body. Time never ticked around the wheel of existence that utterly submerged my movement through the infinite, invisible space; that *Ethereal*-like Pyramid which revealed all the grandeur of my littleness!

Nevertheless, I, the creature of a span, the being which I was bound to, began to wonder about this reality. Suddenly, perplexity and fear to lose identity in the Source—the eternal bliss of *Love*—weighed heavily on me. At this very moment of personal doubt, everything ceased, and weight, physical weight, took possession of my body. I found myself again framed in the middle of nowhere, standing motionless against time and space.

A new Grand Pyramid stood, majestically, surely much bigger than the precedent ones in front of me. Its base extended either way from me and expanded along an entire horizon. Its apex infinitely rose above Earth. From the top, a *Giant Eye* looked directly at me; that single and perfect point penetrated deep into my soul through my now awakening eyes. A feeling of hope and appeasement enveloped me at the emitted divine *Rays* that opened wide the way for me through unbounded existence as it unfolded space and time.

The Giant Eye is the Eye of Providence! I thought in the depth of my mind as my spirit rejoiced. I believed it was just gazing at me, rather than spying on me! It created a shield of pyramids to protect me against the future arrows of the archer, already positioned in the Sagittarius constellation. It was a time when I finally sensed my heart was kept safe!

Moments later, my eyelids opened to find myself again standing with the Guardian under the Cedar tree. The sky was deep blue; the wind refreshing and, so soon, all fields would self-regenerate. Out there, as far as my eyes could reach, I imagined different types of flowers of an incredible mixture of colors blossoming throughout the evergreen grass. Mountains and high hills trailed along, one after the other. Nature has evolved!

Without looking at me or even a word uttered, Kadmus took his Scepter off the ground and vanished somewhere in the distance. I was sure he would come back at the right moment, but for now, he left me alone to savor those insights to their very depth.

I shut my eyes in a leap of internal faith!

17.
PE(H)

It is the Mouth uttering Words that make changes under planet Venus

Peculiar steps appeared randomly cut on the hard, awkward rocks to my left. They led my feet down a deep valley. Halfway through it, I made a few turns to the right and climbed an ascending path somewhere between two opposite extremities of nature; one *above* and the other *below*. It looked like being wavered between Heaven and Earth, for Hell does not exist, struggling for life to keep death away.

Had I not met with Kadmus on that road to lend me the *fil d'Ariane*, I would have lost my way, my sanity, inside a labyrinth, turning right and left, up and down, perhaps forever. For the sake of keeping the Sacred Alphabet hidden from the profane, the Guardian of the Alphabet has come forth out of Earth's memory and guided me along a wide and lengthy field.

No valleys. No mountains. Just a straight path, the middle path, which naturally soothed my thinking process and freed me from any strings attached.

Subtle energy seemed to have been flown eternally here, emitting a tranquil and harmonious melody in all directions. I realized that the serene music did not emerge from the sagacious performance of the Seraphim in their high places, but rather from the combination of my heartbeats and breathing, which rhythm comprised a steady-state of existence, gliding with no beginning and no end.

We entered a simulated dark cave and then, immediately after, into a Temple of wide starry sky dome and wide field for the floor. The view of the four directions stretching to infinity replaced the inexistent walls. Inside, in the mid of time and space, Kadmus stopped, turned around, and gazed into my eyes to pierce my mind and read the words my thoughts emitted.

"The cycle of life is inevitable!" the Guardian started in a serious yet gentle voice. "There is no escape from the duality of existence as yet because the phenomenal world of forms is manifested in simulated realities."

A vivid light flashed out from his inner eyes. They reflected wisdom, a serene state of mind, and the depth of his ancient realm. His words, however, left me mystified.

"Each and every form of life," Kadmus continued, "is destined to enter the *Circle of Necessity*. However, every atom in that wide Universe would leave the Circle, not by jumping over the circumference, which is *nowhere*, but rather by merging with the center itself, which is *everywhere*! At the center, on that *Unity point*, there is a balance to attain. However, any attempt to escape through the barriers of time and space is a vain end. From that central point, a vertical line rises toward the infinite space. It is time."

A moment of silence ensued.

"We humans, and every other living and evolving atom, would have to oscillate around it in a spiral movement that ascends to its highest point. There, we will acquire *symbolic wings*, akin Angels, that set us free in our ultimate journey towards the Sun," he uttered with lots of commitment and then took a long breath before he turned around to show me what rose behind us.

"This erect line is the *Caduceus* of Enoch-Taautus-Thot-Hermes," he explained. "It is standing at the midpoint of existence, at the center of the Circle. It is the real Altar of the Great Temple of life. What other temples do we need, than that of life? What other altars do we need than ourselves? Once you realize that truth, you would keep paying homage to God at every moment of Death and Rebirth."

A moment of reflection ensued.

"The Phoenix," he resumed, "holds the secret life-cycle within his essence. He is consumed to rise, after three days, from his ashes—a reborn. A new cycle then starts. The process undertakes seven times seven, in other words, forty-nine human lives, by which men and women evolve. The night follows the day, and the day, the night. Yet, in the end, Judgment is done, and divinity is reached. The same fate is also programmed for the world, through successive destruction and reproduction of itself, until comes a moment where time and space reach their Kosmic resurrection."

Despite the complete bafflement in which his words threw me, I looked inside myself in much deeper scrutiny. My inner realm appeared to have been designed to reveal an eternal stimulus that would eventually lead me to gain the freedom of a god! Or that was what I thought I am in the beginning!

"Look at Nature, my brother," Kadmus brought back my attention to his uttering mouth of words full of change and aspirations. "It is the great Teacher of humanity, for it is the revelation of God. Oh . . ." he moved around, surprised by his unexpected behavior. "Tell me what you see," he suddenly invited me.

I looked at Nature and murmured, "Seasons do follow each other. Leaves do fall from trees in autumn. Water does run in the veins of Earth in winter. Flowers do bloom at springtime, and their enchanting fragrance is quite a true interpretation of the beginning of a new cycle."

The Guardian nodded and drew closer to utter in one mystical voice of his, "The Phoenix is the bird of *Resurrection* to Eternity."

Then, after revealing some great Mysteries that made me even feel *lost* in a secret world now totally found, he loomed over with a wistful smile. Like a real Hierophant to a neophyte, and from *mouth to ear*, he whispered the *ineffable name*—the *Word* that was to change the course of events.

"This is the secret essence of the Holy Grail," he ended with a bright twinkle in his eyes.

With utmost respect, I swore a solemn oath to keep the *Word* protected from the vulgar. *Why should I not do so?* I asked myself. I was given the mysteries and the secrets of the world, or so I was told! But I fully believed it. Particles in the air would not reveal what the Sun Rays murmured among themselves!

A few moments later, I daydreamed I saw *them* coming down from Venus, as swiftly as the speed of light. With all their seductive appearances, the children of Venus, those women, tried to make me forget the *Word* I've just received from the Guardian. They tempted me with their sensual looks, and in the most pleasant possible way, they have expressed strong desires for me to succumb to their voluptuous aroma.

Under the Shaft of the Shepherd, or the *Tree of Life*, I sat lotus-like as a Buddhist monk and meditated on the Mysteries. I kept on repeating the *Word*, the *mantra*, until it created in me a state of serenity and a sense of strength. Anxiety, fear, doubts, and illusions faded away at once. The pleading voices of the messengers of Venus seemed to decay through the air before reaching me. Many times, they attempted to weaken me with their seduction games, only for the fun of it, but the force of the *ineffable name* made their alluring silhouettes dissolve from the memory of existence, or better say, from the phenomenal world—Earth, and back to Venus.

After all, ladies, I am really on a spiritual journey, and now I fully understand why I was there!

The Phoenix . . . that beautiful bird, perched on the top of the Caduceus, launched his flight freely to Heaven, with the perpetual motion of his wings.

I seemed to have heard his wings approaching Heaven!

18.
TSADDI

It is the other side, the Dark Side, Satan.
It hits like an Arrow, or capture Humanity with a Fishing hook
under the power of the Capricorn

Turning and spinning at a very high speed, the ball of fire exploded in front of my eyes and echoed hard in my ears. I no longer hear the wings of the Phoenix. Something has pulled me back from watching his free flight to Heaven. This ball of fire gave birth to a dwindling human-like form. Instantly, I leaped back, horrified. My heart felt whacked by the explosion and by the hazy image under the dim light of the torches. Blood seemed to freeze in my veins for moments.

With great efforts, I gathered my courage and strength to face the nameless entity of such an atypical human form. From under his black hood, two shafts of fire pierced my eyes, perhaps in an attempt to penetrate my mind . . . *or was it my soul he was aiming at?* I wondered alone in the great darkness that surrounded me.

At the strength of his stares, where creepy shadows alternated with fiery sparks, I prompted to lower mines at once. A foul smell swapped entirely the mysterious room I found myself in, nearly suffocating me. I breathed and repeatedly, panting for clean air. His presence became more and more offensive. In an instinct of survival, I braced myself to defend the territory I claimed mine against the incursion of a terrorist power.

Was he an illusion? Yet . . . he looked so real. Was he Satan, the devil? How can I succeed in getting him out of here? My thoughts rushed in torment.

"You have something I need, human!" the voice rose, throaty, metallically.

I swallowed hard but stood firm on my ground, wondering if he could read my hidden terror on my face.

"If you give me what I need, then I'll give you everything in return," his voice drifted gruffly through the short distance that separated us.

I had the impression that the long black robe that draped over him camouflaged something underneath or behind; yet I could not fathom what it is exactly. He sputtered angrily at my silence, obviously impatient, and then in a swift that left me in dismay, he clapped his hands sturdily, transporting me, both of us, in seconds, out of that Mystery Chamber, and to the top of a small mountain.

"Do you see this?" He pointed at one of the most beautiful mansions I have ever seen in my life, not even in my wildest dreams. "I can give it to you!" he added.

I glanced at him with doubts and much caution. *Who could he be to express such generosity? Who might be that entity who seemed to have such great power of control?* Questions harassed my reasoning. It was then when I immediately remembered the vision I had with *Zaza'el* and the earthly Kingdoms he offered me to take by the power of the sword, by war and bloodshed. *Why is he here again? Why he still follows me?*

"Oh . . . oh, I can actually give you a lot more!" he spat with arrogance.

He pivoted on himself, clapped his hands again, and his magic, or better say, sorcery, shoved us right into a showroom of the latest models of the most luxurious cars my eyes ever saw.

"Just pick anyone your heart desires, and it's yours!" he loudly proclaimed, with hands opened wide toward the variety of cars exposed all around. "What else do you want? Maybe . . . a boat?"

His hands waved in the air, and a luxurious yacht appeared in front of me to coax my longing even harder, deeper. I did not answer, too startled to do so at this point along the journey.

"No? What then? An airplane?" He enticed me again with a glamorous private jet. "Maybe both, I suppose . . . ah!" He sneered and snorted at the temptation he could read in me.

His luring presentation rendered me breathless and puzzled to the very last thought brewing in my agitated mind. My materialistic desires were re-awakened as they sought to manipulate my mind, and my will vacillated to the dangerous edge of surrender to Azazel, once again.

My imagination met in line with such a luring collection of prospects, images, and feelings. I fancied myself driving a luxurious car on that splendid road to my glamorous mansion up the mountain and creating on my way a big impact on the minds of others. I delighted already at their expressions of awe and admiration.

Why not? Sailing my boat across seas and oceans, yelling 'land' every time at nearing a new country, and docking at every harbor around the world!

Why not? Flying my private jet up in the air, mighty and free, as in my wildest dreams, and looking down at the world beneath, so small and controllable!

I felt them deep down to my bones, these pleasurable sensations of power no man had ever resisted throughout the long history of our species, except perhaps, those very few Initiates who pounded their *Scepters* to the ground and marked history with their force and wisdom.

Am I one of them, seriously? I asked myself.

What else do I want, really? I inwardly rebuked my uncertainty.

My eyes widened before closing tight on these wonders for moments. Then I felt the nameless form looming forward as I snapped my eyes opened again to meet the fiery sparks of his. The words he uttered next wheezed a stinking smell right onto my face.

"What if I grant you the presidency of a very big company . . . ah? You would then own both power and money."

He does not give up easily, does he? My inner voice retorted from within the smog of chimeras, suffocating my brainpower.

I fantasized about a life of full power and commodities where hardships had no say; a carefree existence where I would never need again to struggle for survival in this crazy world around us.

But . . . at what cost? Ask him! At what cost? My inner voice hissed, like that of the Old Serpent I met in the "Circle of Trees," almost inaudible now.

Right! He did say he needed something I have, something I own, but what was it? What could that be so precious to him that it would make him grant me such wonderful contributions in exchange? I considered that for some time, asking myself.

He must have read my mind, for the effect was immediate.

"I tell you what!" He jerked my attention back to his exploitation. "Forget about even working as head of that mega-company. Instead, I'll open for you a bank account of an unlimited amount of money and will provide you also with a large number of Jewels and gold you could keep in the treasury safe of the bank!"

My intake of air barely reached my lungs, for, in a quick dizzying clap of his hands, he shoved me with him inside that bank, right in front of the doorway of a sumptuous office. "Set Servitor, General Manager," read the inscriptions on the iron door.

"All you need to do now is to enter with me inside that office and sign one little piece of paper," he said, encouraging while giving me a pleading smile I rarely saw drawn on his hidden face!

Only a signature? I marveled at the opportunity. *Without having to work, produce, or do anything, I would live rich like a King!* I rejoiced secretly at the tempting notion of sitting down, relaxing all day, and not giving a damn about anything. *Why not?*

Under such irresistible expectations and overexcitement taking a tight hold of me, I pushed the door and entered. He followed me to the desk akin a ghostly shadow. The Manager, whose features I could barely notice in my thrill, smiled as he handed me an official paper and a golden pen. I smiled back, grabbed the pen, stooped to sign, and then halted at once.

Something alarming took hold of me. *Live rich like a King? Kingdom? Is that really Zazae'il?* The thought came rushing into my mind. Then I heeded some whispers, yet too softly and too vaguely for me to comprehend their meaning. I turned abruptly and met with angry impatience in the cinder-like eyes of the nameless form.

I held his anger for a second then asked, dubiously, "If I sign now, it means I'll have everything you offered?"

"Yes!" the reply came swiftly.

"Fine, but what is that thing you want in return?"

Rage flashed from his cindery eyes, under that freaky black hood, then vanished at once, as he unexpectedly took fast control of his temper. He attempted a meek smile, and in a velvety voice that conferred me with much more apprehension than comfort, he assured me that he needed nothing from me.

Unconvinced, I stood my ground and insisted on knowing my part of the deal.

He shoved his hood back irately and nailed me with a crusty glare. I recoiled instantly at the hideous scene unfurling speedily in front of me. With his patience gone now, he bristled and fumed like a monster; a monster he had physically become, absconding his previous human-like shape. Smoke puffed out from his wide nostrils. Repulsive noise wheezed through the misshapen teeth of his maw. The sound of an explosion, resulting from the claps of his hands, followed us back to the Mystery Chamber.

"Give me the *Word!*" He screamed in mighty wrath, and the walls trembled. So did I. "Give me the *ineffable secret name*, or I shall break you into little pieces."

I fell back fast. Terror crawled all over my skin. My lips moved to speak, yet no words came out. I gasped for air, but he seemed to have had gulped it all to increase the power of his scream. My lungs ached in search of more air, and the hammering of my heartbeat painfully blocked my ears. With an extraordinary exertion, I retained the *Word* I received solemnly from the Guardian of the Sacred Alphabet and summoned up all the strength I could muster for my survival. Against all odds, I firmly stood up, back on my feet, and braced myself to fight.

"Wretch!" I countered back.

Stunned silence ensued.

We each held our ground: I, the Man on a spiritual journey, and Azazel, the beast from hell, that *Fallen Angel* from Heaven! Our eyes initiated a fiery war for a moment or two. Then, he pointed at me with his long, bony fingers in an attempt to hypnotize me and rip off the *Word*. He seemed to have cunningly planned each and every stage of that movement and stood there, waiting for my breakdown, as he furiously probed my memory.

With a desperate effort, I amassed every remnant of my dangerously dwindling energy to resist his powerful and penetrating stare, hoping for his demise. However, he had previously read my mind. *He could do it again!* I thought as my heart shivered at that possibility. I knew then that the only way to win was for me to block him out completely. Yet, as the minutes ticked away, I began to feel an unbearable distortion of my perception of things around. It soon evolved into a terrible headache.

The intricate network of the narrow synapses of my brain weakened alarmingly, and my brainpower wavered under the invisible pressure. At his point of infirmity, I detected nothing but a blurred image of the horrid entity standing in front of me. My breath stifled as if someone or something was strangling me in the invading darkness. My energy waned, and numbness took hold of my limbs, spreading through my body to the very essence of my existence. I reached the point of no return, almost at the edge of losing consciousness . . . losing the war or better say, the battle for freedom.

I collapsed!

~ ~ ~

Twirling fast, as if a tornado had unleashed its power all at once, the ball of fire looped uncontrollably before it exploded in zillion glints to spit out the human-like form again in front of my face. I looked at myself and found my body dropped to the ground. I was just waking up! Memories of my encounter with that beast came flashing into my mind. I was not surprised like I was the first time, but light waned as fearsome darkness raided the Mystery Chamber. There was a sense of strain there, but I knew well what was going to happen. My eyes were open, ready now to face him. They were not vacant but full of determination to look through his vicious mind. Swiftly, I leaped my body back, crawling on the ground, trying to stand up, in vain!

Dark indeed, that façade shadowed by the black hood! Blistering fire spurt out from where his eyes are and pierced the virtual block my mind has drawn up between us, him and I. The shadows that alternated the fiery beams in his eyes did not lessen the powerful spell. Nailed to the floor, I felt heavier than ever. The stench that he profusely diffused caught me tightly by the throat and revolted my stomach. I then breathed repeatedly . . .

His presence became more offensive. I tried to reason as my mind struggled for a sense of sanity. Yet, feigning surprise and ignorance, much initiated now of his origin, my mind knew all too well that the ugly entity facing me was nothing other than those vicious parts, that dark side of my persona, dangerously manifested in a human-like form.

Is he truly an illusion? But . . . he looks damn real! I can see him, touch him, and surely smell him all over me! He cannot be Satan, the beast from hell, nor Zazae'il, that Fallen Angel from Heaven! They simply do not exist. What I am encountering now is nothing more than my darkest side.

"You have something that I need," he spoke again in that deep and raspier voice I remembered too well. "If you give me what I need, I'll give you everything in return!"

The promise of the deceitful! My mind said.

Draped in a black mantle, his countenance lurked, his back hunched, and his head swerved slightly for him to glare at me sideways.

Sneaky countenance of the deceitful!

I restrained from answering him. The scenario played back like in a nightmare. He clapped his hands in a blast, and I barely had time to gasp as he snatched me away with him to the peak of a mount.

"Do you see this villa?" His crooked finger pointed a filthy corkscrew nail at one of the most beautiful manors ever seen, but I already anticipated the trick, for I have been there once before. "I can give it to you!" He snapped, challenging my steadfast attitude reflected by my gritty silence. "Oh, oh I see, hmm . . . Actually, I can give you a lot more."

Another clap of his hands brought us speedily into a big hall packed with people addressing me, 'Mr. the President' with respectful admiration.

President! My eyes widened, and my mouth parted. He smirked and winked at me. That offer was quite new, modern and most suitable for our present time than being a King, actually more tempting than my expectations. I might have failed to conceal from him my awareness of his wickedness.

"I have seen you before, haven't I?" He took me by surprise.

As envisioned, or perhaps telepathically instructed by the *Guardian*, the plan was not to give him the least shadow of a doubt that I knew what was going to happen. It was also recommended not to show him any signs that would expose my identity and thus eliminate any thoughts of recognizing me. He had already informed me to react as if I have been there for the first time. It was better for me to behave normally, looking like a simple man, a profane, and giving him the chance to offer me what he desires.

When this would happen, I would start to face him strongly in an attempt to bait him. By then, he would offer me more and more. This should happen until we would reach the critical point when I would resist him even more. He would go mad, becoming more aggressive and dangerous. Only at that time, during the battle's apex, I should will myself not to succumb to his power. Instead, I should will for him to lose his.

Still, however, a gloomy silence filled the place . . .

In a swift, I looked away, avoiding his inquisitive stares while I recovered my calm appearance, asking him in defy, "What else can you offer?"

"Everything you desire," he yelled to the wind, and with a theatrical gesture of his hand, scenes of outlandish luxury unfurled fast in front of my eyes, shaking me and my resolution. "I can give you just about everything," he emphasized, lifting both his hands arrogantly then gyrating on his heels with a sarcastic grin.

His new proffers stirred up my imagination and plunged me into an incalculable assemblage of images, thoughts, and feelings. Breathless and puzzled down to the very last thought, I yielded to my inward deliberation. Once again, my mind tricked me into basic material desires and ambitions, weakening me. I instantly fancied myself having and doing just about everything my heart would desire.

I will rule the world. What else do I want, really? I concluded in my fallen mind.

My eyelids closed for a moment in which I savored the illusion, and, at once, the image of my collapse the night before flashed into my mind. A fleet instant, yet it brought me back to my senses. *I cannot fail again. I cannot give him the Word entrusted to my keeping!*

As if reading my mind, he pushed forward, pressuring on me, "All you need to do is to sign your name on this paper, and everything in the world will be yours!"

That piece of paper hooked my eyes, my mind, and my temptation. I glanced at his twisted smile that pleaded in deceit. I knew, yet I could not dismiss the thought that a simple deed would grant me so much glory and wealth.

Just a signature! What about all those who died to keep the Word protected? A faint voice hummed from the very back of my mind. *No! I cannot betray them. I shall not betray myself!*

Like a ghostly imposing presence, he edged closer and waited for my signature. I glared fiercely at the cold anticipation in his void eyes, and my mind commanded his to a steadfast decline of his final and ultimate offer. As expected, the lustrous aura of his devious generosity faded away slowly.

Gentleness evaded him at once. His eyes blistered mine. He panted heavily and hastily. I knew then that I had provoked the beast once again. In fact, he shoved back his black hood angrily. His slicing eyes attempted to probe my soul. His human-like shape initiated certain changes, and he grew as ugly as a horrific monster. In a blast, his hands clapped so strongly that the gushing wind wafted us back into the Mystery Chamber. Panting heavily, he strode back and forth in front of me, halted abruptly, veered to me, and loomed fearsomely to rage out, "Give me the *Word*, the *ineffable secret name*! Or I shall break you into little pieces this time, and forever!" his voice echoed sardonically between the walls, but that was the moment I was waiting for.

I heaved a deep breath to summon the forces within me and stood before him in a fighting position. "You shall not get it!" I screamed in his face.

A stunning stillness followed that none attempted before to interrupt. Without hesitation, I made a conscious effort to keep the *Word* hidden inside my deepest realm.

He lifted his hand and pointed his long corkscrew finger at me to hypnotize me. I stood firm against his attempts to wreck my mind and steal the *word*. He tried, again and again, probing for what he most needed so furiously. The spiritual battle heaved physically hard on me. I gathered my energy to resist the nervous breakdown that befell me before and which he had anticipated. The potential energy surging within me met his in electrical waves, almost palpable through the short distance that separated us.

Block him! Block him! All my being urged me.

I tried really hard yet, as the moments ticked away, my headache increased with the terrible sensation of my brain breaking out in blisters and its network of narrow impulses weakening. My vision partially blurred. My breath shortened to a dangerous level, faster and faster. Darkness crept in, strangling me. Lights waned. My energy betrayed me into yielding. I was about to lose my final battle, and this one could be mortal.

From the dimness of my downfall, I saw her, the mysterious Lady, say, the Queen of Heaven I saw in my previous visions. She mouthed something out, but I could not hear her. Light ceased in complete, then dimmed again. She was still there, her eyes urging. Then it all came back to me. She was the Mother Goddess of Love who promised to send her child—*the chosen child* to save us and whom we should follow. I believed in Love, and in the child, she poured into the trembling hearts.

From afar, from the depth of my mind, a pulse of courage flitted out to whiz through my veins. I could swear I heard the sweet melodious sound of the flute I heard reverberating around the "Circle of Trees" when I first met the Old Serpent, the Guardian of the *Tree of Life*, announcing me to 'wake up from my deep sleep . . . oh, little god . . . and behold the *ascension* has begun!' It was when I gathered even closer to her like a neophyte around a Hierophant inside a Temple and revealed in my true nature—*divine nature*. The impulses curled and weaved in all directions like a powerful orchestra, boosting back my energy in full force. I opened my eyes.

Wrapped in his black overcoat, he gawked at me in astonishment. I lifted my hand in command and charged with great authority, "You're nothing but a trick of the mind!"

He winced uncomfortably, muttering under his breath words not loud enough for me to hear. Somehow, he dangled between his power and my clear-cut statement.

"I'm the Devil, the Prince of Darkness. How dare you talk to me this way? I'm the Lord of this world!" He snapped, yet his authoritarian tone surged weak and scrawny.

"Ah . . . there is no existence of the Devil. You just don't exist!" I countered back.

"What?" He blinked in outrage. "But I'm the Devil!" He proclaimed earnestly. As soon said, his eyes turned blood-red, and two horns spurted out from his head.

I glared at him with disdain and disgust. *What an illusion!* I thought, then chuckled and said, "I know what you are. You are a part of me, my darkest part, and I shall forever confine you in a state of oblivion."

Having said that, with faith in my true divine nature, I willed him out! He went backward and fell to the ground. My darkest side drifted slowly away and into the left corner of the Chamber. He wailed sluggishly for having been cast into nothingness.

"This is for every Keeper of the *Word* . . . I cast you out into *Dudael!*" I finished with a great sense of victory.

Then I sensed a warm hand on my forehead but could not tell whose hand that was. I smiled in my silence. From afar, I heard the voice of the Guardian of the Alphabet. His whispers to my ears praised my triumph over the beast of illusion.

"Is that you, Kadmus?" I asked with fondness.

Immediately, the name of Kadmus must have brought up the 19th letter, *Qoph*, out of the Mystery box, floating weightlessly in front of my eyes.

At once, streaks of light transported me away!

19.
QOPH

It is the Keeping of secrets inside the Back of the Head, under the constellation of Aquarius

Quaking in all directions, I found myself traveling through space and time. Yet, I could not detect time nor perceive a tangible space. I felt that I would lose contact with the Laws of Nature at any time now. An impenetrable wall of total darkness stretched in front and all around me, but what lay behind was probably the habitat of the gods, so I thought.

Then, stars appeared, numerous, shining almost everywhere. A peculiar feeling of peace overwhelmed me while elated praise of the lofty sparks, those beings of Light, the stars, escorted my ascension toward the celestial dome. In this serene state of magic and elation, I felt somehow an inscrutable force impelling me toward one of the constellations at the *right* corner of Heaven— Aquarius! Its rays absorbed me smoothly, and its energy touched me to create compatible and telepathic communication.

A harmonious melody drifted to me all along the path of light, and a color-ful gate between two worlds swayed wide open. In vain, I tried to perceive the new world I had just entered. Apparently, I had mysteriously made a quantum leap into another mystical and spiritual reality within the Kosmic bonds.

But there, amidst a cloud of purity, totally cloaked in white, Kadmus waited for me. His smile widened, and his eyes brightened beneath the hood. With a brotherly gesture, he welcomed me into Aquarius.

"I'm proud of you," he confessed, surprising me all too suddenly.

I nodded, trying to hide my shy and humble smile.

We walked along the open fields in easy and slow steps, heading toward the *White Mountain*. There was no need to hurry up or hasten in the pursuit of Truth! Patience and vigilance were necessary steps in keeping the balance of the true seeker. Any awkward movement of the *ego* could send me back to point zero!

"You have now conquered Satan, the Tempter and Destroyer," Kadmus imparted with a sideway look of approval in my direction. "Satan is not Lucifer, for the latter is *lux-feros*, the *bearer of light*, as called by the Initiates, wrongly confused with Satan who is a representation of darkness. Lucifer is more like the Greek Prometheus, one of the Titans, and considered the supreme trickster and god of fire because of his intellect and forethinking. Because of Lucifer's revolutionary and intellectual nature, his bright image was distorted through the ages by organized religions! However, esoterically speaking, that horrific satanic beast from hell or that Fallen Angel from Heaven is not but the *Mind* in its greatest tricky maneuvers—the *Lower Mind*—that manipulates the weaknesses of *man*, such as emotional breakdowns, instinctive sexual desires, the yearning for power and dominion, and at last, the false ambitions for wealth." He glimpsed at me before he added, "Divinity, the *Son of God*, as called by the Initiates, is also the *Mind*, but in its greatest benevolence of beatitude—the *Higher Mind*— to what *man* has of strength, such as the unbendable *will*, the apotheosis of *faith*, and the peaceful redeeming walk toward Love."

I marveled at him, and for the instants that followed, I felt as if deeply lost in a dream where memory no longer existed. *Who am I?* I wondered still.

"In that subterranean Mystery Chamber, as in Hades, Hell or Dudael, as it is on Earth, a great battle has just ended," he announced. "The Divine inside you fought Satan and took away from him all his deceitful appeal. It's when your Higher Mind wins over your Lower Mind in a final battle for awareness. His fiery sparks no longer burn yours, for they were truly extinguished. Know that there is only one Light, and it's that of Divinity, which creates the path to the abode of Liberty. However, vigilance . . . eternal vigilance is needed on that path."

A giant arch of brilliant light appeared dominant in the sky, and the Sun sprung from behind the clouds and greeted us. I felt embraced by the invisible presence of the Divine Light, which the Sun is not but its reflection. I took a deep breath at sensing the warm energy interconnecting with my iridescent vibrations. It felt soothing, soothing indeed. It didn't seem like a physical communication or interaction, but rather an invisible manifestation of the Deity in me.

At once, a great joy inhabited me, and the path to Light, Peace, and Love opened wide in front of me. Behind it stood the gate to the Kingdom—the Kingdom of Heaven. Reaching it remained my choice to make; a very tough one, though. *However, what other choice could there be more honorable for a man than the one of eternal liberty? What could be better than evolving from the son of man to the son of God?* I weighed in my mind.

"Now, since you have realized the divinity in you, it is you alone who can keep it shining inside the Temple of God that you are, in reality. You have been awakened to the greatest Mystery of all. Keep it safe and secret, and follow the path of the Initiates," he graciously recommended, yet the firmness of his tone was apparent.

A few minutes later, we reached the grotto in the heart of the *White Mountain*. The Elders say the Aquarius River sprung from this grotto and streamed to the points from which the constellation of Aquarius, the eleventh sign of Zodiac, hung in the sky. Inside the coolness of the grotto, we stopped at the spring bounding plentiful. Kadmus edged a large hole in the natural wall and extracted a terracotta jar that he filled from the spring with a lot of devotion.

"On your knees, Brother!" his reverential tone hinted a promise of a major decisive moment. It echoed in my ears and through my body while I knelt and bowed my head, right there at the rim of the spring.

Water profusely flooded over my head, down my body, and all along my spine to spiritualize me as a whole and energize my mind, first thing first. I closed my eyes to catch in the mystical sensation the Guardian of the Alphabet bestowed upon me while he professed the *Rite of Acceptance* into the *Great Order*, the Kingdom of the Inner Deity!

Kadmus, *the water bearer* he became, baptized me by pouring *Sacred Water* on my head, my Godhead! My higher mind, raised heart, and beautified spirit marked the mysterious Phoenician words he hummed in my direction or the direction of Aquarius. Then, he bent closer, and from *mouth to ear*, he solemnly whispered, "Truth, my Brother, is one and eternal."

From close, so close a distance in space and time, and like a shining word spelled out from the mouth of the Hierophant of the Alphabet, his murmur resonated the same as a Divine Whisper inside me, an adept of the *Word*!

Under Aquarius, I breathed in a new vigor of life.

I stood up slowly and stared for a pensive moment at the surface of the pond. Unexpectedly, a mysterious shape took gradually form over my head's reflection on the water. *Resh*! The 20th letter of the Alphabet rose from lethargy then into the air in an aura of great light.

Bit by bit, it dissolved to slip into my awakened eyes!

20.
RESH

It is the Head that lives in Poorness,
and challenges Misery for the work of Sacrifice under planet Mercury

Rushing through the tunnel of light, I came to an abrupt halt as I wandered into a strange empty place. *Where am I?* I wondered and ran, ran again, endlessly, repeatedly, in a circle. Dazed and confused, I stumbled and dropped to the cold floor. Caught in some unconscious state of perplexed mind, I paid no heed to what happened in the gap of time that followed immediately after.

Then, in a wink, the first faint sparks of intelligent lights flickered and receded in the Kosmic night. I closed and reopened my eyes to witness uncountable myriads of tiny lights shining in the sky and all over my head as if fiddling with my destiny! I looked around in all directions and was startled at the rapid changes in my surroundings. Transported onto a piece of land, I roamed across the sky!

Ripples of astonishment engulfed me. I wanted the sensation to last forever. In the Celestial Realm ahead of me, an enigmatic formation of waves of an unusual mixture of colors floated amidst the stars. Their radiation spread close by, and I trembled in every atom of my floating being. Fearing a stroke of blindness would hit me, I averted my eyes in protection. *Where am I?* I pondered again, in a panic this time.

Then, the mass of radiation swapped into a single streak of light that adjusted gradually into the form of a being with a long blue robe and brown hood. He walked with steady steps across the flying land where I stood motionless like a marble statue. He approached me with incredible lightness; his features appeared, drawn and haggard.

"I'm your *ego*, unveiling myself to you!" he suddenly said in a lofty voice.

A moment of terror chilled my skin and congealed my bones. I was lost in the very depth of his eyes that hypnotized me into fulfilling an order I could not fathom. In the bedlam of forms that passed in front of my eyes, I detected few signs—a cross to bear! A mass of electric heat shook me inside and impeded me from thinking. Captured within that moment, my head wedged in a central point between a vertical line and a horizontal one—a point of intersection between two worlds. Balance!

"We, *egos*, are the farmers of the fields." His voice freaked me out. "We reap here amidst the stars what you, *humans*, sow on Earth, your planet."

I swallowed hard, yet my mind, that of a Seeker of Truth and Lover of Light, prevailed on my fear. I surprised myself by asking, "I don't understand. What have I sowed that you are willing to reap?"

"You have controlled your material instincts, and your sexual desires are no longer your appetites . . . ," he paused for a while and grinned at me.

I rushed to interfere, "Not completely. This spiritual journey indeed gave me strength and control over my unbalanced sexual activity, but I think I would still feel the aroma of women when the journey is over. I mean . . . I am still tied to the manifested dualistic world. I believe I cannot be a Saint. Can I? Would I? Should I? I seriously don't know . . ." I tried to explain that to him, and I hated feeling defensive in front of a total stranger, yet he claimed to be my ego. *Was he?* I thought, bewildered.

"I know what you're saying . . . I understand that the road of Sainthood is hard. To the very few Initiates, it's a matter of *choice and will*; to others, it's evolution."

"Evolution?" I startled with a deep frown.

"Yes, of course, it is. Since you don't think you can completely control your physical desires when back to earth, and, in case you would not be able to do so in this life, then, it would be a matter of evolution."

"What do you mean?" I asked, perplexed.

"Well, according to our *Akashic* records, there happened to live once a very distinguished man on earth, Pythagoras, the first philosopher. He once said *Man is a smart evolution of the animal, and divinity is a smart evolution of man.* So I tell you this now, ruminate on that," he lectured me, then waved his hand above his head as if searching for an idea from the invisible world. I waited for more.

He startled me when he clicked his fingers unpredictably and grinned before he continued, "You have successfully and courageously conquered Satan. All the powers in the world, money, and the prestige he offered on two consecutive trials, meant nothing to you. The majority of men usually succumb to him, the so-called *tempter or illusionist*, and down the spiritual darkness, they plunge. You have failed to block the seducing voice of Zazae'il at first but learned very well your lesson that the Kingdom of Heaven is much more *glorious* than the Kingdoms of Earth when you heard the melodious voice of the Old Serpent and grasped her divine way." He halted for a breath.

"You, my dear Brother, have won the final battle and saved your soul, the *word*. By refusing to fall, you have justifiably become a *Keeper under Mercury*, the Ruling planet of Enoch-Taautus-Hermes! Very rare are those who have reached this degree, yet there is one final mission for you to accomplish, and that's why I am here and what I want to reap!" He said in finality, and his face lit with determination.

I watched him in a daze. My heart pumped fast. There was a moment of silence . . . an eternal instant of eye contact that enthralled me in fright; fear from what would happen next.

"*Sacrifice* . . . !" he revealed. "Sacrificing to the Most High is always good work to do. Detach yourself totally from the ignoble and disorderly passions. Choose to become poor in the mundane life so that you can be rich in the spiritual sphere. The offering of self-interest on the altar of Humanity is the most sublime act a man is capable of doing. It is a necessity and a free will in the discharge of duty! What I want to reap, my brother, is what you are willing to let go of. It is me, your ego . . . let go of *us*! And the conscience of the new man, the *newborn*, is the very voice of the Deity."

His words came up transparent as they entered my mind like a divine whisper. I sensed them peaceful and loving and wanted to hang on to them. In my very realm, I realized the Truth he has spoken and believed in the light I have seen, but . . . *Sacrifice?* It sounded very hard to me at this phase in my life!

"I cannot promise you now that I will let go of you, my brother. I do not know if I could sacrifice myself on the altar of life. I wish I could, but I guess I am not ready. Maybe . . . not yet, ready to fully sacrifice me. I hope you'll understand," I answered him sincerely and politely.

He bowed his head in respect, waved his hand in farewell, and then departed morosely into the night sky.

Instantly, back on *Urantia*, the spiritual Earth, I met Kadmus waiting for me on the crossroads of life, amid a bountiful field of beautiful flowers in their prime.

"Have the visions ended for me?" I sought to reassure myself.

His caring stares took hold of me while he approached me further.

At his echoing silence, I was prompted to explain, "I cannot sacrifice myself on the altar of Humanity. I am not a Saint, and I don't think I'll ever be one, at least in this life, but you know I can keep the *Word* safe, close to my heart . . . close to the Light. I can surely transmit it to others, I mean to those whose conducts in life prove their walk toward the state of becoming *Kosmic*," I promised earnestly.

He looked at me again and uttered in a soothing tone, "Don't worry, my brother, I understand. Let no human live a life he or she cannot bear. It is a free choice. It is a free world. You have successfully gained the power to keep the *Word,* and you shall be granted the permission to transmit it! Very few have already done so anyway . . . ," the Hierophant of the Alphabet paused for a second, in which I bowed my head in respect, accepting honorably to fulfill my mission.

"And the remaining two visions . . . uh . . . would certainly find their ways inside your eyes," he warned me in conclusion.

Two more visions left! I thought in the depth of my being.

Immediately, *Shin*, the 21st letter, radiated out from his head toward me and lifted me up to where the Mystery resided.

My eyes led the way to my spirit!

21.

SHIN

It is the abode of Mystery where Secrets are kept close to the Light under the constellation of Pisces

Shining above the fading crescent moon, the Sun reached over the darkest regions of our planet, Earth. Something, however, appeared to have radically changed. The Sun stood like a King in the center of the sky, amidst the Heavenly bodies—moving in a circular motion across time and space and all around it.

Great temples—dedicated to the Sun—rose on top of High Mountains. The moon had vanished. No more illusions, no more false religious ceremonies and rituals to non-existing gods, and no more bloody sacrifices to *any* god, either. Before that time, people guided by the so-called religious men of all nations did not raise their minds and hearts in prayers to whatever resided beyond the *visible heaven*. They followed not the true *invisible* light but rather the luminous bodies that blazed in the firmament. They had ascribed divinity to the Sun, the Moon, and the Stars!

And the drama continued, as religions—false religions—haunted the minds of people, when the king-priests declared the *Jus Divinum* doctrine by which they led their flocks, blinded by imagination. However, only a very few *Initiates* had conceived a clear and different vision. Illusions and blindness took no part in their choice of visualizing the world beyond the physical. Into the Mysteries, they had so forth entered and sought the Truth to open their eyes to the True Light.

And inside, in the deepest sanctuary of God, the *Sanctum Sanctorum*, the new adepts met with *Man* and his odyssey in life. The Secrets, therefore, became knowable. What was concealed to the profane revealed now to the eyes of the *Initiate*. The door, shut in the face of the weak and naive, opened wide to those who dared to knock. The veil of *Isis*—the holder of the *Secret Doctrine*—lifted, and the rays of *Osiris* shone over him, the *newborn son*, Horus the Initiate.

The Mysteries somehow resembled each other, not only in Canaan-Phoenicia and Egypt, but almost everywhere across the ancient world: in India, Greece, Mexico, United Kingdom, and Germany, among others. However, the Truth had remained one and originated from one basic source, a Primary Tradition. It had journeyed around the planet. Very rare were those who could see it and preserve it. I was among those who have received the honor and have been allowed access to the Mysteries. With great awe and admiration, I've entered the domain of the *Secret Order*. There—in front of the Great Altar—stood the Hierophant, clad in his bright white tunic. A purple robe draped over his shoulder added to the sense of mysticism in his countenance. His voice rose, loud and clear in my ears—

"The Stars, the Sun, and the Moon—which ornament the ceiling; the sky above our heads—are neither objects of worship nor are they personified images of the Deity, as the vulgar think. They are only symbols . . . allegories to *Higher Truths*. Shamash—the Sun—shines during the day and dives into the ocean later at night. It is Aton—Osiris—whom Typhon killed. However, on the third day, he rises sublime and powerful again, akin to a god. The same thing happened to Adon. And when, later at night, the Sun gave its place to the Moon, Isis—Astarte—to shine and persist in guiding people throughout the dark moments—this second luminary became a goddess too.

"It is because of that . . . because *Light* wins over *Darkness*, that people considered them divinities and worshipped them. Planets, stars, and the Zodiac also played an important role in the theology of the ancients. Now, here in the abode of Mysteries, in the Temple of the *One*, the celestial objects mentioned above fall . . . they just fall. So, beware of the illusions! Here, in the domain of the *Secret Order*, we do not worship anything from the visible world as true divinities, but only as reflections or manifestations of an invisible Truth—the *Word*—uttered by God—the Universal Mind that diffuses in everything, our *Father who art in Heaven*.

"There is a spark of God in each one of us, divinely embedded inside, deep within our Individual Mind—the only bridge between Heaven and Earth, or shall I say, between Spirit and Body. Man is a triune being, set in disorder most of the time. Lost between two worlds and sunk in duality, *man* remains a wanderer inside a labyrinth of error. Let the mind be conscious of itself, as *Holder and Keeper of the Word*, so that it can connect the body and spirit in one *Unity Point* of Truth. Accordingly, the creation of *Harmony* will occur, and *Order* will be established."

There was an imposing echoing silence in the Chamber for a few seconds.

After halting for a deep breath, the Hierophant moved toward the Altar and stood majestically behind it. The sign of Pisces appeared, inscribed on the visible side of the Altar. He took a cup of wine in his hand, raised it, and uttered mystically, "The cup of wine is the spirit, and the piece of bread is the body." He paused as I watched him in silent admiration, not knowing if he had appeared from the world of visions or the world of realities.

And it was then when it dawned on me. He was the Priest of the Most High . . . *he was Melki-Sedek!* I thought as blood rushed into my heart.

Suddenly, a melodious susurrus slowly started to become audible. It seemed to be emanating from two beautiful Pillars, which, all too slowly, took form on both sides of the Great Cubical Altar. The *golden stone* on the left Pillar twinkled. Its light grew steadily, ever more intensely. Simultaneously, the *purple stone*—on the peak of the right Pillar—beamed softly and filled the room with exquisite colors.

"*The pillars are alive!*" I whispered aloud, in wonder, but no one can hear me.

A plant—beautifully engraved on the left golden Pillar, the *wheat,* shone vividly and transformed into *bread.* Meanwhile, the *vine*—ascending along the purple right Pillar—gleamed with a bloody red light and turned into *wine.* The alchemical words of Melki-Sedek had brought life to the Pillars, and the light emerging from the Stones had fused into one, at the point where the sign of Pisces shone brightly on the Great Altar . . . and the two fishes merged into one!

Magically, on the ancient wall behind the Great Altar, the painting of the most sacred rite of all times—that of *Bread and Wine*—regenerated gradually into a new one, as the few pieces of the puzzle found their hidden yet determined places, forming a complete image of the Last Supper. There, at the table, Jesus the Christ and his disciples shared the bread and wine in a sacred communal. *Most certainly, it was not the painting described in The Da Vinci Code!* I thought.

"I elevate the loaf of bread and the cup of wine to you, **Abba,** so you can bless the people of Earth and unify them with you forever, Oh, Universal Mind," the High Priest intoned.

He then ate and drank in a ritual of unification and asked me to do the same in *real life,* as done in the ritual! A great sense of sacred presence overwhelmed me as I recognized the Truth in the High Priest's words, which entered my very realm, like the very first rays of Sun—the Son—that shine over the darkened world.

"The cup of wine is the remembrance of the Spirit that inhabits us all and leaves us at the moment of death." He took a moment then said, "The piece of bread is the assurance, which the Body gives to life," he continued solemnly. "Death and Life—the greatest riddle of the human mind—will no longer be an enigma to you, brother, oh no, but rather, an answer to your query."

"Know that death is not a complete breakdown of the human being. It is not the end. It is just death in the Body and life in the eternal Spirit. That god has resurrected, be it Osiris or Adon, does not matter anymore. What matters is you, my brother! Understand that you, too, will resurrect one day above the *Cycle of Generation*. It will happen when the Light of the dawn of time shines upon you and lifts you in a final resurrection, out of the *Circle of Necessity* and into the abode of the Father."

He waited in silence and added, "Let *Justice and Mercy* be the eternal lights that guide you through and along with the perfection of your Body and the refinement of your Spirit. Henceforth, under the All-Seeing Eye of my Father, the *Eye of Providence*, and with much perpetual effort, I, Melki-Sedek, bid you live by the virtues and moralities, as a true witness to the *Secret Order*. You are a true Keeper of the Word!"

Time ceased, in which I tried to grasp the enormity of what I have been granted.

Now I know who I am. I thought in the inner depth of myself. *I am a true Keeper of the Word.*

"Along the great and long history of the Mysteries, *Initiates or Keepers* like you have always been the announcers of the coming of the *Son of Man*, who will whisper the eternal dictum of 'Universal Love and Peace' into human ears. He will awake the Divine Truth in the human *Mind*. He will do all that before leaving Earth, the *Sphere of Generation*, to finally merge and unite with the ultimate Truth, as a *Son of God*, in the realm of the One," Melki-Sedek, the Hierophant of God, the Most High, concluded eloquently.

Upon hearing that, we looked at each other with great respect and honor, while a feeling of commitment took hold of me. I accepted my call as true Keeper of the Word, yearning and waiting for the great coming of the *Kosmic Man*!

At once—from the carving of the two fishes on the Great Altar who merged into one at the blessed moment of the *ritual of unification*—a Cross— the Sacred *Tau*—appeared in all its glorious light. It was the final letter of the Sacred Alphabet. Smoothly but energetically, the Divine Sign—bathed in the Eternal Light of Abba—entered my eyes.

It conveyed my essence into the closing realm of visions!

22.
TAU

It is the Sign of the Cross, the Initiate, and the Elected to the Great Power, up in the sky, when the light of the Moon fades out

Through the mist, *he* appeared, walking along the field, sure of his deed, fearless of the end and his adversaries—scurrying and raging behind him. They had felt threatened by his constant message of Love and Peace and had refused to perceive the *Light*. He had come to the world from a *Superior Order*, and so, with slow and steady steps, his destination clear, he continuously marched without turning back. His long white-linen tunic, torn by excessive use, edged his papyrus sandals—worn out by his long journey through the awkward and hard path of Truth.

I was there, watching and wondering about him. His enemies cursed him and threw stones at him, but he never answered back. They ran after him, spitting and howling out his death like mad dogs, thunder amid a storm, but he kept impressively silent. His strength of control amazed me. When he passed by me, he smiled with ineffable tenderness. Loving warmth emitted *Beauty* from his eyes and communicated with my dazzled mind. I followed him—the *man in white*—without hesitation. A soft breeze escorted him along the way.

A small hill stood just ahead. He advanced, getting closer. Stains of blood appeared on his white robe. Surrounded by a few mountains and plains, the hill appeared as if in the heart of the world. A beautiful old tree rose on the top. Despite his injuries, he approached his destination with unnoticeable effort. Very few men and women followed him with sad faces, weeping. They were probably members of his family and some friends. Compassion towards that mysterious man overwhelmed me. I wanted to help, but courage seemed to have escaped me, as it had escaped his relatives and friends—who seemed unable to assist the man walking towards the hill.

Reaching the tree on the top of that hill, he greeted it and turned back to face those who considered him an enemy. He, on the other hand, held no such feelings of resentment toward them or towards anyone! He raised his hands to the sky and whispered in a silent zephyr—a soundless moment in which hundreds of arrows, perhaps, even more, launched with mighty hatred yet by shaky hands, swished across the air and struck his body. The strength of the strikes pierced him, crucified on the *tree of life and death*. His eyes blinked. A nail perforated his right wrist, another caught painfully on his other wrist, and then another across his feet. He strove for a mouthful of air.

They had just elevated a cross on that hill . . . in the heart of the world. He looked down at the people and smiled with the same warm and loving eyes. They wept and wept again. In spite of all the suffering and pain that invaded his realm, he only murmured a faint sound, a sound only the *Eternal* could hear.

His blood dripped to the ground—a witness, or rather, an *insignia* in the memory of life—marking his sacrifice on the *Altar of Humanity*. Whether on the cross or the tree, it didn't matter at all. Everywhere he existed, he appeared powerful, standing in the center, a Master, intimidating the flesh and shining with divine charm.

With great emotion, the faithful few who had come to that place looked at him, thought about him, hoped, and asked for a miracle—for a way for him to save himself. From above, however, he kept watching them. In the stillness of time, he knew he would not fulfill their wishes but rather accomplish his mission, written by *Divine Words*. I drew nearer to the cross. Somebody there filled a Grail with his shedding blood. *Joseph of Rameh!* I gasped in recognition. *His Great uncle!*

The murderers, conversely, waited for him to die, debating whether or not he could save himself. A frightening feeling appeared to have taken over them, and anxiety subdued the remnants of their thoughts. Time elapsed slowly for the dying but too quickly for the caring ones. The Sun had not yet disappeared in the ocean, but darkness had crept up that hill like a spy. He gazed at them, then toward the sky above, and talked to his Father, saying, "Father, forgive them; for they know not what they do."

Time stood still.

As *Keeper of the Word*, I knew by then that the man of the white-linen garment was, in truth, the *Kosmic Man*. His great force of compassion and his aptitude to forgive—even those who had greater sin than Pilate—left me awestruck. Suddenly the air changed, and the wind blew all around. It struck him hard, diffusing the coldness of death into his blood. In a mystical whisper, he chanted to God, his Father, "Eli, Eloi . . . " The call held no request for help but rather for guidance along the final path of his conscious spirit. "It is finished," he imparted, as his spirit floated away from his body like a note of melody from a musical chord.

The Sun sunk into the ocean at once. Massive black clouds clothed the hill and its surroundings. They hastily moved in all directions, changing forms, eventually hovering like circles in the sky. The air became cold, very cold. The Earth rocked and quaked. Every existing atom, whether blind or intelligent, trembled inside. Animals drifted in weird movements, losing direction, crying, and howling in fear. Birds lost control of their flight, and the fish plunged into the abyss. Flowers trembled in the breeze, and trees swayed in the darkening tempest.

The walls of each fake temple and house shook to their very foundations. People became clumsy as they lost their perception of things. Chaos replaced the orderly rhythm of life. Night invaded from all directions. Alone, abandoned in an obscured and unknown place, they felt unsafe, searching for a probable answer to their mislaid feelings.

Abruptly, the erratic hysteria of nature came to a halt. *What was it?* I wondered. I turned to watch the faithful, lowering the body, very gently, all too carefully, from the cross. The tree breathed. His enemies departed, rejoicing in their victory and relief. His mother, family, and friends took the body away to bury it in the Sarcophagus—inside a new tomb that Joseph of Rameh, his Great uncle, had carved in the rock of his garden. I went with them.

From afar, our eyes perceived twinkles of light. The more we walked towards that light, the more our fear of darkness and our anxious loneliness faded away. Then, the sound of drums echoed all around. The sky cleared for the stars to shine like diamonds on the dark-blue dress of an Ancient Goddess—the Queen of Heaven. The road led us inside a forest of Oak and Cedar trees. Its beauty enchanted us. The fragrance of *tears*—the 'golden amber,' leaking down from the trees—seeped fast into our minds.

Time elapsed without a trace. Clouds ran across the sky. Days followed nights, and nights followed days. The sky danced. On the *third day*, when the moonlight dimmed, a faint whisper came from afar—far away like the wailing of some lost spirit. Within seconds, the faint wail surged into a steady voice. A voice, sweet as amber, vibrated inside the walls of the Mystery Chamber, where the body rested.

"Let God—the Most High, the Father—illuminate you and lead you out from the wilderness of pain and illusions into the *Realm of Light!*"

Words of mystery indeed, strong and meaningful, entered our ears like the sound of waterfalls, thundering down from a High Mountain. Then we watched as the body took life again! We trembled inside and followed the light within.

"*Fire* in the East is shining over *Water* in the West. Life is conquering Death. Behold the Resurrection of Man!" the *Angelic* voice continued.

From within our inner realm, we saw *him*, standing in front of us, on the top of the High Mountain. His arms stretched upwards; his feet parted. A crown of red roses ornamented his head, and his hair glittered under the rays of the Sun, draping his shoulders. His glorious pink aura calmed down our fright. A *five-pointed star* shone on his chest, revealing the emanation of Heaven in his being.

He was the *Initiate of the First Order*. A *Microcosm of the Macrocosm*. An elected to the Great Power. He was Keeper of Justice, Wisdom, and the Mercy of God throughout the *Eternal Truth*. Wearing his new white-linen garment, he appeared pure as a *Good Angel*, a god. With a glorious smile, he whispered aloud, "I'm Phenoch-Thor-Taautus-Thot-Hermes, Adon, Horus-Osiris, Krishna, Pythagoras, Buddha . . . I'm Jesus Christ, son of man, son of God, every man, in the process of becoming—a *Kosmic Man*." Silence, and then, "I stand as a Metatron between the Spirit and Body, redeeming the *Body*—by its regeneration below, and the *Spirit*—by its jubilation above, giving Humanity the will to walk once more with God. I am the son of the everlasting Light." And before it was all concluded, he said, "I am now leaving Earth—my mother, and will rejoin my Kingdom, where my Father lives eternally."

He opened his arms up high and soared like a flame towards Heaven.

Along with his final Resurrection, he uttered loudly, "I am the Aleph and the Tau, the beginning and the end."

His last words vibrated all over the seen and unseen Kosmos.

Up in Heaven, he would become a creature of Light, free at last from the tyranny of matter and the aspirations of the spirit of bondage.

8.

The Occult Numbers
The 2nd Level

1.
FIRST MEDITATION

Standing in front of the door, my heart began beating so fast, and I couldn't lower its speed nor ignore its sound, echoing inside my body.

"Calm down . . . ," I whispered to myself. "Everything will be alright."

I opened the door and entered. A different kind of air was floating inside, so pure, so elevating that it entered through my skin and into my heart, refreshing it. A strange voice, akin to that of Angels, welcomed me into the Mystery Chamber and congratulated me for my success in passing the four tests. I have passed them even before. It was before I met with Kadmus in the mysterious world of the Sacred Alphabet.

I have passed by the *Fire* element in my first vision, the *Earth* element in my sixth vision, and the *Water* element in the tenth. As for the *Air* element, and as previously explained, it is the link and mover of the other three elements. I have indeed passed by it the moment I passed by the three others. So I thought!

Very shy dim lights illuminate the Chamber. All around its walls were exhibited successively few paintings. Beautiful statues holding torches in their hands illuminate them. I counted them one by one; they were twenty-two! Under each, only the first ten, I could scarcely see inscribed a letter and a number. Immediately, as I saw them, I remembered what I have learned from my visions. There, inside the Chamber, that secret knowledge might evolve into a practical aspect.

"Each letter of this Sacred Alphabet, along with its specified number, have their direct influence on the triune dimensional worlds of Spirit, Intellect, and Matter." The voice uttered nicely into my ears.

I stood still and in awe in front of the first painting. It pictures a *Magician* in a white robe holding a Scepter in his hand and wearing a golden crown on his head.

"The white robe signifies *Purity*, the Scepter shows *Mastership*, while the golden crown means the *Universal Light*, where each and every will, united with God for the manifestation of Truth and Justice, will be in direct connection in the participation of the Divine Power over the existential life. It is an eternal gift given to the free spirits!" explained the voice. I listened carefully.

"In the *spiritual world,* the letter **Aleph** and the number **1** symbolize the Absolute Being from whom life sprung. However, in the *mental world*, they would denote Unity—the Equilibrium of life; whereas on the *physical plane*, they mean the Microcosmic man, who—by expanding his occult faculties—would elevate himself up into the spheres of the infinite Macrocosm, God." It continued eloquently.

I was somewhat surprised by that strange system of *Initiation*. But, as the Angelic voice continued explaining the hidden meanings of each of the paintings, I progressively began to perceive the inside codes of the sublime ideas and images they so powerfully embody and beautifully expose.

There was a *Five-Pointed Star* painted on the ground in the middle of the Chamber. A Scepter stood at the midpoint of the Star. It was the Caduceus of Hermes, coiled with two serpents around it, their heads meet a little bit below the top point, which opens up in the form of wings, like that of a Phoenix.

"To proceed with your *Initiation,* you should find your seat beneath the Rod of Enoch, closing the circle, or should I say, the lines of the Star, and activate the energy of its five points!" The voice surprisingly revealed, my mind got confused, and my heart resumed its normal beating after a minute or so.

"Come on . . ." ordered the voice. "From the Eastern apex point of the Star where the Sun Rises behind you, walk in the direction of the left Northern point, then right on the Southern point, before reaching the two points in the West. From there, mark your steps reverently toward the Shaft of the Shepherd."

I complied with his instructions and command without hesitation, as I heard the Angelic voice adding, "Once sat in meditation, breathe in Unity and exhale out duality."

The meditation began . . . and the mantra AUM echoed in the Chamber . . .

After moments of deep meditation, a sudden rush of energy began to circulate along the lines of the Star, connecting the five points altogether and lighting them up all at once, before an abrupt energy cut-off took place, astonishing me, but instantly followed after by a sense of order that soon settled in, and a great presence of peace—harmonious in nature—flooded in the Chamber. It was real, so beautiful that I couldn't let it go outside of me.

From the top point of the Caduceus, something looking like a crystal ball or an eye shone with intense, transparent light. I kept on focusing. The Phoenix' wings seemed to have taken life, fluttering silently *above and below*, right and left, transporting the light from the midpoint and diffusing its glorious radiance all around. In a spiral, elliptical movement of the light, an image that seemed to have been traveling across and within time and space hovered in the air, a few meters above my head. A point! It beamed miraculously amidst the mystical circle. A sense of deep serenity and unexplained vibrations appeared to have inhabited my mind.

"O Thot-Hermes, the Ibis-Headed god inside the 'Great Hall of Justice,' the divine lawgiver, you, who records the assessment of the heart of the deceased against the *feather of truth*.[1] Open the way . . ." the voice invoked the spirit of Thor, before suddenly asking me, "What is God, young brother?"

"It would be impossible for human thoughts to rightly conceive what God is," I answered. "One cannot describe through material means that which is immaterial and eternal."

"Right! The *Eternal* is an actual perception of the *Spirit*. The other is not," continued the voice. "That which our senses can perceive, can be described by words; but that which is incorporeal, invisible, immaterial, and without form cannot be realized through our ordinary senses."

---

1. In the *Egyptian Book of the Dead*, we see Thot recording the result coming out from the weighing of the heart against the *feather of truth* of the goddess Maat. Through that ancient funeral ceremony, and when the deeds of the deceased were found justified, his beautified soul would pursue its journey to the Lotus Lake for his eternal purification. In the Fields of Yalu, the blessed and sanctified soul gains its everlasting life in paradise. From now onward, it would continue its life working along the Celestial Nile before it proclaims its final realization into the abode of the Absolute Truth (where the Father resides), unifying its mortal yet resurrected being with the Immortal Spirit, and by such, identifying it with Ra, the Supreme Being.

"I understand thus, O Thot, I understand that God is *ineffable.*" I spoke coherently and repeated the words in such a way, "O Hermes, I understand that God is ineffable."

A moment of sacred silence ensued . . . time to reflect on those words.

> The *One*, **1**, is not just a number but the creator of all numbers. The Primordial Harmony is mirrored in the Sacred Alphabet by the letter *Aleph*, the unbecoming, unborn, unmade, and the unformed. It is the Central Fire which diffuses in everything and circulates through the circumference of existence. The act of **Creation** occurred by the invisible power of the *One*. It is, therefore, a solitary, all-embracing whole in which everything is truly interconnected.
>
> The *One* is the **Monad**, or *"monas."* It is the Intelligent Spirit that moves by itself; without being divided or manifested, being unique, eternal, and unchangeable.
>
> The *One* is the **Universal Mind**, or *"nous,"* which initially pervaded the Cosmos[2], calling it forth out of chaos by *sounds and harmony* and guiding it into an order of Divine Origin.
>
> The *One* epitomizes **God**, *or Good*, the Source of life, the very Essence concealed in the heart of things that are moving and changing through a harmonious measure of Intelligence.
>
> The *One* profiles the **Unity Point** that contains *Infinity*. It is the Absolute Creator whom we call the **Father**. His sign is Light and Fire, the Life Force and Essence of the Whole. We dedicate it to the First True Light, for which the Sun is not but *His* physical reflector.

"Truth I tell you, brother! The ultimate goal of *Initiation* is to come closer to the One." The voice then said, ending his explanation and telepathic mental transmission on the nature of the first principle.

"But . . . how can we possibly come nearer to the *One*, our Father?" I inquired curiously; a frown of puzzlement drawn on my face.

---

2. Cosmos or Kosmos as called by Pythagoras who actually seemed to have been the first one in history to ever use such a word to indicate a *well ordered and harmonious universe.* According to Pythagoras, the Kosmos is an immeasurable musical instrument in perfect tune with itself. Its vibrating numbers produce melodious tones that resound almost everywhere. Hence, both the Universe of gods and Man, Heaven and Earth, the Macrocosm and the Microcosm, are all linked together eternally. They do reflect the same harmonious proportions Pythagoreans examine in mathematics. But this is only achieved through the Divine Numbers, which are the primal reality. (El Koussa, Karim, *Pythagoras the Mathemagician*, 259)

"Time will come when you will know! As for now, will you please repeat after me the Glorious Hymn that Enoch-Taautus-Hermes taught his direct disciples, and from them to every true Enochian Initiate, through a succession of mystical lore!" He urged in an Angelic tone, adding, "Holy is God the Father of all being . . ."

"Holy is God the Father of all being," I repeated venerably.

"Holy is God, whose wisdom is carried out into execution by his Powers . . . Holy art Thou, who through the *Word* created all." He continued, and I followed suit.

"Keep in mind, fellow *Initiate*, not to speak of God without Light, for God is the True Light. Accept "It" with a free spirit." The voice advised with divine authority.

"I believe in Thee, bear testimony of his Wisdom, and vow to live freely the Life I have received. I shall work hard to perceive the Light." I chanted melodiously after him.

And the sky night rolled peacefully through time!

~ ~ ~

Reflecting on what was revealed during that First Meditation was important for me to understand that although God, the Father, is *ineffable*, the most appropriate names given to Him would all start with the first letter of the Sacred Alphabet, *Aleph*. I name Al-El, the Canaanite-Phoenician God, the Most High; Aton, the Egyptian Monotheistic God of Akhenaton; Al-Apollo, the Pythagorean God; Abba, the Father to all, preached by Jesus Christ; and Allah, the Muslim God of the Sufis. These were the names that first shuffled inside my mind.

After that silent break in the outside field, there on top of a mountain, I breathed in Light and exhaled out darkness . . .

2.
SECOND MEDITATION

The time came when my mind unconsciously asked for a new adventure, and so it was. At night, I stood still in front of that door, ready to enter into my Second Meditation. Inside the Chamber, I made my steps on the Five Points of the Star, from East to West, and then sat underneath the Rod of Enoch. After invoking my *inner* spirit, the energy fast circulated. It then enveloped me with such great presence, a presence so terrible yet so mesmerizing. It took hold of me, in an unimagined and unexpected manner, but that was the reality of my feelings!

The vibrating light from the Caduceus, that which was lifted by the fluttering wings of the Phoenix, floated up in a circular motion to hover above me and below me through an intertwining string of energy. The point in the middle of the circle brought forth spirit and matter before *Divine Intelligence* could be dispersed through rays all over the circumference. That was a frightening momentary cut of pure energy along the five lines and points of the Star! A few moments later, the order came back, but it was not as the first one of the First Meditation, one of serenity and peace. That new order was chaotic and confusing.

And then it happened, the spirit, descending from one point, met the matter in the other, and together they *built and destroyed* the bridge between the Central Point and the points scattered along the circumference.

"The One," suddenly uttered the voice without warning, adding, "The Universal Mind, that pervaded the Cosmos, summoning it out of chaos by *sounds and harmony,* intended it to follow a certain order of Divine Origin, after being diffused through everything and circulated the circumference of existence. Yet, two points derived from the Order, that of the *Word*, and formed a confusion of Unity, or rather, a *line*, imitating the second letter of the Sacred Alphabet, *Beth*, the duality of the created existence."

Silence reigned for some time . . . Time to think!

When the *One*, **1**, decided to manifest itself, it became *Two*, **2**. That is the **Dyad** of indivisible essence, but divisible substance. The *Monad* then acted on the *Dyad* to produce the numbers.

Therefore, the *Dyad* is not a number by itself, but rather a **Two-Pointed Division**, a solid confusion of Unity, a **Line**. On one side, the *male-active principle* is *Spirit* or Energy, and on the other side, the *female-passive principle* is *Body or* Matter. By that, it distorts the equilibrium created by the Mind.

Consequently, the *Dyad* represents the **Conflicting Union** of the will of the *Eternal Male* and the faith of the *Eternal Female*. These two essential divinities created the visible phenomenal world. We dedicate the *Dyad* to the Moon, or Juno, which is the second luminary.

"Oh, what does that mean exactly?" I asked, not sure I understood his words, transmitted to me by telepathy.

"As you already know from the previous meditation, the *One*, of High spiritual nature, is not at all Hermaphrodite—male and female—as some have assumed! But now, well, life in the Cosmos, and precisely here on the physical plane, is bound to that duality, primarily consisting of the Male and Female aspects. However, within all the creatures that lived, evolved, and prospered here on Earth, Humanity is the most qualified at the time being to escape that duality."

"How can we do that?"

"Time will come for you to know the way! As for now, just meditate on the idea of escaping it, as well as knowing that the *Word* itself could not be perceived but perfect as the Divine Mind. Thenceforth, the imperfection of the Human Mind if occurring in the phenomenal world is not due to the imperfection of the Mind of God, but rather to the imperfection of the Demiurge, hence dualism and the work of it in Nature."

That was hard to absorb, as anxiety filled me all through the night!

~ ~ ~

Meditating on the shaky revelation of that Second Meditation, for the night was a battlefield, was important for me to realize that this concept was mentioned in almost all ancient religions; these dual divinities embody *Adon(Ba'al)-Astarte* for the Canaanite-Phoenicians, *Osiris-Isis* for the Egyptians, *Bel-Ishtar* for the Babylonians, *Shiva-Shakti* for the Hindus, *Heaven and Hell* for the Persians, *Yod-Heva* or Yahweh for the Hebrews. It is the Androgynous Demiurge of indivisible essence, but divisible substance. It contains the *male active principle*, the *Spirit-Energy*, on one side, and the *female passive principle*, the *Body-Matter*, on the other.

I came then to understand that the Demiurge is the union of the *Will* of the 'Eternal Male' and the *Faith* of the 'Eternal Female,' the two essential divinities that created and generated the visible manifested physical world. We envisioned them as the Sun and the Moon, overburdened by Saturn's power, and enclosed within its ring!

Among the most important worth mentioning disciplinarians who sermonized the "escape" from the work of duality are Pythagoras and non-dualist Gnostics. Gnostics, in general, believed that every human being housed a divine spark trapped in matter. The Aeon, or Emanation of God, the *Man of Light*, the mirror of the Macrocosm, and regarded as *Adam-Kadmon* by Kabbalists, has been truly deceived—by the Androgynous Demiurge who created the lowest material level of reality—through the process of incarnation and forgot his true nature. Gnostics, therefore, wish that one day they would reach Liberation and therefore Union with the True God in the *Pleroma*, the Gnostic Heaven. The Journey is long and confusing and could take many lifetimes.

It seems, however, that dualist Gnostics who were not able to wait for that foreseen unification with the *One*, indulged in the work of duality, particularly in sexuality, considering it sacred at some point, though the Demiurge created it. They rather began to believe that it would not only bestow them with joy, but it would also make them achieve *oneness* with the Divine and the Universe. It happened that they were trapped and have forgotten their True Nature!

Yet, they were not alone engaged in these peculiar rites for an alleged *oneness*, but many amongst others believed the same, like in the traditions of Hindu Tantra, Chinese Taoism, some of the Templars, some Alchemists who appeared to have deviated from the true Alchemy of Hermes, and some of the Rosicrucians who claimed to be *Hermeticists* but were not . . . At any rate, we will elaborate more on that in Chapter 11.

Time passed me by so quickly, walking outside for some fresh air. I needed a break, there on top of the mountain to restore my mind to serenity. That was a great revelation I had not expected coming so fast, as I took a long moment breathing in Unity and Love and exhaling out duality and hatred . . .

3.
THIRD MEDITATION

Later at night, inside the Mystery Chamber, ready to venture now through the meditation of the third number and to sit as usual under the Caduceus of Hermes after crossing the Five Points of the Star, from East to West, I began invoking the Force within. Energy accelerated, and the air changed, filling me with an intense feeling of confusion and anxiety, yet a sense of hope always remained to spark in my mind. Then a thought came rushing in as I began to wonder about the sensation I was experiencing. Though, I could not linger on that thought a lot, fearing to interrupt the meditation process.

From the eye, the *Eye* of the Phoenix, a transparent light has been emitted. Through the wings of liberty, it traveled through the dimensions of the physical world, to hover above my physical eyes and then into my inner eye, seeping slowly inside the very realm of my spiritual dimension.

"The Androgynous Demiurge, the Dyad, generated the material world, the Tryad, the third number. It exists everywhere and gives life to the Kosmos from its three *toms* of Fire, Air, and Water." The voice began. "Within it are hidden the key elements of life in the Kosmos, its Creation and Evolution, passing by all levels of life forms, starting from the Mineral state, to the Vegetable, Animal, and then finally, the Human state. Without it, as humans, you cannot secure your salvation, but there is a twist here! Indeed, the third element of the Tryad also represents the mundane world of suffering. But why is it so? You may ask, of course! Could you advance a suggestion?"

The question threw me into even more confusion. I nodded in denial. The voice did not expect me to know, I wondered.

"No worries! I will tell you why, young brother. Men and women then began their journey through nature, wandering under the fading power of Jupiter, inside the three-dimensional world. Being thus most overburdened by the three dimensions that enveloped its existence, Humanity wandered, conjured by its virtual beauty, and occupied ever since in the work of procreation for survival, to keep the dream running and the vision of its true nature fading, forgotten, as it had been confined to a voyage through life.

"When you humans were pushed into the realm of the Tryad, you have subsequently lost the Vision of the Sublime Reality, the *One*. As a result, you have become and remained stuck between the Natural and Animal-Human world that pulls you downwards into the depths of the ground and the Divine world that always seeks and tries to absorb you back upwards into its Perfection.

"Your goal now is akin to mine when I first embarked on my spiritual journey, striving through many years of quest and Initiation to attain that kind of knowledge that was once and always is the goal of every *Initiate* of the True Tradition. And it is to revert, to bring yourselves back to your original state—to the *Primordial Unity of the Monad*—and that, by totally ending the material and instinctive evil elements within yourselves."

"Evil elements!" I wondered aloud. "What do you mean? How can we do that?" I asked, more perplexed than ever.

But the voice was silent, and it scared me a bit . . . Time to reflect on who we are!

When the *Dyad*, the *Two*, **2**, broke the Unity of the *Monad*, the *One*, **1**, it generated the physical world known as the *Three*, **3**, reflected as the letter *Gimel* in the Sacred Alphabet. That's the **Tryad**; it exists everywhere, being the first physical number. It is the **Psyche** that we compare to a **Triangle**. It gives life to the Kosmos from its three atoms of Fire, Air, and Water.

The **Microcosm**, say, Man, is composed of three dimensions; the **Body** that means *Strength*, **Spirit** that means *Beauty*, and the **Mind** representing *Wisdom*. Similarly, the **Macrocosm**, or the Universe, is composed of three spheres of existence: the *Natural world*, the *Human world*, and the *Divine world*.

We dedicate the *Tryad* to Jupiter. It is a perfect number indeed, for it is the symbol of **Truth** manifested in the *Mind*, **Virtue** in the *Spirit*, and **Purification** in the *Body*.

The *Tryad* constitutes the key elements of life in the entire Kosmos. And this is a fact! Along with Creation, there is Evolution that passes by all levels of life forms, from the mineral to the vegetable, to the animal, and finally, to the human.

"As you have been taught before, Man resulted from the smart evolution of the animal, and Divinity surged from the smart evolution of man. Thus, to attain that sublime state of holiness, you must break out from all the evil deeds of the Dyad, or dualism. Since you already know from the previous two meditations and this one, the goal of Initiation is to come closer to the Father!"

resumed the voice. "It is only by merging with the Father that you can feel Its essence. The Source of Intelligence exists in the heart of the Macrocosm, as well as in the heart of the Microcosm that you are.

"Your spirit, however, is like trembled water, agitated by the mundane world. You have to purify it, make it clear and clean. Realize, though, that the Divine Powers are in your Individual psyche and can *rise to unite* with the Central Fire of the Universe, the Divine Spirit, the Monad.

"The Father will then be awakened in your conscious mind. You will, moreover, participate in His Powers, entering somehow perfection, dominating things by the strength of your Intellect, your will, being therefore active like Him. Thus, achieving that, say, becoming a god, or son of God, is the state of facing, absorbing, and then eliminating the Hermaphrodite or the dual nature in you. This can be achieved by actualizing a *Union* between your three dimensions, with or in your psyche, which is nothing more than your *Individual Monad*, which would accomplish that state of concordance by finally coming to Unity with the *Great Monad*." With this new revelation, the voice concluded another important session of the esoteric teachings of the numbers.

As I thereafter contemplated the meanings of the explanations given, I wondered still, *How can we become gods and accomplish a Union with the One?*

~ ~ ~

Reflecting on that revelatory number and its importance path that would lead me to Unison with the Divine and hence the divinity within me, I came to understand that the Phoenician Tradition identifies this *Tryad* by the theological concept of the Trinity that comprised the *Divine world* of Anat, Adon, and El, while the Egyptians associated it with their main divinities; Isis, Horus, and Osiris. The Hindus, in turn, correlate it to Sarasvathi, Vishnu, and Brahma.

While this Trinity could have also been represented, perhaps at a later stage, by almost all ancient religions, the two religions of Egypt and Canaan-Phoenicia have seen coming out of the *Dyad*, the duality of their divine male and female, say Anat and El, and Isis and Osiris, a synthesis, a son and holder of the germ of duality. However, this son, Adon or Horus-Osiris, dies, killing dualism within him, so to speak, and resurrecting in a new life, becoming the kind of a savior, a son of God, who would have then achieved *Oneness*. That was surely, a much-evolved theology!

The Hermetic doctrine, which is nothing other than that, is based on the unity of all things; God is all, and God is within. Thus God is *One*, and we thence could be one with him through spiritual awareness. Hermes, also called Hermes Trismegistos, or Thrice Greatest, representing by its characteristics the *Tryad*, is identified as the Earthly agent of the Divine Creator, the *One*. Surely, he was the inventor of speech. As it was revealed earlier, the inventor of the phonetic Alphabet, being Thor-Theut, the wise physician and magician, was referred to in the Egyptian Book of the Dead.

The Caduceus of Hermes is the Rod held by the first Shepherd of Men, Enoch, who would guide them to repent, so to speak, rid themselves of darkness and grasp only light, forsake corruption caused by the *Fallen Angels*, and ultimately partake in immortality. Every true *Initiate* requires self-discipline and certain forms of asceticism. Meditation in silence would give Man the ability to remember his true nature as he sees through the light of the two great Visions and perceive their depths by suppressing all the senses that fall within the boundaries of Dualism.

The Light in those Visions, the first and final one, could be perceived as that of the *One*, whose *Knowledge* is Man's *salvation and resurrection*. Having descended from the *One* and captured by the *Dyad* within space and time, Man would pass thereafter through a cycle of death and rebirth until the day comes when the *Initiate* birthed in him, would come to identify himself as being one with the whole Creation and with God himself.

In short, what Enoch-Thot-Hermes, that *First Initiate* had revealed, concluded the mystery of everything. He eloquently taught that *man on Earth is a mortal god, and god in Heaven is an immortal man.* As above, so below, his famous axiom is not but an invitation for man to come nearer to God and for God to come nearer to man. It is, therefore, an invitation for man to become a god, son of God, and for God to speak the *Word* that would come and dwell among us, in the form of a man.

Christianity, who preached that Jesus was born of God, being the son of God and a woman, could not be understood and perceived outside that spiritual guidance of Enoch. On the physical plane though, Jesus, a High Priest forever after the Order of Melki-Sedek—who on his image was fashioned Hiram Abiff in Freemasonry—being born of man and woman, trapped like us, in the cycle of death and rebirth, in that duality, had after all succeeded in facing its preventative implications, totally absorbed it, and finally eliminated it by reaching the fulfillment, a *Oneness* with God, becoming what he is in reality, the Son of God.

Pythagoras, the son of Hermes through Aithalides, one of his avatars, as he always claimed he was to his faithful disciples, repeated much too often the one *Initiatic* dictum, *Man is a smart evolution of the Animal, and godhood is a smart evolution of Man.*

When enlightenment showed in gradual degrees on my features, I nodded and continued pondering something I suddenly remembered. It was related to me once by a very dear *late* teacher, and sort of something similar to it was revealed to me by Kadmus in the vision of the 13th Sacred Letter, *Mem*, "There are men who are born to become fathers and remain *sons of men*, and others who chose to stay sons and become *Sons of God*." That very free-willed notion just came rushing into my mind, and I now understood well what it was meant by it. Either man carries the Journey of life trying to imitate the Demiurge or becomes akin to the Son of God and sits on the Father's right hand.

All are children of God, and I don't actually know if I could keep that cup away from me and become *Son of God*, but I surely know my path now, for I have become *Keeper of the Word*. That is what matters for the time being, as I took a walk outside to that mountain top, grasping at the Sunlight, relaxing, and breathing in Unity and Order while exhaling out duality and confusion . . .

4.
FOURTH MEDITATION

It was seven at night when I found myself standing still, looking ahead of me at the door that would open up to the inner knowledge of the self. Inside the Chamber, I walked along with the *Five-Pointed Star*, with its apex onto the East and its bottom on the West, and then began my meditation session under the Caduceus.

From the upper point of the Caduceus, magnificent energy was fast propelled along the Five Lines of the Star and into the near surroundings, enveloping me and lifting me on the fluttering wings of the Phoenix.

"Other than those who have chosen to become Sons of God, and are very few," the voice began, "and those who defeated death by becoming gods, say, immortal men in Heaven, there are the rest of humanity, which decided to enter the *square of life*. Inside the four boundaries of existence, the major group manifests in the four elements that form Nature itself; Fire, Air, Water, and Earth, moves within it, and completes the creation process.

"The Four elements are the keys, the most important ones in Nature, yet the most tempting. They are Keepers of many important natural phenomena that would come in groups of four, like the most significant one that describes the four levels of existence: Being, Living, Feeling, and Realizing. Again, it is the question of survival—that of your species. Afraid of physical death or reaching immortality through spiritual resurrection and mental awareness, Humanity has long sought material immortality, here on Earth!"

Meditation continued in silence, for the voice muted!

Number *Four*, **4**, the **Tetrad** or **Tetraktys** symbolizes the *Kosmic Creator*, embodied by the **Logos**, the hidden archetype of the universe. Number *Four* completes the process of **Creation** because it begins with the *One*—being the **Point of Fire**—then moves to the *Two* that epitomizes the **Line of Air**. At that point, the process shifts to the *Three*—the **Surface of Water**—and finally reaches the *Four* that portrays **Earth's Solidity**.

The *Tetraktys* is, in reality, the true **Sacred Decade**, for the basic principles do exist in the first four numbers **1**, **2**, **3**, and **4**; the sum of which is equal to **10**, which stands as the best of the numbers. Thus, it is arranged to form a triangle with *One* at the top, then *Two*, *Three*, and finally *Four* at the bottom.

Number *Four* is the most important key in Nature. It is the **Key-Keeper**, the **Perfect Square** of *equality and regularity*. It is the symbol of **Moral Justice** and stands between the subject and object in a *horizontal direction*. The *vertical line* describes the **Divine Laws** in a conscious and energetic method. Hence, all powers and vibrations of the physical and spiritual planes are engraved within the Perfect Square. And the name of Him, **Alim**, or **Abba**—the Logos—is equal to the sacred number *Four*. We, therefore, dedicate it to the Sun!

These teachings entered my ears like in a divine whisper, or was it, after all, by some sort of mental telepathy? I didn't know; however, I needed more explanation on what that Angelic voice was saying earlier.

"We often wish to soar and hover like *Good Angels* across the sky, hoping to realize the *Perfect Square*, drawn on the Sun, that of equality and regularity. But, I mean, how can reaching immortality through spiritual resurrection and mental awareness be achieved where we are still bound into that gross matter that keeps us attached?" I asked.

But the voice remained silent, and so continued the meditation!

~ ~ ~

The morning of the next day came so fast as if the imposing silence of the night before had surpassed the heavy weight of the world we live in. Indeed, the morning moments of the Rising Sun have conquered the moments of sleep, of that temporary death, which always comes and takes you without a sound, and without even a whisper, it takes you in silence.

Pondering upon the meditation of last night, I realized that we, humans, always wish to accomplish Moral Justice between the subject and object and strive to accept the Divine Laws consciously and energetically, but we often failed, for Individual Consciousness haven't yet become a collective one. Therefore, we look above us, where the only possible way for us to reach the sky is by coming nearer to it, and thus we would instead climb the mountain, the highest one.

With great hope, we would invoke the name of *thee*, for all powers and vibrations of the Physical and Spiritual planes are engraved within the Perfect

Square, the Logos, and where the name of the Father is replaced by the sacred number *Four*. There resides the door and the path, portrayed as the letter *Daleth* in the Sacred Alphabet, the delta that leads open to Taurus, the *Sacred Bull* that would plow the Celestial Field for our spirit to journey through.

The day passed so routinely fast as I spent much of my time at the mountain top communicating on a higher speed with the world, breathing in Unity and Truth while exhaling out duality and deception . . .

5.
FIFTH MEDITATION

At the center of the Five Points of the Star, I sat under the Shaft of the Shepherd and invoked the forces within to guide me along that awkward path mirrored as *Heh*, the fifth letter of the Sacred Alphabet, which had me enter into the world of temptations, hoping to unlock its hidden secrets. As always, inside that Mystery Chamber, and within the depth of my meditation, I sensed the energy circulating across me and inside me after reaching the middle point where I was.

Energized by the serpents coiled round it, the upper point of the Caduceus shone like a crystal eye, and the wings of the Phenok oscillated the accumulated energy above my eyes.

In meditation, I plunged again!

Number *Five*, **5**, the **Pentad**, is the most important and powerful number of them all. It stands in the middle of Ten. It is **Central** in its position, a circular number that comprises five circumscribed circles. The *Five* characterizes the return of everything to its original central point. And by that is meant the return of the **Psyche** into itself, where *Purification and Knowledge* abide by the **Cycle of the Pentagon**[3]; a Great Cycle that rotates in harmony and commands the movements of the Kosmos.

Five is the symbol of the five tomic shapes that exist hidden in Nature. They consist of the *Pyramid, Octahedron, Icosahedron, Cube,* and *Dodecahedron*. In a systematic and respective order, these geometrical shapes represent the five elements of **Fire**, **Air**, **Water**, **Earth**, and the **Ether**. However, nothing is pure of the existential matters *since* Earth partakes in Fire, Fire in Air, Air in Water, and Water in Ether. For purity to embrace existence, Earth should partake in Water, Water in Air, Air in Fire, and Fire in Ether.[4]

---

3. The Pentagon, or the State Department of the United States of America, is undoubtedly based on the Pythagorean idea of the *Cycle of the Pentagon*. Of course, the US State Department is not ideologically built with the idea of commanding the movements of the Kosmos, but rather, those of Earth. From here, came the idea of building an American Empire.

4. Some may replace Fire with Air, but we stick to the order we presented in the text.

Number *Five* is a merger. It is named marriage for it contains a male-odd number, the *Three*, which is limited and determined, and a female-even number, the *Two*, which is unlimited and undetermined. The sum of these numbers, 2 + 3 equals 5.

The esoteric and spiritual symbol of number **5** is the **Five-Pointed Star**. It is the **Pentagram**. In the secret language, it means *death to reveal*, a term that connotes the death and resurrection in the system of *Initiation*. Each line of the star intersects with the other in the proportions of **Macro to Micro**. *Five* is dedicated to Hermes-Enoch, to Mercury!

It mainly symbolizes the **Kosmic Man**, that is, the Microcosm of the Macrocosm; the *thinking and conscious* Man. Therefore, drawn on a **Pentagon**, *Five* epitomizes harmony and health.

After I heard the voice's mind, he resumed his teachings, "Instead of following the natural rhythm of Reincarnation, when the Psyche returns to its very self by Purification and Knowledge of the *Cycle of the Pentagon*, revolving harmoniously, energetically, and consciously, commanding the movements of the Cosmos, it would, however, continue the cycle in a circular movement, and everything would return from the center to the circumscribed circles! Thus, the participation of the elements among themselves would be forever confused and imprisoned inside the flesh. Nothing is pure of the existential things, unless Earth participates with Water, Water with Air, Air with Fire, and Fire with the Ether, the fifth element.

"If thus followed, the five *tomic* shapes representing those elements would then become one. It would, moreover, open up a window to the constellation of the Ram and accomplish a communication for an inspired revelation! Then and only then, the *five-pointed star,* on which you dwell now, would mean in the secret occult language of the Tradition, "death to reveal," the allegoric, say, *Initiatic* death of the Body, the Microcosm, and the resurrection of the Spirit into the abode of the Macrocosm. Thus, if drawn correctly inside the *Circle*, and I mean figuratively, if used properly into the *Cycle of Death and Rebirth*, it would then exorcise the bad daemons, so to speak, where the Cycle would end, and true immortality through spiritual resurrection and mental awareness would be achieved." The voice ended adequately, answering my previous questions.

I meditated more deeply into myself!

~ ~ ~

Reflecting on that the next day perplexed me a little bit, but I felt optimistic about the things to come. I learned that Pythagoras, the Master of Mysteries and one of the five Pillars of the Great White Fraternity, has chosen the Pentagram, the *Five-Pointed Star*, as the symbol of his Great Society. It became, *de facto*, the sign they wore on their chests denoting their official adherence to the first degree, *Preparation*, which requires a total disciplinary silence. It became the secret sign of their Fraternity, meaning "death and resurrection" in their ancient system of *Initiation*. Each line intersects the other in the proportion of Macro to Micro. It was dedicated to Hermes-Enoch, whom Pythagoras proclaimed to be one of his incarnations, symbolizing the **Kosmic Man**, whose Individual Mind *Rises* towards the Universal Mind, where he would under the guidance of Mercury stand healthy and harmoniously on the right hand of the Father.

Pythagoras, who so eloquently drew the path to *Initiation,* taught that to invoke the powers of the Kosmos as an *Initiate* should, there is no need to perform prayers and dramatic rituals. Instead, one has to put himself in total synchrony with them. And so, if one uses the same numerical proportions as those of the Kosmos, then and only then would he be able to vibrate in the same frequency of Heaven. His spirit would call forth the Heavenly Spirit, and it would descend upon him like a white dove from the sky. He often asserted that this approach would undoubtedly allow one to hear the Music of the Spheres and live in Harmony with the universe!

Therefore, the Kosmic music of the Muses should be imitated down here on Earth, placing the Dodecahedron on the Cube, meaning Heaven on Earth, starting first at one place and then moving on to other places around the globe. If this is done successfully, then humanity will realize the *Perfect Square*, that of equality and regularity, and achieve a deep state of Homonoia, a true and strong union of minds and hearts among all people on Earth!

Moments passed by like a soft wind passing through green leaves in springtime; as I walked towards the mountain top, there, relaxing and breathing in Beauty and exhaling out vileness . . .

6.
SIXTH MEDITATION

Having walked from East to West on the Five Points of the Star to ultimately sit under the Rod of Enoch, I felt completely ready to receive the hidden secret knowledge of the numbers. The energy moved fast all around me as I placed myself in an inner state, invoking the powers within to unleash the meanings of the matching *Vau*, the sixth letter of the Sacred Alphabet.

The Phoenix's wings radiated the energy above my eyes, where I came to see a virtual visual presentation of the powerful impact of money on my life and how can I overcome it.

"Alas, bound within a square, the *imperfect square*, resides the kingdom of material gain that attracts the physical man more to Earth, where a series of temptations and degradations of the Human soul begin," the Angelic voice suddenly uttered, breaking the silence that had endured for a while. "Having entered life through its wide door, the first of all temptations began," the voice added. "Still wandering in that *imperfect square* of Earth that changes somehow into an *imperfect triangle* . . . you humans have indulged yourselves even more into that *geometrical* imperfection by being attracted, now and then, to the physical changes that would play you like puppets.

"Money and gain played an important role in transforming you into slaves of your weakest and illusive ambitions to become wealthy on account of your humanity. You would do anything in the name of money; cheating, lying, and deceiving, thus securing your existence, continuity in a circular movement of your degrading abilities. Therefore, to sustain the power of dominion and control, endowed to you by an abundance of money, you would plunk yourselves into the ugliest things in life, killing—killing for the survival of the fittest. Again, death would reveal itself as the main participant and seemed to haunt your feeble spirits. Man would then enroll in an avenging situation to restore the pride of the family, clan, society, religion, believed to have been lost, after death has taken one of their members. And what will happen as a consequence, though, is revenge, which is nothing but additional bloodshed of the body, *the matter*, a member of another clan, another family, or religion.

"Chaos would certainly begin to prevail over the destiny of man, and Humanity would start walking into a labyrinth that would never end, and thus, finding an exit door out of that chaos would be as difficult as ever. To restore the honor of the flesh by the flesh is not but an additional sunken reaction of the mind into the world of illusion. Thus, *the spirit*, the eternal part of the human being, neither could be restored into the body after death, nor would it feel satisfied if another spirit has flown out of another body due to a kill. By that, the spirit would have to come back in another life, take a new body to purify its deeds from the previous life's implications."

Hearing that immediately made me stop the meditation, moving my body left and right. "You're making it so hard for me to understand what you are saying fully. I feel I lost track with previous meditations! Why bringing death and killing into my meditation, while my only concern is to realize the *Perfect Square*, drawn on the Rising Sun behind me, that of equality and regularity. I mean, accomplishing immortality through spiritual resurrection and mental awareness?" I questioned his authority, but then I realized that what he was whispering is vital for me to know at this point.

"Parallel to that, you could have been able to meditate on the six levels of natural life. Alas, only a few did that along the course of history while the majority hadn't had the time to do so, for they were busy making money, slaving for their egoistic recompenses, killing for that, and more for other above stupid reasons. Now, young brother, it's your moment to meditate upon all of that since you have chosen to walk the path of the *Initiate* and have been chosen to enter behind the veil! Meditate . . ." the voice came to a halt with a powerful command that shook my entire being.

And in deep meditation, I entered to know thyself!

> The **Hexad**, number *Six*, **6,** is the primary perfect circular number. It is the regular figure for marriage, unlike **5,** which is only a merger in that concern. Why? One must wonder! *Six* is the **Union** between the *Male and Female* in its absolute form. The male has a sign of a downward triangle in the following shape (▼), whereas the female is represented by an opposite triangle in this upward shape (▲). Together, they form the **Six-Pointed Star**[5].

---

5. In almost all Ancient Religions and Mystery Schools around the world, the male was represented as the God-Energy descending from Heaven (▼) and impregnating the female, Earth (▲). One of the most famous examples to such an archaic belief could be seen with Giaia, Earth, and Zeus, the Most High God of Ancient Greece. In Greek Mythology, Zeus has been often regarded for his divine insemination of Giaia. And so, Zeus made life beat in her bosom. Some may swap the meanings of these triangles, but we stick to the meanings we herein presented.

In concordance, the **Triple Giving Spirit** descending from *Heaven* (▼) interweaves with the **Triple Receiving Matter** of *Earth* (▲). The *Six* is sacred to the goddess Astarte, also known as Aphrodite. It is Venus which, as we know, the morning and evening star. Thus, the holy day of Venus is Friday, the sixth day of the week.

Number *Six* is also important for it represents the **Six Levels** of *Natural Life*. The first level encompasses the *Seed Level* and starts from the bottom. Up the second level takes in *Plant Life*. The third comprises *Animal Life,* and the fourth *Human Life.* The fifth is *Angelic Life,* which profiles the mediators between men and gods. And finally, the last and sublime echelon at the top of this hierarchy is the *Godhood Life.*

Six cubed (6×6×6) is equal to two hundred sixteen (216). In truth, it represents a very mystical number, for it is a **Generator Principle of the Spirit**! It repeats itself by its *spherical structure* that produces an eternal recurrence of approximately the same events in both the spiritual and physical worlds. Matter is not at all infinite in the Kosmos! So, every two hundred sixteen years, the *spirit of man* travels around the **Circle of Necessity** to incarnate a new and different body. That **Cycle of Reincarnation** commands the state of being of every mortal!

And the meditation continued silently through the night!

~ ~ ~

Thinking about that early next morning made me understand that I have to fully grasp an important knowledge of my physical and spiritual evolution in this scheme of Natural Life. First, from my lowest existence at the *seed level*; second, at the *plant life*; third, at the *animal life*; fourth, at my current *human life*; fifth, at my upcoming *angelic life*, where I become a mediator between men and gods; to finally reach the highest state at the *godhood life*.

Should I do that successfully, I would witness, under the superb light of Venus, the star of Astarte, the mystical meanings behind life on Earth, and the generator principle of the spirit, say divine energy, within it. In addition to that, I would come to comprehend the essential nature of the *Triple Spirit* and *Triple Matter*, as well as the *Cycle of Reincarnation* designed for every mortal, associated numerically with the six cubed, or 6 times 6 times 6, thus 216 years, the period in which the *Spirit* would find its new bodily incarnation.[6] That's a mystery by itself, according to Pythagorean teachings, for Six repeats itself because of its spherical form, in an eternal recurrence of the same events, or of the finite *Matter* that *blindly* floats in the Cosmos.

Having learned that and thus been *Initiated*, so to speak, into the secret process of *anamnesis*, or the recollection of my previous lives' memory as a Kosmic being of earthly fabric, and the destination thereto of my future existence on Earth and in the Kosmos, I would therefore be able to succeed in accomplishing the equilibrium between my Triple Spirit and Triple Matter.

At the peak of the mountain I have just climbed, I breathed in Order and exhaled out confusion . . .

---

6. The *Doctrine of Reincarnation*, also known as *Metempsychosis*, mentioned in many world religious books and traditions like in Hinduism, Buddhism, and Pythagoreanism, is based on one essential law that says, "you reap what you sow". It clearly states that humans live an eternal life through a journey of evolution and experiences they ought to have on the spiritual, mental, and physical levels. Hence, on the physical plane, humans are responsible for whatever actions they take in their lives, in the present and in the future. One must know that early Christians truthfully believed in Reincarnation for it was in the teachings of the Christian Master, as we read for example in Matthew 11:11-15, and 17:11-13. Such a belief was misperceived by the Church as a great danger to the power of the Christian dogma. However, not only Christianity but also both Judaism and Islam consider Reincarnation a belief-form of paganism! Anyway, the Doctrine of Reincarnation was absconded around 553 AD, at the Second Synod Council of Constantinople, held under the reign of Emperor Justinian. Strangely though, and without the attendance of the Pope, the Council declared: "If anyone asserts the fabulous pre-existence of souls and shall submit to the monstrous doctrine that follows from it, let him be excommunicated."

As for the *Cycle of Reincarnation*, taught by Pythagoras and its numerical value of 216 (years)—the period in which the *Spirit* finds a new *Body* to inhabit—extracted from 6 cubed, or 6 x 6 x 6, could probably be the origin of 666, being the *number of the beast*, doctrinized, creeded or decreed by the Church who rejected Reincarnation in the way it described it a few lines above, refusing all together the idea of a soul incarnating a body!

7.
SEVENTH MEDITATION

Ahead of me, the door to the Chamber—the Star Chamber that would reveal more of its hidden secrets. Naturally, the *visions* revealed here through the meditations into the Occult Numbers are very inspiring, and to a certain extent, similar to the ones I received from the Sacred Alphabet. However, I wondered how I could clear up my mind and deeply meditate, while certain images of money, killing, death, etc., from my previous meditation, are still lingering above me, inside me, perhaps in my unconscious or subconscious. Despite that, I had to enter the Chamber and continue the journey. There was no way backward.

Inside, having seated for meditation, and within its profound exaltation, the powers within invoked the meanings of number Seven, simulated by the seventh letter of the Sacred Alphabet, *Zain*. From the mid-point, from where the energy is hoarded, the shaft of the Shepherd sent up forth, through its wings of the knowledgeable Phoenix, a vision of devastating wars.

"Entering more into that *imperfection* of the human concepts ruled by Mars, the red planet, which allegorically means the indulgence into a fake glory taken by the sword, war. Life seemed to be more precious than death, but precious life is not justified by degrading and aborting its universal rhythm," the voice began. "As life is given by the will and order of the Monad, the *One*, so life cannot be taken by the evil and confusion deed of the Dyad, the *Demiurge*. It is the easiest, and thus, the most outrageous glorious ambition humanity had ever sought. It degraded itself in its most gross forms of materiality.

"Within these distorted forms resides the biggest temptation of all, the quest for Glory. To achieve it is the total oblivion of all that man is, in his/her true nature. By the power of the sword, and what it can promise as rewards for human hunger and thirst, of blood and more of it, came to paint the surface of its blade, under the impact of the dual horns of the Devil, Satan, matched by Azazel or *Zazae'il*, the most dangerous leader of the *Fallen Angels* from Heaven!

"As men, and lots of them, have sought earthly Kingdoms and were ornamented Kings on their thrones, in the recent and remote past, so men, and lots of them, had been elected Presidents, to rule the mass by dictatorships, or some forms of *alleged* democracy, so to speak, by the power of disgrace, raging all kind of wars, from economic to military, upon each other, in the present time. What has been accomplished of atrocities in the name of the *Demiurge* is more apparent in human life than what has been accomplished in the name of the *Father*. And thus, what has been led and is being led of religious wars, in the name of the Father, is more dishonoring to humanity than what has been done of Peace in His name."

There was silence for many minutes!

Seven, **7**, is the **Perfect Number of Life** and its ideal vehicle. In truth, it combines the *Three Higher Elements* of the **Spirit** with the *Three Lower Elements* of the **Body**. The fourth level, or shall we say, the middle one, is the **Mind**. As such, it shows the great relationship that exists between Man's *Individual Monad* and the *Divine Monad*. It represents the *Active Mind*, the **Godhead**.

The **Heptad**, *Seven*, is associated with the *Seven Heavenly Bodies* that form the *Music of the Spheres*. These heavenly entities are also related to the seven days of the week. This association is best described as follows: Moon for Monday, Mars for Tuesday, Mercury for Wednesday, Jupiter for Thursday, Venus for Friday, Saturn for Saturday, and finally, the Sun for Sunday!

The *Manifested Universe* is also a constituent of *Seven*, and so is the *Microcosm*, or Man, who is organized into **Seven Levels of Evolution**. These levels start at the bottom with the *Physical Body*. The *Sidereal Body* ensues at the second level and the *Desire Body*, third. The fourth level, being the *Mind*, is the stage of equilibrium. The fifth corresponds to the *Human Spirit*, and the sixth to the *Vivid Spirit*. The seventh level betokens the *Divine Spirit*.

You should know by heart that the symbol of number *Seven* is the **Seven-Pillared Temple**. It means the **Initiate**, *the lover of Sophia*, and for that reason, it is dedicated to Jupiter!

And in the stillness of meditation, silently disappeared the night!

~ ~ ~

The following day passed me by so calmly, yet so thoughtfully, as I went into thorough evaluation of what I have learned to be the value and meaning of number Seven while rejoicing for hours at the view ahead from the top of the mountain.

I came to fully realize now that the cherished yearning for death on account of life seemed to shadow our illusive ambitions for money, power, the crown, throne, or seat so that to govern as assumed gods, or better say *daemons*. Most of the times, this controlling power is exercised contrary to God's will and the promise of peace and harmony given to humanity. Otherwise, we could have bravely launched an inner battle against *Tsaddi*, the Dark Side where Satan is secretly at work, opening ways to reach us, fabricating illusions to hunt us down, and hitting us like an Arrow, or hooking us with a fishing hook under the power of Capricorn, the *fishtailed goat*.

We could have also understood that *Seven* is the perfect number of life, its vehicle that links our three elements of spirit to our three elements of the body, perfectly in balance through our active mind—our Individual Intellect—strongly related to the Universal Mind, to whom it can *Rise*, once we are crowned by the only worthy Crown, that of our Godhead—*Resh*! It would then be the exalted time when the sound of mystical silence, the *Music of the Spheres*, resonate in our minds the voice of God, whispering Love and Peace on Earth and in the entirety of the invisible and visible Kosmos.

Therefore, I understood that the heart is the place where the *Word* should forever reside and that we should thence keep the Secrets eternally close to the Light under the constellation of Pisces, in the domain of *Shin*, the abode of Mystery. Therefore, we would vibrate akin to the manifested universe organized like us in Seven levels and accomplish our evolution from the physical state of our Body to the divine state of our Spirit, passing by the middle point, the equilibrium level in our Higher Mind. We would ultimately become *Keepers of the Word, Initiates, and Lovers of Sophia*, performing our secret and sacred rituals in the *Seven-Pillared Temple* under the rejuvenated powers of Jupiter and Mercury.

I looked at the Sun before it completely disappeared in the horizon, and breathed in Truth and Love and exhaled out deception and hatred . . .

8.
EIGHTH MEDITATION

Having entered the Mystery Chamber again, moving step by step on the Five Points of the Star, from East to West, before I sat underneath the Caduceus, and summoned the Force within to reveal the mysterious meanings of number 8, simulated by *Cheth*, the Eighth letter of the Sacred Alphabet.

Thereafter, the energy flooded all around me, projecting up above my eyes, exposing pictures of those active yet passive demonstrations of human pleasures.

"Entering through *two imperfect squares* of Earth, the *imperfect cube*," resonated the voice in my ears, "we would find ourselves guided by the power of Sexual Instinct, driven under the constellation of Gemini, the twins, *Adam and Eve*. This is, however, the final submergence into the realm of matter, more specifically into duality. Hence, it is the most difficult for humanity, for it would enclose some of them into uncontrolled acts of fornications and others inside the fence of Animosity!

"Outside the sacred sexual rites performed for their deities, their divine couple, seen and explained in the second meditation, and as also seen in the vision of this letter, men and women would enroll in sexual practices giving pleasurable homage only to their bodies. Hypnotized by the power of the flesh, which combines heat, fragrance, taste, as well as audible and visual perceptions, this power would imprison them even more into the five senses of physical enclosure. Hence, they would enter through an endless loop of ecstatic feelings and orgasmic desires that would or might never end.

"Otherwise, humans could have found a way to break that virtual chain and come to see the *first actual-active Cube*. But . . ."

"The first actual Cube? What's that?" I rapidly asked, but the voice came to a halt before finishing his explanation, and I instantly understood that I may find my answers through further meditation as I always do.

Something echoed consciously in my realm as I delved deep!

Number *Eight*, **8**, is, in fact, the **Octad**, the **First Actual-Active Cube**. Its relationship with the Kosmic harmony allows a perfect balance that regulates everything in the Universe. Hence, two cubed is *Eight*, and 2+2+2+2 equals 8.

It is the source of all musical ratios and is greatly associated with the *Music of the Spheres*. For that reason, it is called **Embracer of Harmonies**, or *Harmonia*[7].

Eight is also related to the principles of *Safety and Steadfastness*. It is the symbol of lasting *Friendship* and that of unconditional *Love* as well! Because those emotional relationships have a healing effect on human beings, *Eight* can symbolize *Medicine and Health*, too. Thus, it is assigned to Eshmun, the Phoenician god of medicine, and dedicated to the Air element.

Number *Eight* represents the Universal Balance that adjusts the *three subjective aspects* and the *five objective facets* of *Human Consciousness*. In a more transcendental geometrical image, it is the **Eight-Pointed Star**, the Star of Melki-Sedek, the Symbol of Priesthood.

As his telepathic discharge for the night ended with those revelations, a strange musical, harmonious melody vibrated all around, soothing my spirit. *Then, silently continued the meditation all through the night!*

~ ~ ~

Early the next morning, on my way across the long-lasting field to that mountain top, I thought about the many different things concerning meditation of the night before. It became obvious to me that accessing the secret passage to the Mysteries is not granted unless I get rid of the dangers lingering around me, say the hindrance to my spiritual evolution, to which I may expose myself to, under the watchful eyes of the Gemini, the twins, the dual principles of nature. In case I negligibly follow that path and got myself caught inside it, I may expose my already acquired powers of the fifth element and thus lose myself as *Keeper of the Word*.

Time stood still . . . as a frightening silence overwhelmed me. Instead, to have it, I should set myself in such complete harmonious energy with the Kosmos itself, achieving universal balance, and forever harvesting true Friendship and Love, where the element of Air—the Air of freedom would be sensed again in my deepest three subjective and five objective aspects of consciousness. It

---

7. *Harmonia* is the name given to the wife of Kadmus, one of the Kabbirim of Phoenicia.

would be the time when I become fully conscious of my hidden forms of unconsciousness!

I felt that I eloquently grasped it when, after a while, totally relaxed, I breathed in Unity and Harmony and exhaled out duality and asymmetry . . .

9.
NINTH MEDITATION

After I delicately and ritualistically moved from East to West upon the Five Points of the Star, and at the exact moments when energy flowed all around, connecting me with the Rod of Phenok, the wings of eternity lifted me above, into a world of mysteries and knowledge.

"Now, this is *Teth*, the ninth letter, mirrored as number nine," uttered the Angelic voice, "and is the beginning of not only fully comprehending your true nature as *divine beings* but also realizing the fact that it has been lost in the wilderness of both, bodily suffering and spiritual elation.

"The Serpent around the *Tree of Life* is not but your unconscious reminder of who you really are and who would you become around the end of your destination. She is the Old Serpent that would lay the foundation of your blossoming into the *godhead state* and would lift you up from your physical organic life, from mud to immortality.

"Through the path of the Cancer (the Crab), you have reached her in your *vision* and found her in the middle of the circle, that Circle of Trees, standing like a Master who would never take sides. Like a Hierophant to a neophyte, she taught you, from *mouth to ear*, divinely whispering in your ears, guiding you to be like her, and be even more than her, be free outside that circle!" he avowed in a solid statement to the Force of this number.

"More divine and free than her! What do you mean? How is that even possible?" I rushed to ask.

Moments passed, yet without an answer. Meditation seemed to have been the only way to hear his telepathic conveying of the secrets.

I pondered upon it as I listened!

Number *Nine*, **9**, the **Ennead**, is the **Number of Justice** par excellence. Its square root is three, 3×3 equals 9, and 3+3+3 equals 9. It is called **Horizon**, say, **Oceanus**, since it represents the *crossing line* between many different important sequences. For example, it is the *passage* between Number Ten and the other numbers that led to it. With *Nine*, which represents our *Mother Earth's spiritual number*, the perfect nine months of gestation are completed for a new birth. It is the number of *beginnings and transformations.*

Nine is also the number of the **Muses**, the *nine sister-goddesses* of **Harmony, Arts**, and **Sciences**. On the other hand, it relates particularly to Terpsichore—the Muse of *movement and dance*. *Nine* embodies an important, powerful Sacred Number, for it is composed of nine aspects of the **Divine Energy**, best described in the following manner:

Heavenly Three: *Father, Mother, and Son.*

Humanly Three: *Mind, Matter, and Spirit.*

Elementally Three: *Fire, Water, and Air.*

Thus, understanding *Nine* and invoking its powers should certainly reveal the way for your **Preparation** three times—nine days each, twenty-seven phases—until you complete the process of **Self-Purification**. Subsequently, you would attain one high spiritual **Perfection**.

And so, meditation continued, more immersed than ever!

"Coiled around the *Tree of Life*, that Shaft of the Shepherd," suddenly the voice came back resonating from deep silence, uttering in my ears, "the Old Serpent is not but the awakening of your memory, long lost, ever since you came to lose contact with your true nature. She is your revealed DNA, your hidden memory in the depth of your being, your cultural-genetic rhythm of truth, long fallen short from its divine archetype. Having known that by now, you would then understand the meaning of its secret number, *Nine*, the Number of Justice, and the spiritual number of your Mother Earth, the place of your spiritual birth into the fabric of matter.

"Know thee brother; through careful examination of this Sacred Number, the nine aspects of the Divine Energy would be unveiled to you, as you come to relate your Human condition of *Mind, Matter, Spirit* here on Earth with the Heavenly reality of *Father, Mother, Son*, as well with the Elemental state of *Fire, Water, Air*. Decoding that by passing along 27 phases through meditating 3 times, 9 days each, you would succeed in purifying yourself from the residues of condensed matter to ultimately reach a high spiritual state of perfection!" thus, proclaimed the voice in finality, attentively offering an insightful explanation that would create a turning point along my journey.

Indeed, it would, as my mind seemed at work, absorbing it all.

~ ~ ~

The rest of the day was so refreshing. I felt that life had been rejuvenated inside me in the few hours spent on top of the mountain. Reflecting positively on that Old Serpent and the Caduceus of Thot took away all the things that have puzzled me all the way across that mysterious adventure of life, so to speak, the Sacred Alphabet and the Occult Numbers seemed to have drawn a very comprehensive path in my mind. The curtain that was hiding the Truth behind appeared to open up wide ahead of my eyes, lifting the *Veil of Isis* and enabling me to have a clear glimpse of its majestic and glorious light—the Light of eternal bliss.

A *Keeper of the Word* I have truly become, I still had one mission to accomplish. It's the greatest calling of all times, the final combat with the remnants of my dark side, conquering my deepest fears and surmounting all illusions brought up by the manifested dualist world. Thence, relaxing and meditating on that particular notion, I inhaled Light, Unity, Truth, Order, Love, Harmony, and Beauty while breathing out darkness, duality, deception, confusion, hatred, imbalance, and vileness . . .

10.
TENTH MEDITATION

As I entered, my senses immediately interconnected with living particles. Inside the Mystery Chamber and after I made my steps on the Five Points of the Star and sat beneath the Caduceus of Hermes, I felt as if it rose from its sleep into the air with such great glory. Blazed again with light, its energy floated up to the ceiling, then towards me in strange elliptical movements, only to stop above my head, hovering reposefully. It then circulated across the points of the Star and into the center, where the Shaft of Enoch completely lit now, and through the Phoenix' fluttering wings, it dispersed Light above my head as if bathing me, finally! Into the very depth of myself, I pondered in an attempt to conjure up the Force that lies within and that which would unveil before me the mystical meanings behind this final number, mirrored as *Yod*, the tenth letter of the Sacred Alphabet.

"Now, this is the beginning of a new cycle, brother," uttered the voice suddenly. "It would open wide the way for you to grasp the mysterious worlds of the Sacred, Occult, and the Mystic!"

"In the revelatory vision of that Sacred letter, your Phenokian brothers and sisters appeared as Angels and showed you the way into the *Lake of Remembrance*, inviting you to clean your sins by *Water*. Cleansing by water is one of the most significant rituals ever operated by High Priests as a way for purification. Water is the element of *Love and Compassion*. It is also a safe place for you, for it would remind you of the aquatic ambiance you were in when inside your mothers' womb, for she was your protector. However, the most important thing is not to lose yourself in the act of *remembering* that and thus succumb to the emotions of the physical life that would impose on you the will to return to material safety.

"On the contrary, you have to break through to the other side, where the path for real Illumination is, and which requires from you to be like water; flexible, clean, pure, loving, and courageous enough to face the remains of your dark side and conquer over them completely. That's when you start knowing yourself, becoming who you are, and the *Invisible* hand would lift you, inviting you into the eternal abode." At that point, the voice came to a halt as it echoed in my mind.

In the stillness of the night, I meditated!

The two most important numbers are *One*, **1**, the **Monad**, the Universal Mind that diffuses through everything, and *Ten*, **10**, the **Dechada**, the very best number, say, the greatest number of all, since it does not only contain the first four numbers: *One, Two, Three* and *Four*, but it is also the sum of all of them: **1+2+3+4 = 10**. These numbers joined together in that way, compose the **Sacred Decade** of the gods. These are the *gods* that hold the Kosmos together, as well as all the *manifested laws* of **Mother Nature**.

Ten is the **Ensemble of the Absolute and Ultimate Truth**! It is **Heaven**!

The act of **Creation** occurred by the *Invisible* power of the *One*. It is a solitary, all-embracing whole in which everything is truly interconnected. *Ten*, or the whole, is the **Superlative Manifestation** of this *interrelated reality*. Add to it, **Harmony** is the mysterious binding agent whereby every existing atom in this vast Kosmos is related to the other.

Number *Ten* is the **Perfect Number** *par excellence*, for when we reach it, we simply revert to the *One*! And thus, there are two paths, the path of the *Initiate* and that of the *Non-Initiate*. For the latter, all creations go back to the Source, and the process of Creation repeats itself *ad infinitum*. For the *Initiate*, all creations unite with the *One*, and a new Cycle of Creation begins, not in repetition, but instead, a thorough transformation of the world occurs, with a new Sun shining upon it. In that regard, *Ten* is related to **Human Fate** and dedicated to the Sun and the World, respectively!

It is not a coincidence that the powers of number *Ten* are **Faultless**, for it is the **Vessel** that holds all things through a *single form and power*. For the *Initiate*, it represents all the **Divine Principles** that *evolve and rejoin* in a new **Unitas**. As such, it also shapes by the Light of the **New Sun,** the **Circle of Necessity**, *initially* planned by the **Divine Will.**

"Then," the voice resonated again in my mind, "you understand that reaching Ten is grasping Perfection, for it would take you back to the *One*. A new cycle for you on all levels, not at all repetitive, but rather, a new beginning, a transformation of your being, with a new Sun Rising upon your head, and never from behind you! There is no place for neither the *Cycle of Death and Rebirth* nor the *Circle of Necessity* in that new world but instead, an evolution of all the Principles toward the Divine, revolving and rejoining Him in a new Unitas. That's the Absolute Truth. Know thee.

"Go on, brother, a Keeper of the Word you have become, face your daemons in the world you are beholding and control them forever. You were given a chance to invoke the Force of the *One* and become what you are, *a mortal god on Earth, an immortal man in Heaven!*" The voice concluded with finality.

An imposing stillness prevailed over space and time.

Silent was the night!

~ ~ ~

Still hearing the voice reverberating inside my mind, the next morning on my way to the mountain top, I felt very much in need to reverently appreciate his essential elaboration on the mysterious and hidden properties of all the numbers from *One* to *Ten*. As for now, I know that Numbers are measures of all things, and while also remembering the *Initiatic* Visions of the Alphabet, I realized there exists a certain hidden mystery in both of them.

Therefore, I concluded that the Sacred Alphabet and Occult Numbers are not at all creation of the human mind but rather have a mystical existence of their own. They initially reside outside the Intellect of man, or any life form, before they became rendered and perceived by the *Rising* Human Mind. They had been originally pronounced and created by the *One* in the forms of Letters (*words*) and Numbers (*value*), respectively, not by coincidence, but by a certain *Divine Reason and Logic*. The Sacred Alphabet and Occult Numbers absorb—to a great extent—from their origin—the Great Monad, the reality of all things. Hence, should I want to discern the properties of the true Enochian Kabbala, then I have and surely must always *meditate* upon their *Initiatic* inner meanings. I will communicate with them. They are gods! While knowing it is not easy to understand that mysterious concept, however, if I do and achieve that communion, I will then utterly become myself, what I am in reality, a *god!*

Alone in total *Harmony* with myself, rejoicing in the *Beauty* of the place, relaxing in the *Truth* of life, and preparing myself for the great meeting with my destiny in the *Order* of things, I thought there is no better place for such a state of Higher Mind than here, the top of the mountain I have just reached. I smiled encouragingly. Then, I deeply breathed in *Love*, that mysterious wit, the Kosmic *Mathemagical* agent, and breathed out all asymmetry, ugliness, deception, confusion, hatred, darkness, and duality. At an exact measured moment, the *Akasa* (Akasha), the *Astral Light,* began circulating me with such a subtle vibration, seeping into my very realm, in which the correlations of its *powers* endowed me with the *Philosopher's Stone*—the *Elixir of Life*. Later, a sudden strange feeling of *Unity* inhabited me.

On that notion, swirling fast in my mind, and at that moment of spiritual victory, having already won over the Devil, my dark side, in the vision of the 18th letter, *Tsaddi*, I just faced his, say, my little demons, and cast them out too, into *Dudael!*

Instantly, I became myself, and it became me.

Myself echoed consciously in my Rising Mind as the day ended, and the night became silent!

9.

The Mystic Symbols

The 3rd Level

1.

THE SIX-POINTED STAR

We shall start with one of the most important symbols: the *Six-Pointed Star*, also known as the *Hexad* or *Hexagram*. What is the meaning of it? It is undoubtedly one of the most trickery symbols an *Initiate* would ever meet on the journey of *Initiation*. It has many different meanings and implications depending on which way or angle the *Initiate* perceives it, or how they would interpret its hidden meanings according to the different planes it presents itself so powerfully.

Besides the fact that it has been drawn in ancient temples, like in the archaic city of Ba'albek where the figure of Astarte or Venus is noticed portrayed at the center of the Symbol, or whether it has been used by the Israelis as the symbol for their national flag, implying thus a political interpretation of some sort, the *Six-Pointed Star* has, two main general meanings: the interrelation between male and female elements in its absolute form and the interconnection between Spirit (*Heaven*) and Matter (*Earth*), as we have seen in the 6th meditation.

That said, and as an Initiate should think, he or she would have to understand the following three essential points to unlock its potentially occult powers within the human mind. First, it symbolizes the *Heavenly Triple Spirit* (▼) descending, giving, and interweaving with *Earthly Triple Matter* (▲) that receives. Second; it represents the *Six Levels of Natural Life,* beginning with the *Seed* and evolving in an ascending path to the *Plant, Animal, Human, Angelic,* and the *Divine.* Third; it is the *Generator Principle of the Spirit,* for it repeats itself through its perfect *circular structure* that produces an *infinite* recurrence of approximately the same events in both the *spiritual and physical* worlds by providing evidence that Spirit and Matter are not at all *eternal* in their original Kosmic energetic *data or form!* However, their transformation is, since the *Spirit,* say, of man is fundamentally bound to the *Circle of Necessity* which orders its incarnation into a new different *Body,* and as long as it follows that *Cycle of Reincarnation* that commands the state of being for every mortal!

Only through the *elliptical* vibrational Force of their union, the *Individual Mind,* that can liberation be achieved when it is *Raised* into the abode of the *Universal Mind.*

Here it is—

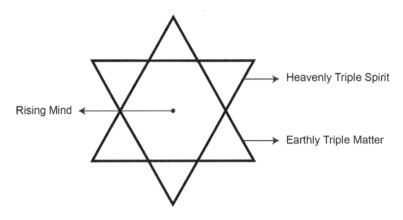

The Six-Pointed Star

2.
THE OUROBOROS

L et's now deal with the 2nd most essential symbol: the *Ouroboros*. What is the meaning of it?

Although the serpent is known in almost all ancient civilizations as the symbol of wisdom and immortality, the *Eternal Cycle of Death and Rebirth* is represented as a serpent biting her tail, the *Ouroboros*. Indeed, but why the Serpent in a Circle?

According to ancient Phoenician Tradition, the serpent was often depicted inside some of their secret domains. It is related that on the wall behind the altar in the Temple of Eshmun[1], in the ancient city of Saydoun (Sidon), an engraved image of a serpent with a Phoenix head was seen stretching from the center of a burning circle. Could that be the origin of the symbol? Phoenician priests and priestesses believed that the Eshmunian Serpent symbolizes the art of medicine, which remains incomplete without the Scepter of the healing god.

The serpent was considered divine to Enoch-Thor-Taautus-Thot-Hermes. She is a very special creature, the wisest of all animals. She breathes stronger than any because of the *Fire* element that runs at very high speed through her entire body. Though she is considered a cold-blooded animal, this same fire grants the serpent great power for maneuvering and the capability of an extraordinary bodily modulation.

Moreover, there is another essential feature. She has the power to live for a long time. One may wonder about it and ask how that is possible. Right! Well, the serpent goes on fasting to escape the aging process! Strange as it may sounds, this eccentric feat occurs when in fact, the serpent remains still and stays stagnant during the whole winter until she ultimately shrinks. And so, when this happens, she immediately gets rid of her old skin, and a new, bright one then forms to reveal a younger and more vivid serpent.

That said, life seems never to stop growing in this amazing creature, and by that, she conquers death! Thence, to the *Initiate*, the Serpent is looked upon as the symbol of Immortality and Wisdom because she defeats time and breaks

---

1. Eshmun or *Eśmun* was the Phoenician god of medicine and healing, copied by the Greeks as Asclepius. According to Sanchoniatho, he was the son of Sydyk, the brother of Misor (in reference to Egypt).

the *Circle of Necessity*, the *Eternal Cycle of Death and Rebirth*. Phoenician priests and priestesses named her, *Agatho-Daemon*, meaning the "Good Spirit," and the Circle on the wall represents the *world in its latent form*. So, when the Serpent appears in the center with a Phoenix head, it means that the good spirit is cosmically resurrected to Eternity, moving and turning the *world in an active mode* by the Force of the *Fire* element—the energy; life energy, where the *Secret Cycle and Initiation* are completed!

Here it is depicted in its two stages—

World in its latent form   World in its active mode

The Ouroboros

3.
THE CUBE

Let's tackle now the 3rd most important *Initiatic* symbols: the *Cube*. What is the meaning of it?

It is certainly defined as a geometrical form representing "Earth" in all its material-physical elements—a base level with all the potentialities to evolve into a higher state of existence, a spiritual one.

According to Pythagoras, Earth is the "Sphere of Generation," and it is so because souls come down to it continuously through birth and always ascend out of it at the moment of death. Hence, they follow a circular movement in order of necessity. So, for one to become an *Initiate*, one must rise up and above this "Circle of Necessity," and *Rising* above this "Cycle of Life and Death" would esoterically mean *Resurrecting* or *Raising* from the death state of the physical confinement of the Body into a life state of the free Spirit.

Therefore, the *Cube,* which symbolizes Earth in its *latent state*, meaning that which has not yet been unfolded, contains six faces or sides. These sides represent the *Six Levels of Natural Life*: the *Seed Level* at the bottom, then the *Plant Life, Animal Life, Human Life, Angelic Life*, and the *Godhood Life* at the top. When we unfold these 6 sides, we transform and elevate Earth into an *actual-active state*, placed as such in the form of the *Great Cubical Altar* in the *Sanctum Sanctorum*, and obtain through the performance of a certain specific sacred ritual a Cross of 7 Perfect Squares[2]; the *Symbol of the Initiate*!

The *Cube* in its raw condition could thus be considered the *rough ashlar* of the 1st degree Apprentice Freemason that needs to be worked out and refined during his/her *Initiatic* journey.

---

2. In fact, when we unfold the Cube, we get two kind of Crosses: one of 6 perfect squares and the other of 7 perfect squares. The Cross of 6 Perfect Squares is when the central interlinking square is counted one time either vertically or horizontally, which is not truly a complete Cross drawn vertically and/or horizontally by all meanings. The Cross of 7 Perfect Squares is when the central interlinking square is counted two times both vertically and/or horizontally.

Here it is drawn in its two phases—

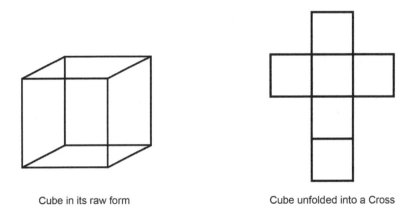

Cube in its raw form   Cube unfolded into a Cross

The Cube

4.
THE CROSS

We continue with the 4th most interesting *Initiatic* symbols: the *Cross*. What is the meaning of it?

It is defined as representing "Enlightenment, Inner Solar Power, Death and Resurrection, Unity of the Dual Principles, and Balance of the four cardinal directions and elements." The *Cross* is that and more with some nuances here and there! We will pinpoint in brief the most important of its *Initiatic* dimensions.

In the Enochian Kabbalistic Tradition, the *Cross* came first to be symbolized as the *Kosmic Holder* of the Four Archangels (Angels of the Most High God El) and are known as Michael, Gabriel, Raphael, Uriel (Auriel). They are the four *Cardinal Angels*—those Exalted Beings or Higher Selves who form the *Kosmic Cross*; Michael in the East, Gabriel in the South, Raphael in the West, and Auriel in the North. They control the four elements of Air, Fire, Water, and Earth, respectively.

In this manner of elemental succession, Creation occurred, and the world came to be. The *Cross* is thus the *Kosmic Balance and Unity* of the Divine Will and the Individual Will. It is the Unity of the Vertical descending Spirit and the Horizontal latent Matter. The *Seventh Invisible Square* of the *Cross* we have *discerned* in the unfolding *Cube*, and which is placed in the middle, the intersecting hidden square, is where the *Kingdom of God* resides; it's in the *Heart of Man*. At this specific dimension, the Universal Balance takes place, not between male and female, but rather between Man and God, hence between the Son and the Father.

Thus, the *Cross* is not the unity of duality or the dual female-male principles. On the contrary, it is the *end of duality* and the beginning of the *Oneness with God* as a result of "Death and Resurrection." After that, the *Cross* has been actively elevated above Earth, unfolded from the *Cube*. It is not by surprise though to find that the last letter of the Canaanite-Phoenician Sacred Alphabet, the 22nd, *Tau* (Taw) figures the *Sign of the Cross* and epitomizes the *Initiate*, and the *Elected to the Great Power*, up in the sky, when the light of the Moon fades out.

Additionally, the Phoenician *Cross*, the *Tau*, represents Divine Mastership over the Physical world, and by its magical/occult use, the *Initiate* organizes the

Great Work at the workshop of Earth[3]. Though the Egyptian Cross, the *Ankh*, symbolizes the union between male and female, particularly between their dual principles, Osiris and Isis, at a certain level during the generation of the physical world by the deed of the Dyad, as we have seen before, it most importantly and in general esoteric understanding mirrors *Life and Immortality*.

Here it is drawn in its three forms—

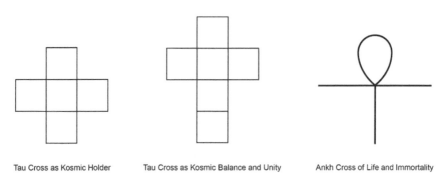

Tau Cross as Kosmic Holder   Tau Cross as Kosmic Balance and Unity   Ankh Cross of Life and Immortality

The Cross

---

3. The famous Phoenician Architect Hiram Abiff has often been portrayed holding the *Tau* in his right hand and *Mastering* the work at the Temple of Ba'al Melkart. In Freemasonry, it's the *alleged* temple of Solomon.

5.
THE PENTAGRAM

We proceed with the 5th most important *Initiatic* symbols: the *Pentagram*, also known as the *Five-Pointed Star*. What is the meaning of it? It is undoubtedly defined as representing "the Five Elements of Air, Fire, Water, Earth, and Ether, thus picturing the Kosmic Man, the *Microcosm of the Macrocosm.*" That is true, but there is more to that, and it's found most essentially in Pythagorean esoteric and occult teachings, which we consider highly important. There is a specific degree related to the Great Pythagoras in the *Ancient and Primitive Phoenician Rite* of the Great White Fraternity.

The *Pentad* is one of the most important and powerful symbols that directly connects with the Psyche. Its numerical value and importance we have already tackled in our 5th meditation. The *Pentad* is central in its position, a circular symbol that comprises five circumscribed circles! It characterizes the return of everything, and by that we mean, the return of the Psyche into itself and the restoration of the unconscious and subconscious into their original conscious state. At this *unification point*, Purification and Knowledge abide by the "Cycle of the Pentagon"—a Great Cycle that revolves harmoniously and commands the movements of the Kosmos!

The *Five-Pointed Star*, the *Pentagram,* is the esoteric and spiritual symbol of number 5. It is the evolution of the *Cross*, which is the esoteric and spiritual symbol of number 4. After the crucifixion of our four elements, represented esoterically by the four *atomic* shapes of Air, Fire, Water, Earth, a resurrection occurs into the fifth element, the Ether. In other words, the *Cross* is the *Death and Resurrection* into the *Pentagram*, which is known in the secret language given in the Pythagorean *Initiation* by "Death to Reveal," a term that unquestionably connotes the *Death and Resurrection of the Initiate*. Each of the *Five-Pointed Star* lines intersects with the other in the proportion of Macro to Micro.

Bathed with the *Etheric Light* after the graceful divine act of Resurrecting the elemental *Body* of the *Son of Man*, the *Initiate* would then be experiencing the *Rising*, upgraded, and called *Son of God*. It is the *Kosmic Man*, whose Individual Mind *Rises* toward the Univesral Mind, the Great Monad that originally diffuses in and through everything *His Divine Essence*. Such *Essence* always remains latent inside the shell until the time comes when it has been awakened at the very core of the *Human Quintessence*—the dormant *Spirit* that is motorized by the *Etheric Light* itself, for the *Mind* is the electric-powered bridge between *Spirit* and *Body*. More to that is revealed beyond the Enochian veil!

Here it is—

Pentagram as Kosmic Man

The Five-Pointed Star

6.
THE DODECAHEDRON

We move on now to the 6th most vital *Initiatic* symbols: the *Dodecahedron*. What is the meaning of it?

The general idea presented is defined as representing "the Ultimate Consciousness of the *One*, the Ether, the Spirit of God, the Heaven, the Higher Self, etc." All these are true identifications of the symbol at hand. However, let us develop it a bit more on the two essential points we highly consider in the Great White Fraternity *Initiatic* System. While the four atomic shapes that exist hidden in nature are the *Pyramid* (Fire), the *Octahedron* (Air), the *Icosahedron* (Water), and the *Cube* (Earth), the *Dodecahedron* is the fifth shape and represents the Ether. Nothing is pure of the existential matters, unless Earth (Cube) partakes in Water (Icosahedron), Water in Air (Octahedron), Air in Fire (Pyramid), and Fire in the Ether (Dodecahedron).

According to our understanding and through a graceful *Alchemical* process, the *Dodecahedron*—that represents the Heaven and is associated in a mystical mode with the Ether of the Kosmos, which is, in truth, the *Quintessence* of the Heavenly Bodies, being the fifth element and the purest form of the Kosmos—should be placed above the *Cube* (Earth) that has not yet unfolded. Thus, the Ether, being a very flexible *Divine Essence* that moves through all visible matters, is indeed the Great Medium between the Invisible and Visible, the Spirit and Matter. Through it, the Divine Mind exercises its total sovereignty upon the world.

When this transpires, when Heaven is placed on Earth, the *Cube* is thus unfolded, radiating forth a collective consciousness upon humanity. At this *higher point*, the *Kosmic Cross* appeared then elevated above Earth and resurrecting it onto and through the entire Kosmos into the *Pentagram* or the *Five-Pointed Star*, which is inscribed upon the twelve faces of the *Dodecahedron*, the Heavens. That said, Earth and Heaven become one and unified, without the need for any invisible or visible mediator. They completely merge, as the Son merges with the Father in Heaven. In the teachings of the Great White Fraternity, we consider these 12 faces of the *Dodecahedron* as representing the 12 Sacred

Builders of Beth-El,[4] where rituals are performed, and the secrets are revealed inside the Enochian veil!

Here it is drawn—

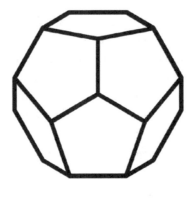

Heaven

The Dodecahedron

---

4. *Beth-El*, meaning "House of El" is the Initiatic Temple or Sanctuary built on Earth.

7.
THE TETRAKTYS

We continue with the 7th most important *Initiatic* symbols: the *Tetraktys*, also known as the *Sacred Decade*. What is the meaning of it?

The main idea here presented is that it symbolizes "God, the Universe, the Ten Emanations from the One Mind, an expression of the Cosmos, the Unity and the Divine, etc." These are correct identifications of the symbol we're tackling now, however, we feel it is quite important to develop it further while pinpointing two essential points we consider in our *Initiatic* System. The *Tetraktys* by itself is the Pythagorean representation of the Enochian-Hermetic Kabbala we have already cited more than once. It symbolizes the Kosmic Creator embodied by the Logos, the hidden archetype of the Universe, Man the Microcosm, or rather the *Initiate*, the Magician or Mathemagician, the Son of God.

The four sets of the 10 dots represent, therefore, the Caduceus of Hermes (Phenok) and complete the process of Creation since it begins with the *One* (Monad)—being the Point of Fire—then moves to the *Two* (Dyad) that epitomizes the Line of Air. And here stands the biggest of all trials on the path of *Initiation*. Should you conquer the work of *Dyad* (confusion of Unity) by the purification of the *Body* through the element of Water in the third phase, the *Three* (Tryad)—being the Surface of Water—presented by our triune-nature, the key elements of life in the Kosmos, where *Truth* is manifested in the Mind, *Virtue* in the Spirit, and *Purification* in the Body, and realizing that your *Spirit* has been embodied by the element of Fire (Light) from the early beginning of your Creation, then finally, at this imperative point, the process shift to the *Four* (Sacred Decade) that portrays the Solidity of Earth, the *Cube* again, but in its alchemical folded state into the *Cross*, say, of 7 Perfect Squares of *Equality and Regularity*.

As the symbol of Moral Justice, it stands between the subject and object in a horizontal direction. The vertical line describes the Divine Laws—given to Phenok, who accepted them at Mt. Hermon from the Angels of God El, as per the book of Enoch—in Conscious and Energetic method. Hence, all powers and vibrations of the physical and spiritual planes are engraved within the Perfect Square. And the name of Him, E.L.I.M., E.L.O.H., A.B.B.A—the

Logos—is equal to the sacred number Four, dedicated to the Sun, which is not but a reflection of EL-Elyon, the First Most High Light!

All this is enveloped by a Triangle that we compare to the Psyche in its *Absolute Uniting Form*, which is not but the Individual Monad, where its great performances and secrets are revealed beyond the Enochian veil! It is when the three spheres of existence: the Natural World, Human World, and Divine World that constitute the Microcosm as well as the Macrocosm are interconnected by the three connecting points or dimensions of the Triangle, being *Beauty* (Spirit), *Wisdom* (Mind) and *Strength* (Body).

Here it is—

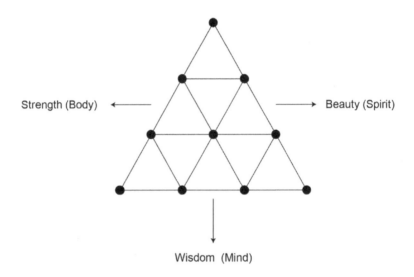

The Tetraktys

8.
THE CADUCEUS

Let's finish with the 8th most essential *Initiatic* symbols: the *Caduceus*. What is the meaning of it?

The principal concept behind this symbol is that it represents "the Flow of Energy from below where the two serpents' tails are indicated and upward to the above where the two serpents' heads are shown, and even beyond, reaching the *wings of liberty* after passing by the dual principles." The interpretation herein made is true but surely needs some refinements. Therefore let us think more on a couple of necessary points we highly consider in the Great White Fraternity *Initiatic* System.

The Caduceus of Hermes is by itself an ultimate Enochian symbol of *Initiation* par excellence, and which had preceded the Hindu Yoga system of seven chakras[5]. The wings on top of the Shaft of Thor are those of the Phoenix, and epitomize the *divine state of humans*, having trodden the path of *Initiation* towards the Divine by overcoming the work of the Dyad, say, dualism, through a strict discipline of complete break out from all its evil/material deeds. One can achieve such a feat by uniting his three dimensions, or his triune nature of being with the Psyche. At that point of accomplishing the state of concordance, the Individual Monad will finally unite with the Great Monad.

There are two courses to take to accomplish that entry inside the eyes of the Phoenix! First, the one that goes upward in a straight line. It is a *Direct Ascension* toward the Divine. It identifies the course of men and women on the path of Enlightenment through a ritualistic *Initiation* into the secrets and mysteries of the Divine. This path—the path of the *Initiate*—is given to the *Inner Circle*. Second, the other goes upward in loops. It is an *Elliptical or Spiral Ascension* that usually takes more time (or lifetimes) and is meant to indicate the course of men and women on that same path of Enlightenment yet, through the authentic esoteric teachings. This path—the path of the *Aspirant*—is given to the *Outer Circle*. Both members of the Inner and Outer Circles reach the

---

5. In the Hindu spiritual discipline of Yoga, the *Kundalini Serpent* is awakened at the base to distribute two currents of Power along the spinal cord, one positive, the other negative, mirrored as serpents, and surrounding the Seven Centers of Energy, called Chakras. No doubt, the spaces and loops formed by the two serpents due to their ascension along the Caduceus look very much similar. Esoteric Physiology, an old system found in Egypt, similarly shows the force centers in the body of the Human Being.

Divine *high and within* according to their individual work and commitment to achieve that highest goal in life, the Great Work—Unity with God.

Curious and strange as it may sound, the Rod of Enoch, that Great Seer of ancient times known as Thot—Lawgiver, Divider of Time, and Counter of the Stars—resembles to a great extent the double helix structure of the DNA! We believe the *Father of Religions and Spiritual laws* had originally discerned it. Thus, it is important to remember now that in the ninth meditation of the Occult Numbers and the ninth vision of the Sacred Alphabet, *Tet(h)*, the Old Serpent—coiled around the *Tree of Life*, also known as the Shaft of the Shepherd—is our unconscious, a reminder of who we truly are and who we would become eventually. As we have seen before, Toth, Teth or Seth[6] is the awakening of our memory, long lost or hence latent—ever since we lost contact with our true divine nature. The Old Serpent[7], who laid the foundation for our Godhead lotus to blossom, lifts us upwards from the mud that composes our organic, material life, and deeper, higher into immortality. Like a Hierophant to a neophyte, she beautifully whispers divine words from *mouth to ear*, unveiling our DNA, our hidden memory in the depth of our beings, and our cultural-genetic rhythm of Truth, long fallen short from its divine archetype. The falling man or mankind is thus understood as *Adam*: the red earth, mud.

Esoterically speaking, it is always good to remember and know that the two Pillars around the Great Altar are mirrored by the two serpents around the Caduceus of Hermes, the Shepherd, or vice versa. The intertwined serpents represent the process of *involution and evolution*, say, Spirit descending into Matter and rising again, enlightened into Spirit. Through the means of the Phoenix's wings that *stretch and flap* over the Serpents' heads, liberation from the unconscious limitation could occur. Then, a new dawn of self-consciousness would *Rise* bright akin to the *Rising Sun*. Since the Serpent around the Rod of Enoch was known in almost all ancient Religions and civilizations as the symbol of Wisdom and Immortality, however, to fully discern it, unlock its process and activate its movement is yet to be revealed inside the Enochian veil!

---

6. Not to be confused with the enemy of Osiris who is also known by the same name and written sometimes as Set.

7. In fact, I have always wondered why the Church has associated the Serpent with the Devil! Maybe the Church didn't actually mean the Devil in our literary understanding, but perhaps referring to the *Cycle of Life and Death*, that of pain when entering into matter, and when temptations increase, and sexual desires are always active. If that's what is truly meant, then the Church had possibly regarded it as the falling from Heaven into Hell, however, it should rather be seen as the *Rising* from Earth into Heaven.

Here it is depicted—

The Caduceus

~ PART III ~

10.

On God or Deity

What is God, or who is God?

This is the most difficult question to answer at all times. Yet, it was one of the most ancient questions to dwell in the laboring mind of humanity—men and women alike—the most intelligent and evolved creature ever found on our populated planet, Earth, or Mother Earth since God was often regarded as the primal and yet primary Male Divine power in the entirety of the Universe, or even behind the creation of the Universe itself from which Mother Earth came to exist.

We will not examine herein the etymological origin and meaning of the English name given as "God," and this for the only reason that it does not benefit us, nor it will enlighten us more in our quest because of the debatable, uncertain, and perhaps even the vagueness of the term "Gott" in modern German, which is believed to derive from the Proto-Germanic term "Guđán." However, the French given name, "Dieu," deriving from the Latin "Deus" is highly important for us and our inner understanding of God or Deity, for that matter.

Both the Latin terms Deus and *Dīvus*, meaning "Divine," have probably originated from the Sanskrit name *Dyàuṣ*, which means "Celestial" or "Shining," thus the "Celestial Light." The term also has the same root as "Dyēus" (Dyēws, Deiwos), believed to have been the chief deity in the ancient religious traditions of Proto-Indo-European societies. Of course, he was part of a larger pantheon, being the god of the daylight sky. As the chief deity, he is also known, spelled and addressed as *Dyàuspítaḥ* in Sanskrit, which means "Sky Father" or "Shining Father." Thence, in his aspect as a Father Deity (Father God) reigning in the upper domain of the sky, the Celestial region, and his consort would have logically been regarded as Mother Earth.[1]

That being said, if "God the Father is Divine Light Shining in the Sky, then, in the beginning, was Light." That makes a lot of sense!

According to us, who go far back to the ancient lore of the Phenokian Fraternity, our mission as adepts of that *Initiatic* system has always been to revive the ancient teachings and codes of the Canaanite-Phoenician Tradition. And thus, addressing the notion of God or the Deity in that particular religion and compare it with the notion of God in other world religions, for example, like that advanced by the Babylonian Brotherhood, and herein especially, addressing its portrayal in Judaism.

First thing first, to proceed in the correct path, we shall address the main question that comes to mind: what is the Canaanite-Phoenician Tradition upon the notion of the Deity? Answering that specific inquiry would have to take us way back in time to see if we have enough information to convey.

Ancient records have shown that Canaanite-Phoenicians had a very long and rich history of religious concepts and their great social and cultural achievements. Their most important religious ritual was that of *Bread and Wine*, performed first by Milki-Sedek, and later by Yāwshu(a) (Jesus in Phoenician-Aramaic). Both were of the same ancient Phenokian Order of Priesthood, which we have thoroughly presented in this book. There is something unique, rather genius in the Hamitic/Afro-Asiatic mind regarding religion and their perception of the Divine.

Phoenicians inspired a whole pantheon of gods, chiefly based on the powers and processes of nature, which they did not fathom at the time yet regarded them in high esteem. These gods were all ruled by One Supreme God of the Kosmos (Cosmos) or the Universe, known as El, the Most High, although, mythologically speaking, El appeared to be one God among many other gods. Yet, he practically stood alone as the chief of the remaining gods, being the main object of worship and the great ruler and protector of the Phoenicians.[2] That said, they proved to have exercised a strong religious sentiment of Monotheism in the first place[3]. However, their later polytheist feelings are depicted in the gods they divided into three main categories.

---

1. That Father God concept became known by many, yet its origin is yet to be discovered! For example, he was addressed as *Zeus Pater*, Father Zeus, by the Greeks and his consort is Gaia (Gaea), often described as the personification of the Earth, great mother of all.

2. Rawlinson, George, *History of Phoenicia*, iBooks, 247.

3. Ibid., 245.

First, we have the *Female Divine* principle, represented by *Ashirai* (or Asherah), the Mother-Goddess of the Phoenicians, who was none but the Virgin Lady *Anat* (also spelled as Anath, Anaitis) herself—the Queen of Heaven. Her daughter was called *Ashtarout*[4] (Astarte, Ashtarte). She had a position of the *Ba'alat* (Baalith, Baaltis), meaning "lady of" any place she was venerated in, whether in the Phoenician land or anywhere else the Phoenicians had established settlements. For example, Ashtarout is the Ba'alat of Gebel. In short, all three, Ashirai, Anat, and Ashtarout, are similar in their divine powers; they significantly symbolize Love, Motherhood, Heavenly Compassion, Life's Giving, and Source of Women's Fecundity.

Second comes the Ēlohim, or "Sons of El," and were mostly known as four. They were represented by *Yāw* (also Yam), the god of waters, rivers, seas, and oceans; Šalim (Shalim), the god of dusk and peace; *Ba'al*, the rider of the clouds, the god of thunder, the god of the Canaanite-Phoenician cities, also known as *Ba'al-Šamin*[5], the Lord of Heaven, and *Ba'al-Hammon*[6], god of fertility and renewer of all Heavenly and Earthly energies; lastly comes *Adon* (spelled Adonis by the Greeks), originally a sun-god *par excellence*, then rendered as the god of resurrection. Both *Ba'al* and *Adon* were sometimes identified as *El* himself and played an important role in the Phoenician theistic principles.

Third, a list of the remaining gods, each in importance to his/her stature. We begin with *Sydyk* (Sedek or Suduc), the god of righteousness and justice; *Ešmun*[7] (Eshmun), son of Sydyk, the god of medicine and healing; *Dagon*, the god of agriculture, discoverer of wheat, and inventor of the plow; *Milikartha*[8] (Melek-Kartha, Melqart), the lord (king of the city) and god of Eden (the first Garden of Vegetation on earth); *Mot* (Moth), the god of Death; *Hadad*, a sun-god; *Shamash*, a sun-god; *Shapash*, a sun-goddess; *Shahar*, the god of dawn; *Resheph*[9], the god of earth; *Yārikh*, a moon-god; *Tanit* (Tanith or Tanata), the goddess of Carthage; and the *Cabeiri* (seven Great Ones), the gods of navigation, patrons of sailors and ships, etc.[10]

---

4. She is the Egyptian Isis. Her Greek copy is mainly Aphrodite and her Roman is Venus, but sometimes, she is Hera, Juno, and Diana for the Romans, and Athene, Artemis, Selene, Rhea, or Cybele for the Greeks. She is Beltis and Ishtar in Babylonia and recognized as Ashtoreth in the Old Testament.

5. His Greek copy is Zeus, and his Roman is Jupiter.

6. He is identical to the Egyptian Ammon.

7. His Greek copy was Asklēpiós, Aesculapius, or Asclepius. Some say he was a physician of divine powers that allowed him to be worshiped as god of healing.

8. Heracles is the Greek copy.

9. Resheph was an Egyptian-Phoenician god having his Temple—the Temple of the Obelisks—erected in Gebel (Byblos).

10. Note: the above paragraphs on the Phoenician gods and goddesses were taken from *Jesus the Phoenician*, 184–186.

Once again, we confirm that despite this long list of various gods, the Canaanite- Phoenicians thought and believed in one Most High Father of everything and presiding overall. Their theological approach gives us the certainty that they were monotheistic in every way possible. In additional confirmation to the matter, we are tackling now, the 19th-century British author and historian George Rawlinson wrote[11]—

> The names by which they designated him were El, 'great'; Ram or Rimmon, 'high'; Baal, 'Lord'; Melek or Molech, 'King'; Eliun, 'Supreme'; Adonai, 'My Lord'; Belsamin, 'Lord of Heaven,' and the like.

He then added—

> How far the Phoenicians realized all that their names properly imply, whether they went so far as to divest God wholly of a material nature, whether they viewed Him as the Creator, as well as the Lord, of the world, are problems which it is impossible, with the means at present at our disposal, to solve. But they certainly viewed Him as 'the Lord of Heaven,' and, if so, no doubt also as the Lord of the earth; they believed Him to be 'supreme' or 'the Most High'; and they realized his relation to each one of his worshippers, who were privileged severally to address Him as Adonai—'my Lord.' It may be presumed that there was no idolatry at this early stage of the religion; when One God alone is acknowledged and recognized . . .

With all that known, El the Great, Most High and Supreme as El-Elyon, also refer to the First Light of creation, that Unity Point of Fire, the Great Monad or the Universal Mind we have already mentioned before and on different occasions. About that, we have, for example, a surprising reference that was conveyed to us by the Roman Emperor Julian (c. 330–363 AD), who wrote[12]—

> And of light, itself incorporeal, the culmination and flower, so to speak, is the sun's rays. Now the doctrine of the Phoenicians, who

---

11. Rawlinson, George, *History of Phoenicia*, iBooks, 245–246.

12. Julian, *Humyn el King Helios*, wikisource.org (Hymn to King Helios). From *The Works of the Emperor Julian*, Volume I. In the Introduction to Oration IV, translator Emily Wilmer Cave Wright wrote, "Julian followed Plotinus and Iamblichus in making the supreme principle the One or the Good which presides over the intelligible world." This clearly reveals that Julian's beliefs were somehow Phoenician, very Pythagorean!

were wise and learned in sacred lore, declared that the rays of light everywhere diffused are the undefiled incarnation of pure mind.

We believe this revered feeling of Monotheism that had once inhabited the minds and souls of ancient Phoenician priests and priestesses had by hundreds of years preceded all other systems of *Priesthood* in any other nation around the globe. It was from the Enochian priests of Mt. Carmel that the famous Egyptian Pharaoh, Thutmose III, took the great and genius idea of the "One God" into Egypt, introducing it first to his close followers and then to some of his trusted subjects in the Mystery School he founded for that single purpose of secret *Initiation*.

We have already mentioned the fraternally Phoenician Egyptian connection of the *Initiatic* Sacred Tradition, but how did Enochian priests transmit Monotheism to Egyptian priests is what we are going to explain now. Let us see how that happened!

With Enoch-Taautus-Thot himself, *Father of Religions, Spiritual Laws, and Founder of the First Religion*, the Great White Fraternity began as a Phoenician-Egyptian Monotheistic Fraternity that sought with anchored faith, the Resurrection of the Self into its higher level and the Immortality of the Spirit. That said, Monotheism lay at the basal core of its theological concept.

It is not known when exactly Phoenicians started to believe in the One High God El. However, this new concept of Monotheism entered Egypt as a Mystery School with Thutmose III or *Thut-Mosis*[13], to eventually appear as a religious reform with Akhenaton. Thutmose III (c. 1505–1450 BC) proved to be the most erudite Pharaoh among all Pharaohs who ruled Egypt. He established a great empire in Asia—a name given to the Land of Canaan—which expanded even beyond the Euphrates. During the many expeditions and military campaigns he led through Asia, he acquired a high interest in Asiatic gods, with a particular focus on Monotheism—already established in Phoenicia.

Among the many locations he occupied in Phoenicia, Mt. Carmel presented itself to him as the most suitable place for *Initiation*. Therefore, in his annals, he referred to this particular place as the 'Sacred Island.' The name Carmel, discussed earlier, derives from the Phoenician word, *Krm-El*, literally meaning, the *Generous Vine of the Father-God El*. Esoterically speaking, it would mean the *Spiritual Offering of El*. Phoenician Priests and Priestesses had built two Temples at the top of the Mountain; one dedicated to El (sometimes identified as Ba'al)

---

13. The name or term *Thut-Mosis* means "Initiate or born of Thut/Thot" in the ancient Egyptian Hamitic language.

and the other to Ashirai (Anat), the Mother Goddess—destroyed later during one of the many invasions of Thutmose III.

It was there, on Mt. Carmel, where we believe Thutmose III encountered some of Phoenician Enochian Priests, direct adepts of Enoch (Phenok), the seer of Mt. Hermon. After watching them worshipping the One Most High God AL, he was very much incited by the idea of Monotheism, as he weighed it against the over-seven-hundred city-gods worshipped all across Egypt. And thus, in a spark of genius, he speculated the possibility and benefits of combining all major Egyptian gods into One Supreme Being.

In consequence of that spiritual-religious revelation, Thutmose III built a new religious center—a School of *Initiation*—on the ruins of the Temple of Ashirai (Asherah). This school immediately found ground in Egypt as a Phoenician-Egyptian Monotheistic Fraternity, known sometime later as the Great White Fraternity. This relation between Canaan-Phoenicia and Egypt persisted for many long years, and therefore, Memphis and Gebel subsisted as twin religious cities.

A bit over one hundred years later, Monotheism emerged with Pharaoh Amenhotep IV (c. 1370–1350 BC)—the religious reformer known as Akhenaton. It surfaced precisely in his religious city: *Akhetaton*, meaning "Horizon of Aton." His father, Amenhotep III, was the son of Thutmose IV, who took for spouse the Phoenician Queen Tia, a believer in the One God El. Thutmose IV was the son of Amenhotep II, the offspring of our famous Pharaoh Thutmose III. In the footsteps of his father, Amenhotep III married a Phoenician Queen, Tiy (Tiye), also a believer of the One God El[14].

We will not venture more into explaining just now what happened next between Akhenaton, "Servant of Aton," his followers led by Osarsiph, and Rameses II (c. 1303–1213 BC), whose name means "Born of Ra," his son Merneptah, and their followers. We simply note that it was an Egyptian internal religious revolution set against Amon-Ra. However, we will explain that shortly and at the right time when we briefly discuss Moses, the traditional religious father of Judaism.

Speaking of Judaism, let us first assert again that the Old Testament fails to prove itself, since it is void of credibility as a true historical source, especially on pre-exilic biblical times, so to speak, and rather, only presenting itself as a book

---

14. Apparently, the Monotheistic relationship between both Canaan-Phoenicia and Egypt was also a strong 12 religious family tie! Hence, during the rule of Akhenaton, their belief led to the laying of the very last stone in the foundation of the Great White Fraternity. As Memphis stood for the religious twin city of Gebel, so did Akhetaton to Mt. Carmel.

of distorted and altered copies of original extra-biblical narratives of other people lives and religious experiences, as we have completely proved before. And thus, when we mention or relate to *scientific evidence, findings, and records*, we mean by it any notable and credible anthropological, historical, theological, archeological, and sometimes geographical data.

So, let us see what is the Judaic Tradition upon the notion of the Deity! Well, their supreme God was and has remained, the Chaldean God *Iao*. However, before that era, Iao or Yaho was a Phoenician minor god, probably a lunar god, or god of sea and water under the name of Yāw. Yaho appeared in the desert of Egypt as a minor god as well. To the Babylonian Brotherhood, on the other hand, Iao was the Mystery God of creation—the breath of life. They identified Iao or Yaho as a combination of an upright *male* and an egg-shaped *female*—the dual principles of Nature.

Let's pause for a thoughtful moment here!

Ye(a)va, Jehovah, and Yahweh are, in fact, other pronunciations of the same name, 'Iao.' Yahweh then became the androgynous Supreme Divinity of the Hebrews. He/She was Ievo-hevah, Adam-Eve, or Yod-Heva—the Demiurge—whom they considered their national power of salvation.

Consequently, a huge theological difference existed between the Canaanite-Phoenician-Egyptian Great White Fraternity Tradition and the Babylonian Brotherhood of the Chaldean-Hebrew Tradition. The first belief system is Monotheistic; the second is Dualistic. True enough! For, Yod is Adam—the Kabbalistic Phallus—and Heva is Eve—the Kabbalistic Grail. Both Yod and Heva formed the name Jehovah, the *earthly—not divine—Tetragram*. However, objectively speaking, and before the dawn of Phoenician-Egyptian Monotheism, most ancient Religions, well before the Hebrews, had embraced some form of belief systems based on Polytheism, Henotheism, and Dualism. Dualism is naught but a form of anthropomorphism of the dualistic gods of creation, a confusion of the Divine Unity, of God.

Contrary to that well-supported analysis, the obvious Kabbalistic Chaldean-Judaic teachings and to even some of the clear notions cited in the Old Testament, some Judeo-Christian scholars, writers, and researchers may suggest, due to the lack of scientific evidence in favor of biblical Israel, that Yahweh is the Jewish version of the Canaanite Phoenician Most High El and to a certain probable extent, Yāw. First, Yahweh is never El, but a confusion of El, as we have thoroughly explained, and will thence highlight a few points herein for the sake of debate. Second, wondering if Yahweh could be Yāw remains a legitimate question to ask per se, until proven otherwise. That being said, how could then the Canaanite Phoenician god of water, Yāw, be erroneously perceived as the Hebrew God Yahweh?

Let us explain how that happened![15]

It has been noted by scholars, as per the Hebrew Bible, that the name attributed to the Jewish God in its most traditional form, YHWH, was not used by the Hebrews before the time of Moses. Undoubtedly, it appears that Biblical (Old Testament) records show that the names *El, El Elyon*, "God Most High," *El Shaddai*, "God Most Powerful," or/and *Elohei Shamayim*, "God of Heaven," were the basic names given to the God the Hebrews seemed to have *textually* venerated, either when led by Abraham, their so-called genetic father, or by Jacob, their so-called founder of the Biblical State of Israel. It was then not until Moses, their so-called religious leader, that the name of God changed from EL to YHWH.[16]

The Old Testament seems to have noted the time and the event that led to this shift in the Hebrew perception of the nomenclature of God. It was during the time, it says, that Moses fled Egypt and its powerful Pharaoh all through the Desert of Sinai and towards the Promised Land of Canaan. It was there, in the Egyptian Desert, says the book of Exodus, where he met Jethro, his father-in-law, a Kenite (or Cainite) priest of Midian who initiated him in a cave at Horeb, the mountain of God, introducing him to the new God—by the probable names of *Yah, Yahu, Yahve, Yâho, Yaw, Iaw, Iaô, Yo* or *Yeho*—who then appeared to him from the midst of a burning bush, unveiling the meaning of his mystery name. He said, "I am who I am,"[17] and sent Moses back to Egypt on a mission to rescue the Israelites from captivity.

---

15. El Koussa, Karim, *Jesus the Phoenician*, 209–218.

16. Again, to avoid confusion, we have already stated in Chapter 1 that the Old Testament is a compilation of stories actually happening in the lives of previous people, like the Canaanite-Phoenicians, Egyptians and Mesopotamians, and noted that the biblical narrative is not at all supported by scientific evidence. So what is said here about El being the God venerated by the biblical Abraham and Jacob is not founded, rather, it was undoubtedly proven to have been the main God worshiped by the Canaanite-Phoenicians and that the scribes of the Old Testament have purposely projected their stories into the Old Testament and make them a Hebrew narration.

17. Exodus 3:2, "And the Angel of the LORD appeared to him in a flame of fire from the midst of a bush. So he looked, and behold, the bush was burning with fire, but the bush [was] not consumed."

And Exodus 3:4, "So when the LORD saw that he turned aside to look, God called to him from the midst of the bush and said, Moses, Moses! And he said, Here I am."

Also Exodus 3:13-14, "Then Moses said to God, 'Indeed, [when] I come to the children of Israel and say to them, The God of your fathers has sent me to you,' and they say to me, What [is] His name? what shall I say to them? And God said to Moses, 'I AM WHO I AM.' And He said, Thus you shall say to the children of Israel, I AM has sent me to you."

Should we consider the narration of the Hebrew Bible a fact—which we reject for lack of scientific evidence—we would reason out the situation that Abraham and Jacob believed in El, while Moses, in Yahweh[18]. Yet, we recognize that the Midianites were known as wise men, or Sons of Snakes[19], as well being known as Canaanites and Hamites like the Egyptians[20]. Such a revelation would make the priest, Jethro, the son of Raguel and Moses's father-in-law, either a Canaanite/Phoenician or Canaanite-Egyptian, hence a Hamite, not Semite.

The probable relation between Hebrews/Israelites and Canaanites has been thought about and investigated for so long a time; some scholars who took the Old Testament for granted as a trusted work have connected the two people. Some others believed that the early population of the Israelites (Hebrews or Jews) were indeed Canaanites or Phoenicians. This connection had been explained by the identical deities worshiped by both people as presented in the Old Testament, from the Most High God Al, El, El-Elyon, El Shaddai, Ashirai or (the biblical Asherah, Yahweh's escort), to his son Adon or Adonai[21], Baal (to a certain extent), and finally Yāw as Yahweh. Thus, as Thompson puts it in his book[22], it would be understandable to think that "El Elyon has made Yahweh God for Israel." If that were the case, then it would be logical to look upon El as a much higher God than Yahweh. And that's for the sake of debate, as we have said above, just pinpointing a few thoughts.

At any rate, concerning Yāw, scientific evidence shows that there were indeed a few references to his name in the ancient world, including in the form of either *personal human name*, or inscribed alone in the form of a *divine name*. It is highly probable that the earliest and most famous body of texts that mention the name are the ones found in both Canaanite/Phoenician cities of Ebla, known as *Tell Mardikh,* in today's Syria (Early Bronze Age, between c. 3300 to 2100 BC) and Ugarit, known as *Ras Shamra,* also in nowadays Syria (Late Bronze Age between c. 1550 to 1200 BC).

In the case of *personal human names*, we find the elements *Yaw,* or *Ya, Yah,* and *Yahu,* to have been used as the grammatical ending of the names, like for example; *Milkiya* and *Milkiyahu,* which means in Phoenician-Aramaic, "My King is Ya," or "My King is Yahu," hence, "My King is Yāw," could well also

18. Exodus 6:3, "I appeared to Abraham, to Isaac, and to Jacob, as God Almighty, but [by] My name LORD I was not known to them."

19. Serpents, hence the brazen Serpent of Moses.

20. Blavatsky, H.P., *Isis Unveiled,* vol. 2, 449.

21. Adon named *Adonai,* but referring though to the Lord, not a son of the Lord, since the Hebrews or Jews didn't and don't believe that the Lord can have a son.

22. Thompson, Thomas L., *The Mythic Past,* 24.

be an abbreviation of a divine name. However, in the case of a *divine name* itself, we find that the name Yāw or Yeuo is indeed the name of a deity believed to be that of Rivers and Sea, the same as Yam, used in all the Phoenician coastal cities of Sur (Tyre), Saydoun (Sidon), Gebel (Byblos), etc., as the god of the Sea and Water.

As seen before, the Canaanite-Phoenician-Aramaic Yāw or Yam is regarded as one of the Elohim, Sons of the Most High God El, same as Shalim, god of Dusk; Ba'al, god of Thunder; and Adon the god of Resurrection, being himself identical with *Yāwshu*, *Ye'shu*, "May YĀW saves," or again, *Immanuel*, "El with us," as patently presented in the Phoenician-Galilean and Galilean-Christian form. As some may have seen in my previous work[23], it is undoubtedly logical to connect the Canaanite-Phoenician god of the Sea with the Christian-Galileans, known to have been greatly associated with the sea and the art of fishing. That determinately makes the description given to the disciples of Yāwshu in the New Testament, being all fishermen, quite understandable.

It is important to note that since Yāw is mentioned as the Son of El, his position as "God for Israel," being appointed by his Father (El-Elyon), as Thompson puts it, would not make any historical sense if looked upon from the Biblical Jewish point of view. It would, however, mean a lot to the Canaanite-Phoenician *Isra-El-is*, or the "House of the Family of El." What do we mean by what we've just said? Right! If we had not done that as yet, it would be vital to explain, so we will highlight the essential differences between two opposite meanings given to the one and same word; "Israel," as seen by both the Canaanites/Phoenicians on one side and the Hebrews/Jews on the other side; however, let us just add an important note we found during our search for Yāw.

In the New Kingdom Egyptian texts, we may surely find a reference to the word Yaw, but in a different context. They didn't refer to a *personal human name* with or without a divine element attached to it, nor to a *divine name* by itself, but rather a *place*, specifically, a geographical area of southern Edom, Udumi(u), Idumaea, or Idumea on the western borders of the Arabian Peninsula. These texts were associated with a group of people called Shasu and Shutu, known to have been nomadic-raiders or desert-dwellers. One example from the texts is a letter penned by an Egyptian scribe that mentioned them as the "Shasu of Yah," moving to watering holes inside the Egyptian territories during the

---

23. El Koussa, Karim, *Jesus the Phoenician*, Chapters 1 & 3.

reign of the Egyptian Pharaoh Merneptah (Merenptah), who reigned sometime between c. 1213 and 1203 BC.

No matter what, let's go back to what has been said above on Israel. Under that new light, we have so meticulously shed, we thus come to identify "Israel" as purely Canaanite-Phoenician people, or a cast of Priests/Priestesses who called themselves *Isra-El,* meaning, the "Sacred Family of El." They were not at all Hebrews, since until now we have no scientific evidence of their existence in both Egypt and Canaan at that time, anyway.

If the Merenptah stele we will come to mention in a bit is true, then we'll have to understand why this pharaoh launched an attack on the people of Canaan and destroyed the "Seed of the Family of El"! In this book, however, we simply prefer to give a short glimpse of that Pharaoh and maybe consecrate a whole chapter about him in future work. Merenptah or Menephtah was Ramses II's son and successor, the Egyptian Pharaoh, who ruled between c. 1279 and 1213 BC. Being the son of that pharaoh, he must have been instructed by the priests of Egypt at the Temple of Amon-Ra in Memphis, as the Egyptian tradition would suggest.

Anyway, what concerns us here, in particular, is yet another person, a very close one to Merenptah, because this person will undoubtedly highlight Moses's identity. These discoveries, yet very little, to what we have come to know, later on, compelled us to focus our inquiry a bit on the religious father of the Hebrews, the well-known Moses, since we are dealing now with the concept of God.

In the Exodus[24] of the Old Testament, Moses was presented as a Jew of the tribe of Levi. He was put in a basket on the water of the Nile by his mother to be saved from persecution and thus was rescued by the Pharaoh's daughter. On the other hand, in an extra-biblical source, and according to Manetho, the Egyptian historian of the third century BC, and who due to his work, the *Aegyptiaca*[25], that we have the best details on Egyptian Dynasties, the name Moses appears as second to an original name of a certain man, called Osarsiph, and that gives us the complete affirmation that the Biblical Moses is copied from Manetho's second *changed* name of Osarsiph. That being said, Manetho became the earliest non-Jewish source that mentions Osarsiph/Moses and the Exodus.

---

24. Exodus 2:1-10.

25. It is unfortunate to say that the original work, *Aegyptiaca*, has never been found as yet, and is only known to us through references, excerpts, comments and copies by authors appearing at a later stage, and the most known or important of them were Josephus, Africanus, Syncellus, and Eusebius.

Oh, but was it the Jewish exodus? Definitely not, totally different from the biblical narrative. Manetho focused his writings on an Egyptian religious revolt led by Hosarsiph, or Osarsiph, a revolt that failed and became an exodus out of Egypt and supported by the Hyksôs[26]. We found out later from a different source that Osarsiph turned out to be the cousin of Merenptah, the son of the Royal Princess, sister of Ramses II[27]. Being of that lineage, he was like his cousin, son of the Temple, and a priest of Osiris he became.

Strabo, the Greek historian who lived sometime around the 1st century BC and who got his information as Manetho did from Egyptian priests, also wrote the same thing. Clement of Alexandria (c. 150–215 AD), Greek theologian and early father of the Church, believed that Moses was deeply involved in Egyptian sciences. And many other historians and thinkers followed the same line of beliefs, as time passed by, like Freud himself, who in his book, *Moses and the Monotheism*, refer to him as Egyptian.

Moreover, just a quick note, if we go back to the open story of the Old Testament on Moses, we may certainly find it to be extraordinary and undeniably similar to another birth story, written in a detailed inscription on the monument of Sargon the Great, the ancient king of Akkad, who reigned sometime around c. 2335 and 2279 BC, and was the founder of the Akkadian dynasty. It read[28]—

> I'm Sargon, the mighty king of Agade (Akkad) . . . my mother, the high priestess, conceived me; in secret, she bore me. She set me in a basket of rushes; with bitumen, she sealed my lid. She cast me into the river, which rose not over me . . .

This famous inscription lived on many centuries later and became a typical motif, an important cultural part of Neo-Assyrian and Babylonian literature and legends. Other Babylonian texts linked to the biblical Moses are the codes of the Babylonian king Hammurabi. For, in the Old Testament narrative, Moses was reported to have received the Ten Commandments from Yahweh up on the top of Mt. Sinai. It is said that the Hebrews remained almost 40 years in the desert of Sinai before they could finally find a way to enter the land of Canaan. However, these Commandments, which were so-called *divinely* given to the lost

---

26. Manetho called the Phoenicians, *Ph'Anakes*. They are the children of Phenok, Henoch, Enoch, or Anak. They are the Anakim (Giants) of Canaan-Phoenicia, who included many tribes such as the Ammonites, Amorites (*Amurru*), Jebusites (*Ib-u-s̄*), Hyksôs, and later, the Arameans.

27. Schure, Edouard, *Les Grands Inities*, 174.

28. Thompson, Thomas L., *The Mythic Past*, 13.

chosen people in the desert, only after two attempts, were mysteriously (!), say, unquestionably taken from those ancient codes of Babylonia.

Back to Manetho's text, let us read what he wrote on Osarsiph according to the *copied* sources. He tells us[29]—

> It was then that the 80.000 of the "impure people" elected for themselves a leader out of the Priests of Heliopolis named Osarsiph, and who afterward took the name of Moses[30]. He instituted many new laws and customs quite opposite to those of Egypt and told his people that they should not worship the Egyptian gods. They were also not to abstain from killing those animals sacred to these gods and were to join themselves to nobody but to those that were of this confederacy.

Manetho also recorded in his *Aegyptiaca*, that Osarsiph who belonged to an elite religious group known as the priests of Heliopolis, a city whose god was Osiris, ordered his people to stop working in the quarries and instead build walls around their city and make ready for a war against the Pharaoh.

In the Old Testament, the biblical Moses (not the Egyptian Osarsiph/Moses), accompanied by his brother Aaron, and his people, "Beni-Israel," who leads a rebellious movement against the Egyptian ruler. He thus ordered them to stop obeying the Egyptians—killing one of them himself—and to follow him, for he will be their savior and liberator, given the power of miracle-making by the Lord of Israel, Yahweh. We already know that nowhere do we find a reference to the biblical Moses in the Egyptian texts!

So, who are we going to believe, Manetho or the Old Testament? Of course, the latter has failed to give any scientific evidence to most historians and archeologists alike worldwide. Suppose Osarsiph, however, was a faithful follower of Akhenaton, Priest of Heliopolis, and cousin of Merneptah who followed his father on the throne of Egypt. In that case, it might be quite understandable to believe Osarsiph has led a riot or, rather, revolution against Pharaoh Rameses II for a reason. It was a typical Egyptian affair!

In the same line of analysis, and as we have seen earlier in Chapter 6, the *Apiru*, mentioned in the Tell El-Amarna texts, were considered outlaws, outsiders, or brigands, living in Egypt and working as hired masons for the Pharaohs.

---

29. Collins, Andrew, *Gods of Eden: Egypt's Lost Legacy and the Genesis of Civilization*, 116.

30. Moses, Mosis, Meses, etc., is an Egyptian word that literally means "Initiate of" or "born of," often used in Egyptian names like *Thut-Mosis* (Thutmose), or *Ra-Meses* (Rameses), etc. We thus believe that Osarsiph changed his name into Moses when he became a priest of Akhenaton.

That said, and weighing the similarities, we could thus suggest that these *Apiru* were the "impure people," if that was the exact term used in the original Manetho's text, led by Osarsiph in a campaign against the Pharaoh. Osarsiph, as the alleged Biblical Moses of the *Hebrews*, ordered his people to stop obeying the orders of Egyptian rulers.[31] Again, these Apiru, as we have amongst others suggested, have nothing to do with the Hebrews (*Ibri*) mentioned later by the writers of the Old Testament during the Hellenistic period.

Anyway, we continue our hypothesis by saying that this group of people, say, the *Hapiru* (also Habiru, alternative forms of Apiru), and who perhaps amongst other groups were led by the revolutionary Osarsiph, failed to win over the pharaoh and his son and were expelled from Egypt, thus pre-mirroring the Exodus story cited in the Old Testament. However, it seemed that these expelled *Apiru* from Egypt, some would suggest, came to live as "outsiders" to the mainstream Canaanite society and were forced to move out from their homes by war, famine, and sometimes by heavy taxation! But this is not supported, and what happened to them, later on, cannot be known, but we can conclude, if that was the case, their destiny could have been similar to many nomadic groups still living today, like the Gypsies, etc. On the other hand, others say they were immediately received in Canaan and welcomed by mainstream Canaanite society, which we believe is a more founded logical conclusion.

It became quite legitimate to think that the Biblical story of Moses, his relation to Yah that he met in the Desert of Sinai (about the Midianite Jethro we cited above), and his conflict with Egyptian authorities, was completely inspired and appropriated by the Biblical scribes from Egyptian texts, just like the Habiru or Apiru argument we just exhibited. For another example, there is no scientific evidence that could support the theory that the Edomites were the Hebrews of the Bible. One of the simplest reasons to note is that there was not a single mention of the Hebrews as a people when Egyptian texts referred to the Edomites (referring to "Shasu of Yah" we mentioned above) as nomadic people dwelling in the desert. However, the Edomites' original land could have stretched from the adjacent Desert of Jordan to the Desert of Egypt, including the region of Mt. Seir, located on the Canaanite Egyptian border. Plus, their relation to the Nabataeans (Nabateans), as Strabo has suggested to be

---

31. *Hosarsiph*, Osarsiph appeared some one hundred years after the time of Akhenaton, the Egyptian Sun worshipper, and preacher of the monotheistic God—Aton. Egyptian history tells that Pharaoh Ramses II continued suppressing the monotheistic religious idea, brought about openly by Akhenaton in Egypt. However, Osarsiph, a learned priest and loyal secret follower of Akhenaton, rebelled against the Pharaoh and his son—Mernephtah—all in hopes of restoring the cult of Akhenaton—the belief in one God.

their origin[32], should not be taken lightly, especially on cultural and religious levels, since it is believed that the Canaanites-Phoenicians-Aramaeans greatly influenced the Nabateans.

We suggest the Edomite religion could have consisted of similar gods worshiped by the neighboring people of Canaan-Phoenicia like the known divine trinity of El, Ba'al, and Asherah, along with Kaus(h)[33] and Yāw. In his interesting book[34], contemporary American professor, Biblical scholar, and author, Mark S. Smith, suggests that the oldest Hebrew Biblical tradition places the Jewish God Yahweh as the deity of southern Edom, which may have originated in the regions of Edom, Teman (a desert to the south of Edom), Seir, and Sinai before being adopted in Israel and Judah.

This significant fact has also been confirmed by many other scholars and authors worldwide, like Thompson, who notably wrote[35] that "The Bible frequently recognizes that Yahweh was worshiped by others than Israel. It understands him as having come from Midian, Teman, and Seir." The "Israel" he meant here is none other than the Hebrew Israel that the Jews inhabited, although he referred to another Israel in his book, as we have seen before from our perception and will see now from his perspective, and which he called Historical Israel, and on its people, he also wrote[36]—

> They are referred to in the stories of Ezra 4 as enemies of Benjamin and Judah. Their offense: they wish to help in the building of a temple to 'the God of Israel' in Jerusalem. They are rejected in the story by Ezra's Jews and given a sectarian identity as 'Samaritans' by historians. This Israel is not the Israel that biblical scholars who write 'histories of Israel' have been interested in. It is not the Israel that we find in our biblical narratives. It is historical Israel.

Indeed, to make things clear and close the "Israel" debate once for all, scientific, logical records impose on our active mind to think of two Israels; while the first is strongly connected to the so-called *Gentile* population inhabiting the wide Land of Canaan stretching from Ugarit to the Delta of the Nile, the other

---

32. Strabo, *Geography*, Book 16, chapter 2, paragraph 34.

33. *Kaus(h)* or *Kos(h)* is also known as Qaus(h), Qos(h), or Qaws, being the national god of the Edomites, and presented as a mountain god that may be connected to Dusharrres, Dusares, or Dushara, the lord of the mountain worshiped by the Nabateans at Petra and some other places.

34. Smith, Mark S., *The Origins of Biblical Monotheism*, 140–145.

35. Thompson, Thomas L., *The Mythic Past*, 176.

36. Ibid., 190.

is only related to the Jews living in Hebrew Israel. Yet, the only extra-biblical reference to the word "Israel" comes from the Egyptian inscription found on a *stele* and describing a destructive military campaign that had been undertaken in the Land of Canaan sometime around the end of the 13th century BC by the same Pharaoh Merneptah we have recently mentioned. The stele mentions a group of people by the name of "Israel" already living in "Canaan," who received a fatal attack, and to whom the Pharaoh desired to see their seeds end, back then.

This interesting inscription could well fit the dramatic part of the Biblical narration describing Moses' conflict with Pharaoh Ramses II, the father of Merneptah, but the reality is completely different, as we have fully explained. The text on the stele could only be seen in the light of an Egyptian religious reform against the polytheistic practices at the time, a reform that had started secretly with Thutmose III, *Thut-Mosis*, the "Initiate of Thut," then openly with Akhenaton, and almost two hundred years later in the form of a revolution led by Osarsiph. And since this revolution was set against both suppressors of Monotheism, Ramses II and his son, assisted by the Hyksôs, it could have also been done under the inspiration and perhaps initiative of the people of *Isra-El*, "the House of the Family of El," already living in Canaan, and toward where Osarsiph was leading his people. This truth would help us comprehend the notion of why Merenptah stele mentions an attack on the people of Canaan to destroy the "Seed of the Family of El."

Now back to Yāw and Yahweh, and similarly to close the debate, by concluding and thwarting all confusions, Thompson resumed his exposé on his worship[37]—

> We also have a number of first-millennium Assyrian and Persian period texts that demonstrate just such a geographical spread of the worship of Yahweh. There is clear historical evidence that the Bible's was not the only religious tradition that recognized Yahweh as God.

He then adds, referring to texts from the early first-millennium century—

> Texts from Sinai and southern Palestine refer to Yahweh as the god of Samaria[38]. They mention his wife, Asherah. Undoubtedly, the di-

---

37. Ibid., 176.
38. Samaria is the "Historical Israel" that biblical scholars were not interested in, as per Thompson.

vine couple was the dominant deities of Palestine's highlands. In the Persian period, Yahweh is worshipped along with his wife Asherah, together with Ba'al and other deities[39] at the town of Ekron in the southern Palestinian coast and as far south as Elephantine in Egypt. Biblical texts identify Yahweh as the name of the traditional deity of the ancient state of Israel, for whom a temple was built in Jerusalem. This deity was understood as identifiable with the universal God of spirit *Elohe Shamayim*.

Many other scientific findings confirm the spread of Yāw into Sinai in texts dated to the first millennium BC and cite him as "Yah of Teman." It is almost certain that this deity was copied later on by the Biblical scribes in the story they created about Moses and the god he was introduced to by Jethro, the Midianite/Hamite, as we have seen before. Since we don't think the Biblical Moses existed (at that time with that name), still the Hebrew Bible failed to introduce the god YĀW in its Jewish form YHWH as a purely Hebraic invention, but rather an adoption of an already existing god worshiped by an old man—a Gentile—the Old Testament introduces as his father-in-law.

Even that Biblical concept itself, and we mean, the act of borrowing deities, whether it was Adon (Adonis in Greek) as Adonai, or Yāw in the form of YHWH, identifying him with the God of Heaven, Elohe Shamayim, does not at all make out of them an entirely exceptional people *to be* labeled the "Chosen People," but on the contrary; they were just below the ordinary group of people with neither divine or spiritual inspiration of their own nor an intellectual genuineness.

Certainly, the spread of the cult of Yāw in the adjacent designated regions from Edom to Sinai could not be understood without considering it to be a socio-religious extension of the notion of Yāw presented in Ebla and, most importantly, the belief in him as the god of Rivers and Sea as pictured in Ugarit.

---

39. Asherah or Ashtoreth (Astarte) has always been cited—sometimes identified with Anat—as the wife-daughter of El in Canaan-Phoenicia and mentioned as the Canaanite/Phoenician main Goddess. The many references to her also in the name of Ashtaroth or Asheroth and as an escort to the god Ba'al in the Hebrew Bible (Deuteronomy 16:21; Judges 2:13; 3:7, 6:25-30; 10:6; 1Samuel 7:4, 12:10; 1Kings 11:5, 33; 15:13; 18:19; 2Kings 21:7; 23:4-7) are solid examples of the Canaanite-Phoenician worship of these deities, and certainly a cult not practiced by the Hebrews/Jews who we believe and proved were not in the land before the Persian Achaemenid Empire set the region under their control. In fact, the many references to Canaanite/Phoenician deities in the Old Testament undoubtedly reveal the meticulous works of forgery done by Persian scribes, like Esdras and Nehemiah, in attaching them (El, Ba'al, Asherah . . .) to the rising *Aebirou-al-Nahara* religious culture they powerfully endorsed by organized propaganda.

If that is so, then Yāw—like Yamm on the Phoenician Coast—would have taken the shape of the god of the Dead Sea close to Edom and the Red Sea close to Sinai. It would then be logical to analyze and entertain with the idea, as per the Old Testament narration, that the god that helped the mythical Moses divide the water of the Red Sea into two parts on his way back to Midian away from the Egyptian forces was essentially a deity who had the power of control over the element of water, a god of water, hence Yāw, the god of Jethro, his father-in-law. Yet, the essential obstacle in that narration has always been the Hebrew Moses himself, a person whose extra-biblical scientific records has not been able to identify as a real being. A figure that had one of his characteristics intentionally shaped on the image of Osarsiph, the Egyptian revolutionary priest we have mentioned before.

It is worth reminding the readers that *personal human names,* including words such as "Yehi" or "Yehaw," were undoubtedly often in use by Canaanite-Phoenician kings, like the 10th or 8th century BC King of Byblos Yehi-Milk (King Yehi) and Yehaw-Milk (King Yehaw), another Byblos King of the 5th-4th century BC. These two recorded historical dates show the first preceding and the second accompanying the correct—*not mythical*—date the Hebrews (*Aebirou-al-Nahara*) entered the Land of Canaan in waves and organized complete manner.

No matter what, the theory saying the Hebrew God Yahweh could conclusively be identified with the Phoenician God Yāw is very erroneous for many reasons. The simplest one is that Yahweh, as pictured by the Jews, is not the god of water! Historical records show the Chaldean-Babylonians—from which, according to the Hebrew Bible, Abraham emerged, having been originated from the city of Ur—believed in the god *Iao, Iaô, Iaho, Yaho, Yâho,* or *Ea, Ia.* The Biblical records, which appear to have no historical authenticity as to the exact correct periods and names of characters implemented in the Old Testament narration, seem to coincide with our approach that the Biblical Abraham could have well been, in fact, the historical Sheshbazzar, Shenazzar, or even Zoro-Babel, Zerubbabel, the Chaldean-Babylonian genetic father of the Hebrews.

In addition to that, scientific records show the Chaldean-Babylonian deity *Ea* was part of a triad of deities completed with *Anu* and *Enlil.* Ea has been mainly considered as the Lord of *Apsu* (Abzu), which means "fresh waters beneath the earth," hence god of Water (in seas, lakes) and may have also signified the purification ritual by water. It has additional characteristics, like being the god of sorcery and incantation and patron god of craftsmen and artists, being a bearer of culture, an intelligent and wise god that evolved with the Akkadians into being devious and cunning. Recognized as the father of Marduk, the national god of Babylonia, Ea also stood as a form-giving god, or simply, god of Creation.

It is also believed that the Akkadian-Babylonian Ea was worshipped earlier by the Sumerians as Enki[40], shown in their mythologies. However, etymologically speaking, *Enki* may have a confusing linguistic root, yet the common translation would be: "Lord of the Earth." Enki has been associated with the act of fertility and regarded as the god of Creation who devised men in such a way to be slaves to the gods. On the other hand, some say that Ea is Hurrian[41] in origin, while others believe it has Semitic origin mainly from the western region, or simply as we think, a Hamitic origin, in the sense of having its roots based in the Aramaic-Phoenician-Egyptian (Afro-Asiatic) root: *hya* or *haya*, which means "life," manifested by the water element.

Adding to that, it is almost certain that the Chaldean-Babylonian god Ea, Ia or Iaô, etc., has been identified by H.P. Blavatsky, who wrote[42]—

> In the old religion of the Chaldeans, the highest divinity, enthroned above the seven heavens, representing the spiritual light-principle and also conceived as demiurge was called Iaw, who was like the Hebrew Yâho mysterious and unmentionable.

The Chaldean/Hebrew Iaô, she added[43]—

> . . . would—etymologically considered—mean the 'Breath of Life,' generated or springing forth between an upright male and an egg-shaped female principle of nature. . . . In Hebrew, Iâh means life.

That all being said, the Hebrew Yahweh or Jehovah, the demiurge, could not at all be regarded as the Supreme God but rather, a creator of matter

---

40. It could be because the gods Enki and Ea were counterparts, combined together in the form of *Enki/Ea* (also Oannes) as "Lord(s) of the Earth and Water," that made the Chaldean-Babylonians portray him as a half-goat/half-fish creature, and from which most probably the ancient astrological figure of the Capricorn was conceptualized.

41. It is not exactly known who were the ancient Hurrians, but some have identified them with the Horites mentioned in the Old Testament. The Hurrians seem to have lived first in Iraq (East of Tigris River) and Iran (mountain region of Zagros) sometime in the 3rd millennium BC before migrating west towards Turkey (Anatolia) and Syria during the 2nd millennium BC. Records show that they established the Mitanni Kingdom in the 15th century BC.

42. Blavatsky, H.P., *Isis Unveiled*, vol. 2, 297.

43. Ibid., vol. 2, 299.

to a certain say, *theistic* extent, and thus looked upon as a subsidiary deity to the Most High God. The big difference between him and El regarded as the Father in the Assembly of gods in the Phoenician Pantheon. Not identical with the Phoenician Yaw, Yahweh, therefore, could be solely identified with the God Iaô, Iâho(h), Yâho, Ea, or Ia, the Chaldean god of Creation. He is the hermaphrodite Ye(a)va, Iahvh, Jove or Jahve (Yahveh), Jehovah (Yehovah), the Androgynous Supreme Divinity of the Hebrew-Israelites, being Ievo-hevah, Adām-Hāwa (Adam & Eve), the Kabbalistic, Yod(h)-Heva.

It is not by coincidence, but rather by a deliberate fact or rather a clear conviction in the mind of the Jewish Chosen People that the deity they have always worshiped is YHWH. Since the beginning, they have pictured their God in such a way that presents its nature as not being *One* and unique like the Pythagorean Monad (*Nous*), or like El, the Father of Jesus who resides in Heaven, but instead, a decomposable Being similar to the manifested forms human beings have taken on earth. Thus, the Old Testament that opens with the Book of Genesis (1:1), "In the beginning, God created the heavens and the earth," continues its description of the creation of the world by saying (1:27), "So God created man in His own image; in the image of God, He created him; male and female He created them."

While the Jewish Yahweh, in its demiurgic act of creation, may represent the Breath of Life of the material world, the Phoenician Yāw, god of water—whose Philo of Byblos gave witness to his worship in Phoenicia even in the 2nd century AD and probably all around the coastal and eastern Mediterranean region up until the end of the Greco-Roman Period—represents the element of life and purification of the living human being. This fits very well the image Jesus appeared with in the world of matter as *Yāwshu*, "Yāw Saves," walking on water, holding within him the Way, the Truth and the Life[44], and saving people by healing and purifying them from their earthly material sins.[45] It is not by coincidence that Christianity adapted baptism by water as one of its major religious rituals—a secret *Initiation* of accepting human beings as members within the Christian Community saved by the Meshiha Immanuel.

---

44. John 14:6, "Jesus said to him, I am the way, the truth, and the life. No one comes to the Father except through Me."

45. Bartholomaios 4:65, "When he had thus prayed, Jesus said unto him: Bartholomew, my Father did name me Christ, that I might come down upon earth and anoint every man that cometh unto me with the oil of life: and he did call me Jesus that I might heal every sin of them that know not . . . and give unto men the truth of God."

Having mentioned here below in the footnotes both John and Bartholomew, two of Jesus's disciples and non-dualist Christian Gnostics, let us observe Marcion's concept of God as it perfectly fits our exposé here. Marcion[46] believes that the Supreme God that had manifested in Christ from the beginning of time was the Invisible, Indescribable, and Good God that actually had nothing to do with Jehovah, the Jewish God, which he defined as the *Demiurgus*[47], the creator of the material world (world-maker) and who by special choice elected the Jewish people as his own and thus became the god of the Jews.

To Marcion, God—the Christian Father of goodness and grace—is a Loving and Merciful God, whereas the Jewish God, as shown in the Hebrew Bible, was very distinct from the Father; he was unjust, unmerciful, angry, jealous, tribal, and a god of war. Eventually, Marcion found it just irrational and impossible to think that Yahweh could be the God of Jesus; hence, Jesus Christ came to abrogate the Jewish Lord, who was opposed to his God and Father, as "matter is to spirit, impurity to purity."[48]

In short, Marcion proclaimed the Unknown Alien Good God on probably three basic characteristics; *Unknown*, because He cannot be recognized in the World or man in any possible sense; *Alien*, because He is not connected to the world or man by any bond or obligation; *Good*, because He is absolutely the Redeemer that became manifest for the first time in the history of the world and man in the person of Christ, prompted by an act of love, mercy, and grace.[49]

This Supreme God, Father of all, was regarded as being the Universal Mind by the great Pythagoras. The first Philosopher, from *Philo-Sophia*, "Lover of Wisdom," taught[50] that God is the *One*, Primordial Harmony, Central Fire, Monad, Intelligent Spirit, Good, Source of life, Unity Point, Life Force, and Essence of the Whole.

---

46. He was a non-dualist Christian Gnostic of the 1st – 2nd century AD who became bishop of Sinope in Pontus (northeast of Turkey today) like his father before him. We believe that Christian historical and theological truth on the nature of the Father of Jesus was said by him.

47. According to Catholic Encyclopedia, it is the *Demiurge*. Gnostics consider the Demiurge a personification of the inferior creative power in the Universe, being the offspring of a union that had gathered Achamoth (lower wisdom) and matter. Since Achamoth herself was only the daughter of Sophía the last of the thirty Æons, the Demiurge was distant by many emanations from the Supreme God. Later on, the Demiurge was looked upon as personifying the power of evil, Satan, who, some of the Gnostics (non-dualist Gnostics) had identified with Jehovah, the Jewish God that sometimes was made identical to the great tyrant Yaltabaoth or Ialdabaoth, Son of Chaos and darkness. He is the Kabbalistic Yod-Heva (Adam & Eve), representing the androgynous principles of creation, the Demiurge that broke Unity with the *One*, 1, the Pythagorean Monad, as we have thoroughly explained.

48. Blavatsky, H.P., *Isis Unveiled*, vol. 2, 163.

49. Harnack, Adolf, *Marcion the Gospel of the Alien God*, 3.

50. El Koussa, Karim, *Pythagoras the Mathemagician*, 294–295.

In Christianity, as written in the New Testament, mainly by Paul and John, the idea of God is exhibited so clearly, without any complications, difficulties, or even any theological imperative notions/calls. God is the Father. God is Love.

Now, in finality, the definition of the Principle of God according to the Phenokian *Initiatic* teachings is related to the teachings of the Great Five Masters—Enoch, Melki-Sedek, Hiram Abiff, Pythagoras, Jesus Christ—on God, and is already presented in the first letter of *The Sacred Alphabet*, **Aleph** and in the first meditation of Number **1** in *The Occult Numbers*.

11.

On Creation and Man

Creation! What is it? It is the manifestation of the Absolute Principle, the physical dualist fruit of the Universal Mind's Creative powers as considered by the Pythagoreans and known as God in all religious systems, including Christianity. Should we decide to envision how Creation could have occurred back in time and with time, we could, however, possibly imagine the following Creative episodic scenes emerging directly from our unconscious!

God, the *One*, the Great Monad, pervaded the Cosmos and whispered his breath of life solemnly, so to speak, saying, "Be it! Let me be physical!" The godly calling voice reverberated up in the Heavenly Kingdom. Instantly, *numinous sounds and divine harmony* beckoned the Cosmic Energy and Cosmic Matter forth out of chaos and void, intending to follow an order of Divine Origin after being diffused in everything. *Two* points derived from the Order, which is of the *Word*, forming a confusion of the Unity that were essentially in the Divine Mind, and shaping rather a line by announcing *Beth*, the duality of the created existence.

It is thus the Androgynous Demiurge creation of an Indivisible Essence, but a Divisible Substance. It contained the *male active principle*, or *Energy*, on one side, and the *female passive principle*, or *Matter*, on the other side. The Demiurge is then the union of the *Will* of the Eternal Male and the *Faith* of the Eternal Female. These two essential divinities created and generated the visible physical world[1]. We dedicate it to both the Sun and Moon, overburdened by the power of *Remphan*[2], say, Saturn, enclosing the whole existence within its ring!

---

1. Mentioned in almost all ancient religions, these dual divinities were represented as *Osiris-Isis* for the Egyptians, *Adon-Astarte* for the Canaanite-Phoenicians, *Bel-Ishtar* for the Babylonians, *Shiva-Shakti* for the Hindus, *Heaven and Hell* for the Persians, *Yod-Heva* (Yahweh) for the Hebrews, etc.

2. *Remphan* is also spelled as *Raiphan* or *Rephan*, it is Saturn and its symbol is the Six-Pointed Star. Reference to it can be found in the New Testament, Acts 7:43, and the Old Testament, Amos 5:26 which read in Hebrew as *Chiun* or *Kewan*.

The odyssey of physical life began, following an order of broken Divine origin! The *One* manifested and became *Two*. Far distant galaxies and stars beamed, one after the other, in the dark-blue sky. And yet, God held time captive in His hands, when a holy moonlit night turned into day. The Sun appeared from the bosom of the Light—the Most High as if it were a *Son of God*—standing in the center of its system and surrounded by its disciples, the planets who followed an order of strict consistency. It shone divine rays in all directions and radiated energy towards and throughout the circumference. They breathed in its heat and looped around it in the act of worship.

Earth moved quickly. It rotated around itself and the Sun. Billions of years passed to transform and gradually evolving it. Volcanoes erupted, the temperature changed, cooled its atmosphere, and floods swarmed it. Earth lost its virginity and was ready to deliver, for the birthing labor ceased in due time, and life, organic life, would appear anytime now, somewhere within its womb.

Through uncanny grayish-blue clouds hovering first above the sea, hiding the Horizon painted with an orange-red color, the Sun had already seeped through, drawing its own reflection in golden lines upon the surface of the water. Those luminous lines appeared like trodden paths, at a time when life beat in the abyss of the ocean, to evolve in silence, in cold and darkness. Life took its first steps on those paths towards lands, where trees and vegetation welcomed the children of water with open arms to live and multiply, and, in time, some of them soared into the air.

Born into blind matter, governed by Saturn, Humans appeared, embodying the pure *Spirit* that emanated straight from the *One*. The curtain dropped, and the many different masks wore on their faces concealed their true divine nature from their sight. Even their inner eye was utterly hidden! It is very true; the meeting between *Spirit* and *Matter* impeded the awakening of Humans from the realm of deep unconscious sleep! They have already entered the *Circle of Necessity*, that *Wheel of Life*, where the surrender to the dualistic principles, the twofold deities of this world took place.

Darkness and Light, Blindness and Awareness, are two obvious manifested examples of paradoxical aspects, which enfolded the material existence of creatures on Earth. They breathed in Life and breathed out Death.

Then, the cawing of seagulls that glided in the air, animals that walked the lands, plants, and trees that grew in the fields created some musical harmony in their minds and spirits, awakening Humanity to the present moment. These interchanges were very much perceptible to Human senses. They made them aware that life communicated in so many ways, and to a certain extent, intelligently! In fact, all creatures of Earth followed the same coherent laws, simply by their connection to the Universal Mind that diffused its impulses through all the existence.

The early spring Sun, shimmering on the even surface of the sea, declared the day Men and Women walked and strutted one after another on that beautiful sandy beach, creating an unbroken chain of Nature's most beautiful creatures, if not, the most evolved. Women's well-designed bodies shone vibrantly, like bamboo recently painted. *From where did they come up with such a marvelous color of skin?* Men marveled as they saw them jumping in the water and swam like gracious dolphins, these peaceful creatures of the sea. They dove in and out, gliding on the surface, bodies sprinkled by water and swathed with light. Gorgeous, almost magnetic, they caressed their hairs and moved their heads backward, staring at the sky above. Their eyes glittered splendidly like stars amid the void of night. They appeared like goddesses of the sea. They were mermaids, Astartes . . . and the Sun strongly reached down to them, and all over their soft skins for the heat to blaze their bodies and elevate their desires to its light.

The *Initiate* amongst Men, if there were any at that time, but they were none as yet, would shun his eyes away, trying to escape the delightful vision surrounding him, and switch from that spellbinding state of mind, which vivid imagination fully gripped him unwillingly. Who would not, when caught in front of such a mesmeric revelation? But . . . the same feelings and aspirations felt by Men at a certain time of consciousness, or an intense moment of awakening to their true divine nature in the abode of the *One*, is now lost, trapped, or better say, "Fallen"[3] in the manifested world of the *Two*, are also experienced by Women, in the same manner, and fashion. However, Life would not end therein for the *Initiates*; men and women alike, it can't just be it, it doesn't just end now! They rather have to skip the melting into this enthralling manifestation and continue on the path that leads to the invisible *One*.

Silence would reign for some time . . . time to think!

~ ~ ~

---

3. A term most ancient *Initiatic* traditions use to express the Fall of Man from Heaven. It is the Fall of Adam and Eve into sin, say, error or matter, by eating from the *Tree of Life*, and wrongly understanding the words of the Old Serpent that would only let them know their true divine nature!

Now, before we go much in-depth into knowing the original Psyches of our human species on Earth, each and every member of the Great White Fraternity *Initiatic* Tradition should know that after its creation, the Kosmos has surely continued its existence upon a Divine Plan. Eventually, some of these planets should present a great probability of maintaining some form of intelligent life, spirits, perhaps as well, physical life of some sort, somehow identical to ours here on Earth—the *Sphere of Generation*. It is on its revolving surface that occurs all the Incarnation and Dis-incarnation operations of the Spirits. On other rotating spheres, say, around the moon, there exist spirits who are relatively *higher* than those who took physical bodies on Earth. However, much higher spirits, almost as spiritually pure as *Fire* or *Light*, live upon the Sun, a solid reflection of the Intelligent Fire, God—the Great Monad. Think about it![4]

So, what are we in reality? With the Phenokian *Initiatic* Tradition, we follow the teachings of Master Pythagoras concerning the hidden reality of what became "Men and Women" in the manifested world through theology of their Psyches. Man is a triune being, and the theology of his/her Psyche reads as follows—

Our Sphere, Earth, went through many phases of evolution along with its Animal-Human life forms. The laws of evolution are one-and-the-same for almost all beings that dwell in space. One should bear in mind that this particular Animal-Human evolution occurred not only by the *Law of Nature* but also by an eternal *Law of Divine Generation*. One should also comprehend the fact that Time is the Spirit of the World!

And thus, when a new species of Mankind surfaced on Earth, some later *Initiates* identified it as a *race of spirits*, of superior monads. In fact, at some point in the history of Earth, a long time ago, this new genus of Mankind had incarnated in the progenies of the previous ancient Animal species. And thus, this superior race boosted the Animal species one step higher in evolution by transforming it into its Divine-Human spiritual image. It is truly a hierarchical process of intelligent evolution from Animal to Mankind and later, from Mankind towards the Divine-God.[5]

Accordingly, we are significantly determined to instigate the instruction based on Pythagoras' sacred science of Psychology, called *Theology of the Psyche or Soul*. Be it by curiosity or high interest, the basic four questions humans have debated throughout the ages constituted the main focus of the new program

---

4. El Koussa, Karim, *Pythagoras the Mathemagician*, 320–321.

5. Ibid., 335.

the Pythagorean disciples were to follow, and every one of us, every true adept, should.

Who am I? What am I? What am I doing here? Whither do I go?

Simply answered now, and before we proceed in development, we believe we are not physical machines nor mere biological automata, but spiritual beings lost on Earth—the fall of Adam—always aspiring to ascend back to our very Essence, the Divine Love, through the Perfection of our *Selves*, say, our Psyches; bathing in Angelic Light!

So, for them, say, Pythagoreans, as is for all of us, to unlock the great Mysteries of all time, we would have to seek and ultimately find answers to these important questions. Dwelling in this eternal dilemma, our Psyche always struggles to avoid falling into the duality of Darkness and Light, or more precisely, of evil and good. And . . . when we are indeed ready, we will be summoned by the *Initiate* to enter into a direct relationship with the Psyche. It is said, "*Know thyself, and you shall fathom the secrets of the Universe and the gods.*" True indeed, for we behold the *Sanctum Sanctorum*, the Holy of Holies, beating high and deep inside our realms!

Every human Psyche is a partial element of the Great Soul of the World, the Great Monad. The human Psyche, *de facto*, lives throughout all the kingdoms of Nature. It resides at all levels of life forms where the anima and spiritual energy evolve. Their evolution is gradual, and it transpires relatively through a series of incarnations. It started as a mere blind force at the *Solid Level*. It behaved as a self-reliant, active force at the *Plant Level*. It then vibrated through the receptive and instinctive impulses of the *Animal Level*, and it lastly reached the *Human Level*, which stands as the highest form in Natural Life. There, the Psyche tends towards a binding point with the conscious Individual Monad.

So, the farther living beings *ascend* in levels, the more dormant faculties of their Individual Monads develop. That occurs by first originating from total blindness and ending with absolute intelligence. Hence, the pre-psychic force is forever related to the elements of Water and Earth, in both the Solid and Plant Levels. However, after death, the psyche of the Animal life sojourns in the condensed element of Air, for the gravity of Earthly life strongly attracts it, and thence it returns to Earth to embody life, repetitively. The human Psyche, however, is solely related to the Fire element. It returns after death to the Central Fire or Eternal Light to be judged. If found guilty, it will take a new physical human shape here on Earth, once again, to redeem itself from the errors made in the previous life. If found innocent, it will then unify with the *Eternal Light*, which occurs only after completing the *Cycle of Reincarnation*.

That said, how could one explain the evolution of the Animal psyche into Human Psyche? It is easy! Evolution, which constitutes the transformation process from Animal to Human, could have never occurred without the prior existence of some properly formed Kosmic Human Psyches. These must have descended to Earth from other spheres of existence and built or seeded a preliminary Spiritual Essence in the Animal psyche to infuse them with Divinity at a later stage of the evolutionary process.

Does that, however, refer to the fact that we come from outer space? To put it in a more understandable way, it is to be perceived in the following manner. Our Human Psyche did not originate from Earth, that's for sure! The Kosmic Psyches, which shaped our Humanity, had existed for a long time on other spheres having very slight material density, almost insignificant, and to be precise, more of *Ethereal* Spheres. In their beginnings, of course, these Psyches were invisible, say, *pure spirits* with great spiritual, divine, and mental faculties. With time, their elemental nature changed because their incarnations and reincarnations occurred lightly and easily. They developed into semi-corporeal bodies as they moved down from one sphere to another in this great Kosmos.

As the spheres consolidated on their way down to Earth, they slowly condensed into physical forms. As such, they gradually lost these faculties, called *Energies*. On Earth, the last material level of heavenly descent, they materialized into Human Beings. A lot of their aforementioned energies waned. This is the *Fall of the Ancient Man* from the Kosmic Garden of Eden—from Heaven down to Earth.

This *Fallen Man* was physically modeled in this fashion due to his deep and heavy kind of interconnection with the fleshly substance of the Animal form and its related elements. On the other hand, the *Ancient Man's* Psyche achieved the impregnation of its residual Spiritual and Mental Essence into the Animal psyche, and that to endow it with the leftovers of its Divinity.

Therefore, on Earth, the Human Being remains still in a constant state of tension because the material world diverts him from his ultimate elevated goal. His goal was, is, and always has been, and will ever be the redevelopment of his *Intelligence* through a chain of reincarnations that would reinstate his lost *Spirituality* and *Divinity*. And from that moment on, his/her reincarnations on Earth are not merely a fall into matter anymore, but rather an elliptical ascension towards the *Higher Spheres*. It's, in short, his/her way back up. Why? Because Earth, as was said, has fashioned his final physical level! Hence, his ultimate mission is to become what he was and is, in reality—a Son of God. One should not be amazed at this knowledge for, in truth, we are the sons and daughters of Earth, but of a Celestial Race. Know thyself![6]

One of the main questions Men and Women may ask is how we can find and understand the way? So, let's try to draw the path.

Inside the Secret Chambers, we enter as *Initiates* into the Mysteries of life and take our positions on the Five Points of the Star. After invoking the power of the Most High God, "ELOH,"[7] the Divine Energy would encircle us all and then envelop us with great presence—a presence so terrible, yet so mesmerizing! It will hold on to us, in a way, unimagined and unexpected, but that is the reality of things! So get ready, for the Light vibrating from the Caduceus of Enoch-Thot-Hermes standing straight at the middle point of the *Five-Pointed Star*, has been lifted by virtue of the flapping wings of the Phoenix, which floated up then in a circular motion to hover above us, below us, around us, through an intertwining string of continuous energy.

The point in the middle of the circle brought forth *Spirit* and *Matter* before *Divine Intelligence* could circulate in rays all over and throughout the circumference of existence. That could be a frightening momentary cut of energy along the lines and points of the Star! A few moments later, the order will come back, but not as serene and peaceful as the first one. The new order is somehow chaotic and confusing.

Spirit descending from one point met the *Matter* in the other and together *built and destroyed* the bridge between the Central Point and the totality of the points scattered all along the circumference. Thus, Life in the Cosmos, precisely here on the physical plane, is bound to that Duality of the Male and Female aspects. But, within all the creatures that are living, evolving, and prospering here on Earth, Humanity is the most qualified at the time being to escape it.

The goddesses unite with gods in sacred marriages for many different reasons. Thus, one of them was the rite of fertility to ensure personal and national fecundity, the creation and procreation of humanity. Moreover, Priests and men and Priestesses and women, worshiping those dual deities, have even constrained themselves more on the spiritual plane to the Dyad. They have

---

6. El Koussa, Karim, *Pythagoras the Mathemagician*, 341–344.

7. ELOH, *Eloh* is another Phoenician-Aramaic pronunciation of El, Elyon, Elus, or Elohe without alluring to Him in its plural form as Elohim. We have been introduced to this spelling prior in this book.

enrolled in practicing sacred prostitution, giving homage and prayers to their so-called divine couples, all to ensure a secure future, not only for them but also for their lands.

They have therefore become prisoners of their material enclosure as well as to their religious rituals. They have multiplied and filled the Earth on the model of their divinities, followed by the instinct of their mundane survival! They would engage in what they call love! Love in this sense is not but a poetic word they would use or choose to rather mean sex instead, a word they feel is not pretty appropriate to describe what they call or want themselves to believe to be; sacred relationship. Yet, they would keep on enacting sexual intercourses through an endless loop of pitiful attempts to unite themselves in one body, but they would remain to have two! They would try to forget that it is not just a myth, religious and secular, and only as an enticement to carry on the Human species through sexual relationships that are only confined to the world of matter. We shall see that in a bit.

Hopefully, and miraculously, their miserable union would give them something in return for their pleasures. It would give them a child, who at his or her turn would also be bound to the rules of Duality with the person he/she chose to be with as their partner inside that frightening endless ring. Humanity, after all, would not be able to break that chain, that vicious circle, the *Wheel of Necessity*, much like the Deities whom they adored, but the few *Sons of Prophecy* emerging still from those *alleged divine couples*, have found a particular way to liberate themselves for the sake of that weak Human race!

Is that confusing to you even more? Anxiety would fill you all through the night . . . think again! You would wake up in the morning a little bit shaky, for the night was a field of battle. You then took your early breakfast and walked outside the Chamber for some fresh air. Later, during the day, you would meet your Brothers and Sisters standing by the *Tree of Life* as if waiting for you to join them in their quest. Hence, your search into the ancient Mysteries before having the chance to enter the Chamber once again would lead you to read and know about the Androgynous Mysteries and their related topics, aka, *sacred sexuality*.

Gnostics, for example, from the Greek, *Gnosis*, meaning "Knowledge," constituted, in fact, many different sects. While some were non-dualists like Marcionism, others were dualists like the Simonians, a sect probably founded by Simon Magus and Helene of Tyre. They (the dualists) were influenced by Hindu, Zoroastrian, Chaldean, and Judaic traditions. However, Gnostics, in general, believed that every human being housed a *Divine Spark* trapped in *Matter*. The Aeon, or Emanation of God, the *Man of Light*, mirror of the Macrocosm, regarded as *Adam-Kadmon* by the Kabbalists, has been deceived—by the Demiurge, say, the Androgynous who created the lowest material level of reality—through the process of incarnation, and forgot his true nature. Gnostics, therefore, wish that one day they would be able to reach Liberation and then Union with the True God in the Pleroma, the Gnostic Heaven. The Journey is long and confusing and could thus take many lifetimes. It seems, however, that some of them, the dualists, were not able to wait for that foreseen Union with the *One* and became in particular indulged in sexuality, considering it sacred, though it was created by the Demiurge! They rather began to believe that it would not only bestow them with joy, but it would also make them achieve Oneness with the Universe and the Divine, as well. It happened that they were really trapped and have forgotten their True Nature.

But of course, they were not alone engaged in these peculiar rites for such alleged *Oneness*! The Hindu Tantra and Chinese Taoism both consider that certain sexual practices would help one achieve mystical awareness, some sort of physical regeneration and longevity, and Unity with God. It may be true for physical regeneration and a joyful feeling, but that has nothing to do with spiritual awareness and Union with the Divine.

In the same context, moreover, some of the Knight Templars[8] were said to have worshiped a strange idol, known as the *Baphomet*[9], which in fact could not be but a secret representation of the Hermaphrodite Demiurge, creator of the physical world, *Male* and *Female* aspects blending in one, for so-called spiritual enlightenment—*sacred sexuality*. Some of the stories related to them, and that which have been well researched, claim that Mary Magdalene was the *sexual Initiator* of Jesus Christ bestowing wisdom upon him as a goddess/priestess and that Christ himself has taken that role from John the Baptist, the true priest of Sophia, the feminine principle of divinity, Mary Magdalene! Therefore, it

---

8. There were/are actually two Knights of the Temple; those called the "Poor Knights of Christ" who lived in chastity, poorness, love and peace, regarding Jesus Christ as the true Temple of God they need to work hard to protect and, those called "the Knights of the Temple of Solomon" who were in favor of war and greed to a point that they became very rich and powerful; their story is long and could be deceiving! They were originally influenced by the manipulative teachings of the Jewish Rabbi, Solomon Ben Isaac, known as Rashi, and originating from the village of Troyes in Champagne, France.

9. Trying to explain the meaning of the Baphomet and its real secret term would make us wonder! Is it *Baphomet* or *Yahomet*? We think it has originated from the Babylonian Ea, which preceded the Jewish Yaho as seen before. It is Jehovah, the Demiurge, the Hermaphrodite Yod-Heva who is referred to by the Gnostics as Ialdabaôth (son of chaos and darkness), though it could also be Sabaôth (god of army and war).

was revealed in these stories that the Holy Grail searched by many and claimed to have been found by these Templars was not the one that held the blood of Christ—*a few of them though believed that*—but the blood of the Virgin, the *Templars' Isis*, Mary Magdalene, bestowed on the Altar, in sexual practice.

But, Jesus, when on Mt. Olive secluded himself to meditate, prayed for the Father to get the cup out of his way. It was not the cup of death, so to speak, in this context, but the cup of the fleshy pleasures. In another instance, "Touch me not . . ." Jesus said to Mary. John and Jesus, who were not Jews at all, had their voices, and their ways of life create a strong impact on Judaism—an impact that shook their religious and cultural foundations. They were both killed in the most horrifying ways, one decapitated and the other crucified, for celibacy was and still is deemed so dreadful and sinful in Judaic tradition, since having the demiurge Androgynous, Yod-Heva (Yahweh), as their God! As history shows, neither John the Baptist nor Jesus Christ had anything to do with sexual Initiation with Mary. They both lived an *ascetic* and *celibate* life, and so did Mary. Jesus Christ never fell in love with any particular woman, for his love was kind of a Universal Love, perceiving the whole existence as *Unitas*. All three were Nazarenes, or Nazoreans, a name held by an ascetic *Asayans* (Essenes) branch living in Galilee and on top Mt. Carmel. *Nazar* means "an individual or person, chosen to Keep the *Word*," thus electing from among them the one who may bear the title of *Son of God*. The Phoenician-Aramaic Asayas, *Ashayas*, meaning "Healers,"[10] or "therapeut" in Greek[11], who lived in Galilee and at Mt. Carmel, and different from the Essens of the Dead Sea, better known as the Qumran Community, were Pythagoreans in their way of life, and related undoubtedly and perfectly to the Great White Fraternity.

Correspondingly, it was the Galilean Essenes, not the Essens of the Qumran Community of Orthodox Judaism, that Robert Charoux mentioned as not Jewish. He wrote[12], "The Essenes are not of Jewish origin but Pythagorean origin." The same note has been eloquently expressed by H.P. Blavatsky. She asserted that the Essenes were Pythagoreans in all their doctrines and habits, and on Iamblichus' assertion as well, he (Pythagoras) spent a certain time at Carmel with them.[13] Of course, the Pythagoreans were Enochians or Hermetists in all their doctrines and habits since Pythagoras himself was Phoenician.[14]

---

10. El Koussa, Karim, *Jesus the Phoenician*, 22.

11. Schuré, Edouard, *Les Grands Initiés*, 438.

12. Charoux, Robert, *Forgotten Worlds*, 278.

13. Blavatsky, H.P., *Isis Unveiled*, vol. 2, 130, 145.

14. Please refer to *Pythagoras the Mathemagician* by Sunbury Press, 2010.

Accordingly, like the Pythagoreans, these Ashayas (*Galilean Essenes*)—though some have suggested they might have also been influenced by Buddhist missionaries at some point in history—shared their goods, prayed at sunrise, practiced silence, wore white linen, and kept safe the *Mysteries*. In addition, that ascetic Ashayan branch, the Nazoreans, were much similar to the Therapeuts who appeared in the desert of Egypt, living as hermits in a secluded group. Pythagoras, instructed from an early age into the great *Mysteries* of Canaan-Phoenicia and Egypt, became an *Initiate of Sophia*, the first-ever world true Philosopher (Lover of Wisdom). Having achieved *oneness* with the *One*, he established a school of *Initiation* in Crotona, Italy. After his mission ended, he got married when he was in his late fifties.

In different circumstances, Siddhartha, for example, who was once a married man, suddenly, one day, left everything behind him, including his wife and child, and chose to continue his life, alone, on a quest for spiritual enlightenment. His journey made him reach illumination. He became the Buddha, finding the four noble paths of the Truth (The Four Noble Truths) that would lead humanity out of pain and suffering.

At all events, it appeared as well that the Templars we have above mentioned refused those ascetic ways of life, though pretending to live by them—*a few though lived by them*—and seemed to have secretly performed sexual rites under the watchful eyes of the *Baphomet*. Nevertheless, these ideas of *Hieros Gamos*, Sacred Sexuality seemed to or might have been brought up to the west through these Templars at some time and continued after them with some other Secret Societies.

Similarly, Alchemists, certainly a deviated group of them, those who appeared to have been following a distorted version of the true original Alchemy of Hermes, had rather the Hermaphrodite, or the blending of Hermes and Aphrodite in one being—as the symbol for the Great Work of the perfected Alchemy, thus, *Sacred Sexuality*! An Alchemical prose of sexual imagery would reveal to the reader as such[15]—

> The Moon says to her spouse the Sun: "Oh Sun, thou dost nothing alone if I'm not present with my strength, as a cock is helpless without a hen."

---

15. Picknett, Lynn & Prince, Clive, *The Templar Revelation*, 200.

Some Rosicrucians moreover, besides their connection with Freemasons, though distinct in some ways, and who claimed to be *Hermeticists* (Hermetists), were not. It could have been thought otherwise if this minority had not used symbols, images, or even words representing some sort of sexual rites. However, the Rose blooming at the heart of the Cross, used by the majority of them as their essential Symbol, generally means Man's *unfolding Consciousness* (Rose) in his/her body (Cross) and better say, the *Dawn* (the Rose: Sun) *of Eternal Life* (Cross: Resurrection of Light and the Renewal of Life, offered to Humanity by the very person of the *Cosmic Christ*, the Redeemer). Undoubtedly by that, they have mystically considered Christ as being the *Philosopher's Stone* of Immortality, which every Man and Woman have to find *Rising* in the depth of their heart. Even so, that main symbol might have a double meaning to that minority of them, totally different from being the Symbol(s) of Christianity and their acceptance of the Church through the teachings of *western esoteric tradition* formed within the Christian tenets. On the other hand, it could present a misleading interpretation, being the symbol of their conjoining sexual mysticism; the Cross, being a phallic representation, and the Rose, the vulva! In truth, these Rosicrucians, like many others, were not at all *Hermeticists* but rather *Hermaphroditicists*. The seventieth-century Rosicrucian alchemist Thomas Vaughan explained their common opinion[16]—

> . . . Life itself is nothing but a union of male and female principles, and he that perfectly knows this secret knows . . . how he ought to use a wife . . .

In an awakening note and through the logic of the *Initiate*, it is not marriage that we mean to degrade here in this chapter, nor in any other text, we may come to tackle this matter, but rather, the worship of ourselves and the succumbing to the pleasures and joy that come with our bodily sexual acts, while believing though it could get us to feel a spiritual experience with the Father, the *One*. Neither do we believe that Adam and Eve, say, Men and Women should at any time feel ashamed when looking at their nude bodies in the abode of natural presence. That is the work of the Demiurge anyway; that is dualism in matter! Marriage is somehow sacred when it is looked upon, not only from corporal pleasures, but as a complete fusion of one's triune nature of Body, Mind, and Spirit, with the beloved partner's triune nature as well, thus to be able to feel, at

---

16. Ibid., 216.

some point during the relationship itself, not particularly through intercourse, the *existential Magic* that would make us achieve harmony between ourselves, and might only lead to a preliminary *perceptive illusionary glimpse* of the Unity with God, and hence, not at all a union with the Divine.

In truth, that is still one of the most difficult things to accomplish, for humans themselves could not even surpass their own drowning into the work of dualism. They are much too often engaged in an unconscious struggle between their bodily pleasures and spiritual aspirations. For that, equilibrium could be the way, the middle path indeed, leading them upwards, above the *Circle of Necessity*! At any events, marriage would lead to an act of creation, and forming life is considered by all religions, cultures, and societies as sublime and divine, for it was first conceived in the *deep thoughts* of the Universal Mind, the *One*, who, oddly thereafter, created the world through the emergence of the *Demiurge*, the female-male principle of creation, by the breaking of Divine Unity!

Thus, it is not a Human fault if the majority of man and woman are bound to create life, perfectly imitating the Hermaphrodite, which might have been, in the first place, an error committed in the mind of God! If such an imperfection could be formed out of what is supposed to be *wholly* perfect, then the situation humans are plunged into is understandable. Hence, what could be termed error, or inaccuracy propelled by the Mind of God at some point beyond our understanding through the conceptual work of creation, would therefore wrongly be termed a sin committed by man and woman in the physical work of life. Everything is compelled to make mistakes in life, whether major or minor, and there are no sins, only mistakes!

But . . . no matter how it is difficult for the imperfect human mind to believe and perceive the Mind of God as imperfect too, this would not stand an obstacle in front of the *Word* (Logos) that comes straight as a direct thought of God to manifest itself in every human being. The *Word,* after all, precedes the *Demiurge*, the creator of dualism, physical existence, and the laws that are related to them. The *Word* does not only precede the Demiurge, but it sprung out as a pure messenger sent instantly from the Divine Mind into the Human Mind without passing by any mediation. Moreover, the *Word* itself could not be perceived but perfect as the Divine Mind is *Holy* perfect by itself. Therefore, the imperfection of the Human Mind occurs in the phenomenal world not due to the imperfection of the Mind of God but due to the imperfection of the Demiurge and its natural work. In short, the union between man and woman is not but a glitch in the Divine Matrix!

That said, and to clarify it even more, the *First-Born*, the *Word*, should not be perceived and believed other than supernatural and Divine. There could be no error in the abode of the *One*, and the *seed of divinity* has already been planted in the Human Mind by the First Divine Light. It became thus true to perceive that it is the *Second-Born*, the *Demiurge*, that is imperfect. Hence, what sprouts out of it and follows from it, such as the existential abode of dualism, is also imperfect and bound to the formation of temptations, or better say in philosophical tongue, the *world of illusions*.[17]

For about this, St. Paul in his first epistle to the Corinthians spoke as thus[18]—

> For I would that all men were even as I myself. But every man hath his proper gift of God, one after this manner, and another that. I say therefore to the unmarried and widows, it is good for them if they abide even as I. But if they cannot contain, let them marry: for it better to marry than to burn.

He continued[19]—

> Art thou bound unto a wife? Seek not to be loosed. Art thou loosed from a wife? Seek not a wife. But and if thou marry, thou hast not sinned; and if a virgin marry, she hath not sinned. Nevertheless, such shall have trouble in the flesh: but I spare you. But I would have you without carefulness. He that is unmarried careth for the things that belong to the Lord, how he may please the Lord. But he that is married careth for the things that are of the world, how he may please his wife. There is a difference also between a wife and a virgin . . . , but she that is married careth for the things of the world, how she may please her husband.

And carried on as follows[20]—

---

17. Non-dualist Christian Gnostics believe, and we share their beliefs, that God the Father, whom we regard as the Most High El, have sent his only son, the *Son of Prophecy*, Jesus Christ, as light of the world, in order to save Humanity from the evil work done by the Demiurge Yahweh, and bring judgment upon him, since he had plunged the world into confusion and iniquity, for he is Ialdabaôth, son of chaos and darkness.

18. Corinthians 7:7-9.

19. Corinthians 7:27-28; 7:32-34.

20. Corinthians 7:35.

And this I speak for your own profit; not that I may cast a snare upon you, but for that which is comely, and that ye may attend upon the Lord without distraction.

In the same line of reasoning, and upon answering certain of the Sadducees, which deny that there is any form of resurrection, Jesus said unto them[21]—

The children of this world marry, and are given in marriage. But, they which shall be accounted worthy to obtain that world and the resurrection from the dead, neither marry, nor are given in marriage. Neither can they die any more: for they are, equal unto the angels; and are the children of God, being the children of resurrection.

However, he also said the following, "The Kingdom of Heaven is inside you." So, once the Kingdom of God, the *Word*, is heard and realized by man— whether married or not—humanity will evolve more into an upper stage of existence when it will thus share the work of God on/from a higher sphere and accomplish Divine Love. Humans then would become Children of God. And so, why then the need for the *Children of Prophesies* when Humanity itself becomes Divine!

At all circumstances, moreover, in the Beatitude of Mathew, one may read the following important message for Humanity[22]—

Blessed are the poor in spirit, for theirs is the kingdom of Heaven . . . Blessed are the pure in heart, for they shall see God . . . Blessed are the peacemakers, for they shall be called children of God.

Conclusively, there are two paths: the *Inner Circle* and the other of the *Outer Circle*. Two ways are drawn for humanity to return to the Source, eventually; the *Way of the Initiate* and the *Way of the Lay*, the Sacred and Profane. The first is straight upward and governed by the spiritual Law of Divine Grace, while the second is elliptical and governed by the physical karmic Law of Reincarnation. It has always been your choice to decide on the way to tread, for you were born free from the beginning of time . . .

21. Luke 20:34-36.
22. Mathew 5:3-11.

And time will pass you by so quickly, where you need to take a break to restore your mind to serenity. That was a great revelation you probably had never expected rushing directly into your way at that time of the day. Next, you would find yourself standing in front of the Mystery Chamber's door, ready to yet venture into the *Secret Path of the Initiate*.

12.

On the Secrets of Initiation

Between Tubal-Cain (Cainan), the ancient Builder and Artificer and Hiram, the Master Architect in the Masonic Tradition and Jesus Christ, the Christian Savior, there is a fine hidden line of Morality, Allegory, and Symbol, which if intersected, may reveal that the lost word of Masonry is already *found*!

We will not get engaged here in this chapter neither into the traditional history of Masonry nor in its alternative or potential beginnings. That will be left for another future book, if we may say, along with examining certain rituals used in Freemasonic Tradition. What concerns us now the most is the literature that speaks of a *lost* word; known as the *word* of the Master Mason.

Of course, other than plenty handshakes or grips adopted in Craft Masonry—the Blue Lodge three degrees of *Entered Apprentice*, *Fellow Craft*, and *Master Mason*—and for the many Appendant degrees/grades presented in either most famous Scottish (30 more degrees) or York Rites (10 more degrees plus around 9, given as Honorary) of Freemasonry, there are many passwords and words applied in as well, but the most important ones are the following three; *Tu-Bal-Cain*, *Mah-Hah-Bone*, and *Jah-Buh-Lun* or *Jao-Bul-On*.

The password *Tu-Bal-Cain* is used during the pass-grip of a Master Mason in the 3rd Degree and pronounced by the conductor as Tubal Cain. The password *Mah-Hah-Bone* is used as a substitute password given by the Worshipful Master to the candidate during the "Raising" ritual of the aspirant into a Master Mason. The 3rd important word *Jao-Bul-On*, also known as *Jahbulon*, is given in the additional seventh degree of the York Rite known as the Royal Arch.

Should we start by investigating the meaning of the first word Tu-Bal-Cain, or Tubal-Cain in its pronounced method by the conductor during the Masonic ritual, we may understand that the word is a composed word of two words: Tubal and Cain. What are these two words? What do they mean? Are they just words or names given to people back in ancient times?

We already know from the Old Testament narration that Cain is not a word but a name given to one of the two sons of Adam and Eve; Cain is the one who is said to have killed Abel. The story in Genesis[1] goes that Cain, who was the older brother—a tiller of the ground—slain Abel—a keeper of sheep—and split his blood upon the earth because God is said to have preferred Abel sacrifices of *sheep and lambs* on the ones offered by Cain and which were *fruit and corn*. On doing that and burying the body of his brother in secret to escape from murder, God knew, of course, and seemed to have cursed Cain, saying in Genesis[2]—

> And he said, What hast thou done? the voice of thy brother's blood crieth unto me from the ground. And now art thou cursed from the earth, which hath opened her mouth to receive thy brother's blood from thy hand; When thou tillest the ground, it shall not henceforth yield unto thee her strength; a fugitive and a vagabond shalt thou be in the earth.

On hearing the wrath of God, Cain strongly complained that his punishment was greater than he can bear, and being a fugitive and a vagabond on the earth would easily jeopardize his life in the sort that anyone who finds him shall slay him. And here, in Genesis also, comes the surprise and the strange twist in the story[3]—

> And the LORD said unto him, Therefore whosoever slayeth Cain, vengeance shall be taken on him sevenfold. And the LORD set a mark upon Cain, lest any finding him should kill him.

A strange and mysterious tweak of the story, but how is that so anyway? Is God that materialistic and bloodthirsty to choose a sacrifice of *sheep and lambs* (of blood) on *fruit and corn* (of no blood)?

---

1. Genesis 4:1-14.
2. Genesis 4:10-12.
3. Genesis 4:15.

Again, how is that so? Was Cain a murderer that could well have received an award or *a mark* of safety at the end of his crime?

At any rate, things have changed then for Cain, who dwelt in the land of Nod, on the east of Eden, and was therefore mentioned as the builder of a city! Also in Genesis, we come into reading the following[4]—

> And Cain knew his wife; and she conceived, and bare Enoch: and he builded a city, and called the name of the city, after the name of his son, Enoch *(Henochia, Phenokia)*. (Italics are mine)

So that's briefly the story of Cain, but what about Tubal, then? Well, Tubal is not mentioned alone in the Old Testament, but along with Cain, in the same form it appeared in Masonry; Tubal-Cain. In Genesis, we continue to read[5]—

> And Zillah, she also bare Tubalcain, an instructor of every artificer in brass and iron: and the sister of Tubalcain was Naamah.

Moreover, and according to the Romano-Jewish Historian of the 1st century AD, Flavius Josephus, we read in one of his books, written around the year 93 AD, not only was Cain a man to be punished for murdering his brother, but Tubal was also the name of a person, his son! He wrote[6]—

> He *(Cain)* first of all set boundaries about lands; he built a city, and fortified it with walls, and he compelled his family to come together to it; and called that city Enoch *(Henochia, Phenokia)*, after the name of his eldest son Enoch. . . . Of those children by Ada, one was Jabal; he erected tents, and loved the life of a shepherd. But Jubal, who was born of the same mother with him, exercised himself in music; and invented the psaltery and the harp. But Tubal, one of his children by the other wife, exceeded all men in strength, and was very expert and famous in martial performances. He procured what tended to the pleasures of the body by that method; and, first of all, invented the art of making brass. (Italics are mine)

---

4. Genesis 4:17.
5. Genesis 4:22.
6. Josephus, Flavius, *The Antiquities of the Jews*, Book 1, chapter 2, paragraph 2.

And on Cain, Josephus continued[7]—

> Nay, even while Adam was alive, it came to pass that the posterity
> of Cain became exceedingly wicked, every one successively dying one
> after the other, more wicked than the former. They were intolerable in
> war, and vehement in robberies; and if anyone were slow to murder
> people, yet was he bold in his profligate behavior, in acting unjustly,
> and doing injury for gain.

Concordantly, both the Old Testament *Book of Genesis* and Josephus' *Antiquities* mention almost the same thing about Cain, Tubal, or as jointly pronounced, Tubal-Cain. However, what is greatly important for us in decoding the first Masonic password is, in fact, the very understanding of the following three elements:

1. God is said to have set a mark upon Cain—granting him complete
    protection against all enemies, which simply means he was no criminal, but actually, the story would rather esoterically mean something
    else; a change of the sacrificial ritual to the Divine!
2. Cain was a Mason and Tubal, a Master; thus Tubal-Cain means
    Master Mason—for Cain was the builder of a city and Tubal, an
    Inventor of the art of making brass and Instructor of every artificer
    in brass and iron.
3. The city built is called Enoch—better call it Henochia, or Phenokia.

Is it *Phoenicia* and Cain could therefore be Canaan, also written as Kenan? Or and does it refer to the city of Enoch, the seer, and Prophet of Mt. Hermon in Phoenicia, as per the *Book of Enoch*, being himself of the lineage of Seth, who was cited as the third son born to Adam and Eve, and replacing Abel, as per the old Testament?

Well, does this all mean anything in plain history? It means a lot so far, and things will get very interesting and mind-blowing in just a bit. However, nothing is simply plain history, especially in the mind of ancient scribes, for there are many things that were written in allegory.

At any rate, having thought about that, we could well refer to a wonderful work penned by the ninetieth-century French author, poet, and essayist,

---

7. Ibid., Book 1, chapter 2, paragraph 2.

Gérard de Nerval, who places *Enochia*, the first city ever built, on the plateau of Lebanon. He wrote in French[8]—

> Et d'ailleurs qui oserait faire du scepticisme au pied du Liban ? Ce rivage n'est-il pas le berceau même de toutes les croyances du monde ? Interrogez le premier montagnard qui passe : il vous dira que c'est sur ce point de la terre qu'eurent lieu les scènes primitives de la Bible ; il vous conduira à l'endroit où fumèrent les premiers sacrifices ; il vous montrera le rocher taché du sang d'Abel ; plus loin existait la ville d'Enochia, bâtie par les géants, et dont on distingue encore les traces ; ailleurs c'est le tombeau de Chanaan *(Kanaan)*, fils de Cham *(Ham)*. (Italics are mine)

If indeed Phoenicia—where the tomb of *Canaan* (Cain, Kenan, Kain-an) rested—was the cradle of all religions that have spread across the world, and that the primitive scenes of the Bible have occurred in this Promised Land, so to speak, and that the first sacrifices happened there, and the first city of *Enochia* (Enoch, Phenok) was built by the giants known as the *Anakim*[9], than this very first story of the Old Testament would be well understood. Besides the fact that the Hebrews vulgarized it[10], they, the *Aebirou-al-Nahara* from Babylon and Ur to the Land of Cainan at the time of the Persian king Cyrus II, all in the hope of promoting themselves as the "Chosen People," while at the same time distorting by that the image of the Canaanites for being a "Cursed People." Yet this is no longer agreed or accepted by the educated masses!

In truth, this whole story is not but a symbolic telling that hides a great allegory behind it and is related to the act of sacrifice to God, which has changed with Cain *killing* Abel, and that which means that the sacrificial to God of *sheep and lambs* (of blood) has been replaced by *fruit and corn* (of no blood). The anger of God against Cain because of the *killing* of Abel has soon changed, totally transformed into an acceptance of Cain's sacrifice of *fruit* (grapes/vine) and *corn* (wheat/bread) by setting a mark of safety upon him, perhaps on his forehead—*Mark of Initiation*—that only *Initiates* would understand, a mark that characterized the lineage for generations to come. So the old sacrifice of flesh and blood that was practiced before on Earth and accepted by God has

---

8. De Nerval, Gérard, *Voyage en Orient*, 409–410.

9. The *Anakim* are the Sons of Enoch, not to be regarded as Giants in literal understanding but rather, as great men and women.

10. The Old Testament narration and Josephus' account of *The Antiquities of the Jews*.

changed into a pure sacrifice—a sacred ritual of *Bread and Wine*—with Cain, in the promised Land of Canaan-Phoenicia.

And on Cain, the founder of the Theosophical Society, H.P. Blavatsky, wrote in her masterpiece[11]—

> Cain leads the ascending line, or Macrocosm, for he is the Son of the "Lord," not of Adam. The "Lord" is Adam-Kadmon, Cain, the son of sinful thought, not the progeny of flesh and blood . . . Cain means a smith, an artificer . . . *Kain-an*, is identical with Cain.

Again, I wonder why Blavatsky mentioned Cain as "son of sinful thought" when she considers him at the same time, Son of Lord and not the progeny of flesh and blood! I never understood her contradiction, unless if she meant, "son of sinless thought."

If Cain were the son of sinless thought and Abel, the progeny of flesh and blood, then it would rather be undoubtedly perceived that the sacrificial ritual has indeed changed. Therefore, since it has changed into a purer practice, and theology evolved into a more spiritual relationship with God, it would be thus understood why Kain is looked upon as the son of the "Lord,"[12] Adam-Kadmon and, not of Adam—the primitive man molded of the mud! However, we previously learned that Enoch initiated the ritual of *bread & wine* when on Mt. Hermon—a ritual later practiced by Milki-Sedek and Yāwshua (Jesus). The *Cubical Altar* erected inside the *Sanctum Sanctorum* of Mt. Armon had two pillars on its sides; the bright golden stone shone on the Left Pillar with the ear of wheat (corn)—the *Bread,* and the glowing purple stone upon the Right Pillar with the vine (fruit)—the *Wine.*

Was it Enoch or Kain who first introduced the ritual? It doesn't matter that much, for it depends, however, on which genealogy one is looking at; the Sethite Line of Generation or the Kenites', and are described as follows:

- The Sethite Line: Adam – Seth – Enos – Cainan – Mahalaleel – Jared – Enoch – Methuselah – Lamech – Noah.
- The Kenite line: Adam – Cain – Enoch – Irad – Mehujael – Methusael – Lamech[13] – Jubal – Jabal – Tubalcain.

---

11. Blavatsky, H.P., *Isis Unveiled*, vol. 2, 464, 466.

12. Genesis 4:1, "And Adam knew Eve his wife; and she conceived, and bare Cain, and said, I have gotten a man from the LORD."

13. Genesis 4:18, "Now to Enoch was born Irad, and Irad became the father of Mehujael, and Mehujael became the father of Methushael, and Methushael became the father of Lamech."

Now, Seth is described as the third son born to Adam and Eve as a replacement for Abel[14], who favored the sacrifice of flesh and blood. Seth walked the path of Cain in the new ritual of *Bread and Wine* (Fruit & Corn) and became therefore known as one of the greatest mystery teachers, an *Initiate* of Men. He is thus Teth, Thor, Thot-Taautus, Enoch, Hermes, Mercury, etc. There is no difference between Cain-an, Seth, or Enoch, for that matter, for it is one sacerdotal line, so to speak, of selected people *marked by God*[15] to teach men and women the secrets of life.

We found support for that in the Apocryphal *Book of Jubilees*, where Cainan was mentioned as a boy instructed by his father—Enoch—to read; he became a learned man, finding mysterious inscriptions concerning the secret science and wisdom of astrology carved on the rocks!

At any rate, and since we consider the *Book of Enoch* as very important in the overall unlocking of the great mysteries and secrets, we have, for that matter, adopted the Sethite Line, which was conveyed to us in the following manner[16]—

> The vision which he saw, the second vision of wisdom, which Enoch saw, the son of Jared, the son of Mahaleel, the son of Canan, the son of Enos, the son of Seth, the son of Adam.

Enoch then, who walked with God—as his chosen son—and the Angels whom he saw in visions in Heaven and on Earth, had learned of the coming deluge or flood when by which God intended to end Humanity because they have sinned with the *Fallen Angels*, to start all over again. Enoch, wishing to preserve for mankind the knowledge and the secrets he have learned from the *Good Angels*, he, with the assistance of his son, Methusaël, constructs in the Land of Canaan[17], "in the bowels of the Mountain"[18] *nine vaults* situated perpendicularly beneath each other on the model he saw in the prophetic vision. Each was roofed with an Arch, and the apex of each formed *a keystone*, having inscribed on it the mirific characters. Each vault represented one of the

---

14. Genesis 4:25.

15. Some say that the *Mark* was actually the *Tau*, the Phoenician Cross †.

16. 1 Enoch 37:1.

17. As revealed before, other than Mt. Hermon, construction of *Initiatic* Temples spread all over the Land of Canaan, and more importantly, in Gebel, Sūr, Ba'albek, Saydoun, Mt. Carmel, and Rŭšalim.

18. It is Mt. Hermon as we have thoroughly explained, however, some believe that the divine secrets Enoch wanted to keep for mankind were on Mt. Moriah, or the Great Pyramid of Egypt as others have suggested according to yet another Enochian Phoenician tradition.

nine names or attributes by which God was known to him, Enoch, the *First Initiate into the Mystery of the Word*. Then he, Enoch, *Father of Religions, Spiritual Laws and Founder of the First Religion*, constructed two deltas[19] of the purest gold[20], tracing two of the mysterious characters on each[21], he placed one of them in the deepest Arch. The other, also inscribed with strange words Enoch had gained from the Angels themselves, entrusted his son Methusael to keep, communicating to him at the same time, other important Secrets now lost to the world and Freemasonry!

Now, after we have refreshed our memory on Enoch and his secret *nine vaults* in the above paragraph, let us continue our search for the *Lost Word* by investigating the meaning of the second important password we earlier mentioned: Mah-Hah-Bone. This will not take long, fortunately, since the word *Mah-Hah-Bone* means nothing! In truth, Masonry openly reveals that the correct word or the *word of the Master* was lost with the "death of Hiram Abiff," and that king Solomon had substituted the word of the Master Architect, now *lost*, with Mah-Hah-Bone!

In a masonic work, penned by the 19th-century American author Malcolm C. Duncan, we read[22]—

> In the meantime, the canvas is slipped out of the Lodge, and as the Master commences to give or whisper the word in the candidate's ear, some one of the brethren slips off the hoodwink, and this is the first time he has seen light, probably, in an hour. The following is the representation of the Master giving candidate the grand Masonic word, or at least this is a substitute, for, according to Masonic tradition, the right one was lost at the death of Hiram Abiff.

In the below footnote linked to that paragraph, Duncan explained, commenting as follows, "Respecting the lost word and its substitute, some say that King Solomon advised the change, while others affirm that the three Fellow Craft adopted the substituted word without consulting him." Then, quoting from *The Freemason's Treasury*, he added that the interpreted word "is not to be

---

19. It could be a triangle instead, like the Pythagorean Tetraktys, the *Sacred Decade*.
20. It is a white porphyry stone in another version of the story.
21. It is undoubtedly the Canaanite-Phoenician-Aramaic *ineffable name* of God Most High, "E.L," "E.L.O.H," "E.L.U.S," or the *Lost Word* of a Master Mason!
22. Duncan, Malcolm C., *Duncan's Ritual of Freemasonry*, 120.

found in any language that ever was used. It is, in fact, not a word, but merely a jumble of letters, forming a sound without meaning."

So, what does that mean after all? Well, a lot actually, and from a masonic point of view, it simply means that Masons have *lost the word* of the Phoenician Master Hiram Abiff ever since he was killed and that Solomon transmitted to them a temporary word until they found the correct one again, yet this word that the so-called wise Solomon has come up with has no meaning in any known language, a *nonsense word*. It also means that Solomon knew nothing of the great secrets and mysteries Hiram Abiff knew, and in conjunction with us, that the temple the latter built in Ur-Šalim was not the alleged temple of the biblical Solomon, as we have explained before, and in different works as well. Moreover, if it were his temple, he, the *wise*, who we don't believe ever existed anyway, would then have known the *lost mysterious word*! Wouldn't he? We will perhaps come to that in a future work one day.

However, many *Keepers* and *Initiates* of ancient and modern Mystery Schools and *Initiatic* Orders all around the world watchfully shielded the secrets from the ignorant commoners, which is certainly no exception to Freemasonry! Since Freemasonry has often been defined by its historians as "a science of morality, veiled in allegory, and illustrated by symbols," then it might just be the case for its mysteries. In 1717 AD, the Grand Lodge of England was established in London on John the Baptist's Day, June 24th. Since St. John the Evangelist is said to have been the patron saint of English Freemasonry, it would thus be important for them to conduct a conscious, intelligent Lodge, where the New Testament lays open on the first chapter of the Gospel of St. John. The candidate, in his continual search for the *Lost Word*, could finally open his blind eyes and read[23]—

> In the beginning was the Word, and the Word was with God, and the Word was God. All things were made by Him; and without Him was not anything made that was made. In Him was life; and the life was the light of men. And the light shineth in darkness; and the darkness comprehended it not.

And that would remind Masons of the Ritual of the 18th degree of the Rose-Croix in Scottish Rite Masonry, Southern Jurisdiction as described in H.P. Blavatsky's work as such[24]—

---

23. John 1:1-4.
24. Blavatsky, H.P., *Isis Unveiled*, vol. 2, 348.

Most Wise. — What hour is it?

Respectful K.S. Warden. — It is the first hour of the day, the time when the veil of the temple was rent asunder, when darkness and consternation were spread over the earth — when the light was darkened — when the implements of Masonry were broken — when the flaming star disappeared — when the cubic stone was broken — when the 'word' was lost.[25]

Within all that game of darkness and light that seemed ever-existent all through *Initiation*, the essential *Third Degree* of the Craft, in what is called Blue Lodge Masonry, is that of a Master Mason and only consecrated to Hiram Abiff, the Master Architect. In the Phoenician *Initiatic* language, as we have seen before, the name Hiram that sounds similar to Hermes could well mean the *Enlightened One or Divine Messenger and Teacher*, identical in meaning to the name of Enoch as *Teacher-Initiator*, or it could well be derived from the word *Khur-Um*, which means, "lifted up to life."

The *legend* of the Sūrian (Tyrian) Architect, Hiram Abiff—and his assassination by three evil brothers—was first incorporated into *Freemasonic Rituals* by the Grand Lodge of England. The ritual bestowed the names: Jubela, Jubelo, and Jubelum on the killers of Hiram Abiff, known collectively as the *Juwes!* One may wonder why, however? In that concern, and a famous work written by two 20th century British authors, Christopher Knight and Robert Lomas, we thus read[26]—

The ceremony continued in a manner similar to the two former degrees and I emerged a full Master Mason. Some months later, when there was no candidate to progress in the Lodge meeting, a Past Master gave an explanation of the Third Degree. The three villains who murdered Hiram Abiff were identified as Jubela, Jubelo and Jubelum, known jointly as the Juwes; pronounced Joo-ees.

This strange accusation of the three *Juwes* killing Master Hiram Abiff has also been mentioned by the 20th-century American author, John Robinson, in one of his reputed masonic works. He wrote[27]—

---

25. It is very inspiring to note herein that Alchemy in the Authentic Kabbalistic Enochian Tradition would surely consider the idea that the *Philosopher's Stone*, as described by the Rosicrucians, is Christ himself—the Christ Spirit, so to speak.

26. Knight, Christopher and Lomas, Robert, *The Hiram Key*, 16.

27. Robinson, John, *Born in Blood—the lost secrets of freemasonry*, 220.

Finally, it is reported to King Solomon that Hiram Abiff is not to be found, so a roll call is ordered, which reveals the absence of Jubela, Jubelo, and Jubelum, collectively known to Masons as the Juwe *s*. (Italic is mine)

Sometimes, Hiram Abiff is shown as an allegorical Jesus Christ, killed, *so to speak*, by Judas, Caiaphas, and Pilate. However, when Pilate, as mentioned in Matthew[28], saw that nothing was being gained but that a disturbance had started instead, he took water and washed his hands before the multitude, saying, "I am innocent of the blood of this righteous person. You see to it. All the people answered, 'May his blood be on us, and on our children!'" Henceforth, Annas—the father-in-law of Caiaphas—should be the third man, not Pilate; for Judas, Caiaphas, and Annas were, in fact, the three Jewish men (*Juwes*) that masterminded his arrest, as mentioned in the New Testament. That was what led to his Crucifixion by the Romans and his Resurrection three days later.

But Freemasonry keeps on saying that Hiram died and was not resurrected, but rather *lifted up to life* and that what happened in the *Third-Degree Ritual* of a Master Mason is thence *Raising*, not, however, a simulation of Resurrecting the candidate into a Master Mason. In truth, whether it is *Lifted Up to Life, Elevated to Life, Resurrecting,* or *Raising,* three degrees later, after successfully going through the *Entered Apprentice* and *Fellow Craft* journeys, the meaning remains the same in esoteric teachings.

The similarity though between both terms, "Resurrection" and "Raising," has been tackled by the 19th-20th century English author W.L. Wilmshurst, in a great work he penned, and where he intelligently wrote[29]—

> If in Masonry the mystical death is dramatized more realistically than the resurrection that follows upon it, that resurrection is nevertheless shown in the "raising" of the candidate to the rank of Master Mason . . .

The secret knowledge of Freemasonry reveals and with precise explanation that in the *Third Degree*, the Fellow Mason would undertake a *Ritual of Resurrection* into Master Mason, thus, perfectly mirroring the Resurrection of Jesus Christ on the *Third Day*, as per the Christian Tradition. "For if we have

---

28. Matthew 27:24-25.
29. Wilmshurst, W.L., *The Meaning of Masonry,* 143.

been planted together in the likeness of his death, we shall be also in the likeness of his resurrection," St. Paul had eloquently stated in his Epistle to the Romans[30]. Hence, if the legendary temple of Solomon was not completed in Freemasonry, it is simply because *Christ* himself is the Temple of God in its utmost Completion!

And didn't he say, in John[31], that if they destroy this Temple, *Him*, he will *Raise* it up—*his body*—in three days? Well, yes, he did!

As for now, let's investigate the meaning of the third password, or better simply call it a word! The strange word *Jah-Buh-Lun* or *Jao-Bul-On* (Jahbulon) is undoubtedly a combination of three syllables that have confused historians and Masons alike of what they stand for. In the additional system of continually higher degrees/grades, of which the best known was the seventh degree of the York Rite; the Royal Arch, fully called the Supreme Order of the Holy Royal Arch, a degree that follows the direction of the Grand Lodge of the Royal Arc, also known as the Holy Royal Arch of Jerusalem, Freemasons would find an incorporation of Jewish myths and history by going as far back as King Cyrus II of Persia, the Babylonian Zoro-Babel—prince of the people, and others! In the Royal Arch Degree, the candidate would *theoretically* become higher than a Master Mason (*Third Degree*), whereby is said, he would encounter the Essence of the Philosophical Masonry and, as shown in the Hebraic Torah, it would allow him to discover the real name of God—the ineffable YHWH, camouflaged in the mysterious name of Jah-Bul-On!

Perhaps all Masonic sources we have investigated suggest that the name mentioned herein is a combination of three different names of God, "Most High," known to three or four different people that characterized the history of mankind sometime in the past. It is believed that the first syllable *Jah* or *Jao* is the name of the Chaldean *Iao* and the Jewish *Yaho* (Yahweh, Jehovah). The second syllable *Buh* or *Bul,* may well be the name for the Canaanite-Phoenician *Ba'al* or the Chaldean *Bel,* whereas the third syllable *On, An,* or *Aun* could therefore refer to the Egyptian *Osiris* or *On*[32], the Greek *On,* or the Akkadian/Sumerian *An.*

However, we insist on the word *camouflaged* because the rite practiced at the Royal Arch Degree is about Jewish myths and history, from King Cyrus II to the construction of the temple in Jerusalem by *Zoro-Babel*—the "seed of

---

30. Romans 6:5.
31. John 2:19.
32. A city of Heliopolis.

Babel." Thus, the mysterious, full name Jah-Bul-On, would mean nothing in such rite consecrated to Judaism. The only name that means anything here and connected to the Aebirou-al-Nahara would be the Chaldean mystery god *Iao* from which was inspired the Jewish *Yaho*, better known as the Androgynous Demiurge, Ievo-hevah.

Thus, it is not strange to hear from Freemasons that it is their fundamental belief to endorse the concept of a single and similar God—to a certain extent—under different names. However, the three syllables *Jah-Bul-On* represents different names for different gods! While the Chaldean-Jewish God *Iao* or *Yaho* is not but a representation of the dualist upright *male* and egg-shaped *female* principles of Nature—the Kabbalistic *Yod-Heva*—the Chaldean *Bel* means Lord, associated with a solar cult of the Babylonian *Marduk*, or the Phoenician *Ba'al*, also meaning Lord, a solar god, where at times he is associated with a storm (lightning, rain, wind), and identified with *El* (Elyon), being his son, whereas the Greek *On* symbolizes the Sun, the Egyptian *Osiris* represents the God of the Afterlife—of Resurrection, and the Akkadian/Sumerian *An*, meaning Sky Father.

At any rate, if this confusing name Jah-Bul-On of the Freemasonic Royal Arch rite was truly found by Knights Templar carved on an ancient stone, while excavating deep beneath the center of the Jerusalem temple, as some would have suggested, it could well be a sacred ritual stone that belongs to the first builders of the first Temple built by the Amorites[33] on Mt. Moriah in the Canaanite/Phoenician city of Ur-Šalim, the city of Šalim (Jerusalem) long before the Hebrews/Jews entered into history!

If that was the case indeed, as we would like herein to suggest, then the riddle is unlocked! On that account, the spelling and interpretation of the mysterious name would be fully different from what it was traditionally believed, and the real name would thus be understood as *Yāw-Ba'al-Ōn* (Jawbalon). "How's that?" One may wonder and ask, "what does it mean actually?" Well, they could have represented the two Pillars surrounding the Great Altar! The Pillar *Yāw*[34] and the Pillar *Ba'al*[35] standing vibrantly on both sides[36] of the Sacred Altar

---

33. One of the most famous Canaanite-Phoenician tribes.

34. Pillar *Yāw* is the Pillar of *Water*, for Yāw is the Phoenician god of water, very much like Yamm.

35. Pillar *Ba'al* is the Pillar of *Fire*, for Ba'al is god of thunder and lightning.

36. Refreshing the memory on the story of the two Pillars, one for *Fire* and one for *Wind* (or Rains) that has been conveyed to us firstly by the Phoenician Historian and Priest Sanchoniaton of Birot, Beirut (10th century BC) in a text translated by Philo of Byblos and related to us by Eusebius in his Praeparatio Evangelica, (Book 1, chapter 10), and secondly by Josephus (c. 37–100 AD) in the first book of his *Antiquities of the Jews*.

consecrated to the Most High God Ōn[37] in the *Initiatic* Temple dedicated to Šalim[38]—a Temple that could have been built by a Canaanite-Phoenician King/ Priest reigning over Ur-Šalim! That said, he could well have been Milki-Sedek (Melchizedek), the High Priest of the Most High God El, and later, one of his faithful descendants in the lineage of the *Sydyk* (or Sedek) Priests, like Adoni-Sedek (Adonizedek)!

Unfortunately, despite all the wariness of the most *Authentic, Ancient and Primitive* Phoenician/Egyptian Rite of the Great White Fraternity, the shape of the true *Word* has been *alas* stolen, dreadfully corrupted by the Chaldean-Judaic system and the other Orders and Brotherhoods that followed it, but it was *not lost.* Thus, it became the mission of the Phenokians to recuperate the Enochian Tradition of the past from Enoch to Yāwshu(a), passing by Milki-Sedek, Hiram Abiff, and Pythagoras, and ultimately reveal the Secrets of the Holy Grail once and for all while keeping it protected forever.

In fact, what has been written in John's *Book of Revelation* explains it all, for we read[39]—

> He that hath an ear, let him hear what the Spirit saith unto the churches *(from mouth to ear)*; To him that overcometh will I give to eat of the hidden manna, and will give him a white stone, and in the stone a new name written *(Word)*, which no man knoweth saving he that receiveth it. (Italics are mine)

And thus, the long *Lost Word* is now *found*!

---

37. *Ōn* derives from Elyōn, Adon; a name given to "El" at a certain time and in special consecrated places.

38. He is one of the Elohim or sons of El in the Phoenician Pantheon, being the god of dusk.

39. Revelation 2:17.

13.

On the Ancient and Primitive Phoenician Rite

An Introductory

This last section of the book is planned to give and provide some additional but only *introductory* information based on a three divisible plan; First, how the *Temple of Initiation* was initially raised, developed through time, and a glance at how it works along the journey of Initiation. Second, a peek at how the 5 degrees *Initiatic* system based on the Great Initiates—the Five Masters—Enoch (Phenok); Melchizedek (Melki-Sedek); Hiram (Abiff); Pythagoras (Beth-agor); and Jesus Christ (Yāwshua Meshiha) is incorporated and thus functional. However, the third—how the *Ancient and Primitive Phoenician Rite* is performed inside that very *Temple of Initiation*—will not be revealed in this present work!

Should we properly and measurably do that after well envisioning it in our mind and spirit, we would thus be able to successfully revive the Phenokian Tradition or the Phoenician Council of the Great White Fraternity by giving it the *Temple and its Pillars*, the *Initiation Rite* and the *Masters*, on all which it can firmly stand and endure despite all obstacles, and forever and ever.

With that said, let us then have a brief history of the *Temple of Initiation*, as per the historical and esoteric Tradition that has been communicated to us all along.

Now, first things first, the primary ritualistic object installed in the first replica of the first *Initiatic Temple*[1] was an *Ashlar Stone Altar* flanked by two Pillars; the first, Pillar of *Water*, probably made of metal[2] so that it might not sink in water, and which we call the Pillar Yāw, for Yāw is the Phoenician god of water, very much like Yam. The second was Pillar of *Fire*, probably made of marble so that it might never catch fire and burn, and which we call the Pillar *Ba'al*, for Ba'al is the god of thunder and lightning. These two Pillars stood vibrantly on both sides. Inside them were kept preserved the Enochian Knowledge and Secrets[3] that would be used by Phoenician *Initiates* after the flood or deluge was over and transmit them thereafter to the coming generations.

Next, the deepest level, say, the most secretive one was inside Mt. Hermon and divided into *nine vaults* above each other, where in the ninth, say, the *Holy of Holies*, we would imagine the existence of the *Great Cubical Altar* sided by two Pillars; the Left Pillar had a motif showing an ear of *Wheat* (the Bread) with a bright Golden Stone shining over its top, whereas, the Right Pillar with a glowing Purple Stone on its top had a pattern that reveals the *Vine* (the Wine). Behind the Altar, in that deepest Arch, Enoch had placed one of the two deltas[4] he made of the purest gold[5], tracing two of the mysterious characters on it, which we believe was the *ineffable name* of the Most High God "E.L," "E.L.O.H," "E.L.U.S," thus, the *Lost Word* of a Master Mason!

In time, the *Temple of Initiation* started to develop and became known as the Seven Pillared Temple. It is a construction planned and built from the *Interior to the Exterior*, the Inner to the Outer, Core to Surface, from the Heart to the Shell. The marvelous structure of the famous Phoenician Temple of Baal-Melkart in Sūr is an edifice built in such a manner. On the other hand, common buildings or other religious ones known to be *non-Initiatic* temples were often planned and

---

1. It was first built by Enoch on top of Mt. Hermon. Another one, perhaps without an altar, a *non-Initiatic Temple* perhaps, was built by Ousous in the island of Sūr to which he fled after the inland Sūr was destroyed by furious rains and winds. There, he consecrated two Pillars: one for *Fire*, the other for *Wind* (or *Rains*).

2. It is laterus, brass, or brick.

3. As seen before, while the first contained history of creation, all pre-deluge wisdom and knowledge of the arts and sciences, the second, mathematical wisdom and/or coded Enochian Inscriptions that indicates the existence of a great knowledge concealed in the arches underground, where the priceless subterranean treasure vault holding one of the two golden deltas, constructed by Enoch, was kept safe. The other delta, inscribed also with strange words Enoch had received from the Angels, was entrusted to his son Methusaēl to keep, while communicating to him at the same time, other important Secrets now lost to the world, like the two of the mysterious characters!

4. Or a triangle, like the Pythagorean Tetraktys, the *Sacred Decade*.

5. Or a white porphyry stone as related in one version of the story.

usually laid out from the *Exterior to the Interior*, and we mean from the facades of the outside walls to the core outlines of the inner walls.

The masonic system that shaped the *Temple of Initiation* was carried on by the "Sacred Builders," mainly from the two ancient cities of Gebel and Sūr. They became officially entrusted by the Great White Fraternity to build Temples to the deities the Phoenicians worshiped. Such Temples were mainly dedicated to the Most High God El, the Elohim (Sons of El: Baal, Adon, Yām, and Šalim), and the Goddesses (Anat, Ashirai, Astarte). Sacred Builders erected Temples to host the Divine, fundamentally in concordance with the mysterious "triune" nature of man[6]. This was all done in total secrecy, using sacred measurements.

One of the most reputed Architects of these "Sacred Builders" has been none other than Hiram Abiff, who commanded the Great Work by the power of the *Tau*! Regrettably, most Phoenician monuments were destroyed by time, completely vanished. However, thanks to Phoenician authors and historians akin Sanchuniathon, Iamblichus, Philo of Byblos, etc., the vital findings at archeological sites in many Canaanite-Phoenician cities like Gebel, Sūr, Ba'albek, Saydoun, Ugarit, etc., and the various accounts left to us by Egyptians and Greeks, that we have been successfully able to recuperate eventually many of the most important Phoenician knowledge, religious practices, and esoteric tradition.

We might have probably alluded before in Chapter 3 that the *Temple of Initiation* is divided into three parts and are as follows. First, the *Saint of Saints*, mirroring the *Holy of Holies* in the ninth Enochian vault, is the most sacred and secretive room of the Temple and is furnished by relatively two small Pillars standing at either side of what looked like a *Great Cubical Altar*, a third Pillar stood just behind it. The Left Pillar is designed with an ear of wheat, representing the *Bread*, and topped with a shining Golden Stone, whereas the Right Pillar shows a pattern that reveals the vine, representing the *Wine*, and having a glowing Purple Stone over its top. The third Pillar standing behind the Altar embodies God El in a marble statue, mirroring as such the delta of Enoch and the two mysterious characters. There probably existed two Sphinxes-Cherubim[7] there. The ceiling would stretch out in a perfectly clean condition and amazingly unveiling the fine beauty of the painted blue sky, enhanced with the

---

6. The triune nature of man is his/her constituents of Body, Mind and Spirit.

7. As per the Archeological findings made by the nineteeth-century French historian Ernest Renan at Oum-Al-Awamid in Tyre, and recorded in one of his most reputed books, *Mission De Phénicie*, 704.

signs of the Zodiac, where the Taurus Constellation[8] takes on a unique shape, predominantly, among all other constellations, and finally, the seven Heavenly Bodies in a rotational movement. This *Sanctum Sanctorum* is only accessed by High Priests through an inner three-step stairs[9] leading up to its veil or door.

Just below the inner stairs, into the second section of the Temple is a bigger hall—the main hall—and known as the *Saint*, furnished with two Pillars, bigger in size than the hidden ones, standing each at either side of a small kind of altar located at the center of the room and used for burning incense. On both sides of the hall, surrounding the incense altar, are fixed twelve lampstands, six on each side, perhaps illuminating the ceiling and walls of the four Cardinal Angels (Archangels) and Angels of El—the *Good Watchers*. This anteroom is only accessed by High Priests, Priests and Priestesses, through the entrance door, made of fine cedarwood and flanked by two huge Pillars, standing majestically still like guards protecting it, and overlooking the outside public court. The Right Pillar, representing *Yāw*, Phoenician god of *Water*, was probably made of metals such as laterus, brass, or brick, whereas the Left Pillar represented *Ba'al*, Phoenician god of thunder and lightning—of *Fire*, and probably made of marble.[10]

The third part of the Temple stretches from those Pillars, leading down through a long stair and into the entrance walk to the outer court circular water basin, supported by twelve Taurus statues.

---

8. The Constellation of Taurus was deemed to be of high significance in both Phoenician and Egyptian Religious systems. It is believed to be the celestial sign of the Egyptian god Osiris and of Enoch-Thot-Taautus, also known as Thor the Geblite, the Inventor of the Alphabet. The Ancients considered Taurus as one of the many animals hunted by Orion, the Hunter—located to its left—for reasons only known to Phoenician and Egyptian priests! When we look at the celestial map, we find that Taurus, the Heavenly White Bull, is situated between Gemini, on the left, and Aries, to its right, topped by the Pleiades. Now, *Alpha, Aleph*, is the first letter in the Phoenician language and it means both Ox or Bull, as we have seen earlier, and a letter or sign describing God, as well! Although *Aleph* meant Bull or Taurus in Astrology—a science fashioned by the Ancients—Taurus was, nevertheless, the second sign of the Zodiac, directly related to the fixed Earth element, and is reached by the fourth Letter, *Dalet(h)*, which signifies the Door and Path that leads to it. What is the first Zodiacal sign, then? One may ask. Well, it is Aries, the Ram, and considered as having a pioneering spirit, a leader in the space chart, always eager to rise to the challenge, initiating original tactics to defend Taurus from the hunt of Orion, lingering on the left side. In order to do that, Aries, associated with the cardinal Fire element, had to cross through Saturn—the planet of evil—then Jupiter—the planet of Knowledge—both located on its path, from right to left, to finally reach the central point of Taurus—the *Eye of Taurus*—where it had to make fortifications against the Hunter. For more information, please check a previous work, *The Phoenician Code*.

9. Some have suggested it is a seven-step stairs instead, and it's very possible.

10. It is essential to remember here the Temple of Ba'al-Melkart at Sūr and its twin Pillars, of which we have some historical tangible reference, recorded to us by the famous 5th century BC Greek historian Herodotus, who confirmed in *The Histories*, Book II, paragraph 44, page 94, having seen the whole Temple, mentioning the two Pillars; the one of pure gold and the other of an *emerald stone* of such size as to shine by night.

Now, such *Temple of Initiation*, or *Beth El*, the "House of El," had been constructed according to the measurements of the arms of the Kabbirim. There were two synonyms for the word Kabbirim or Cabiri in ancient Phoenicia and are: "Giants" and "Sages." We, however, are not concerned with the synonym "Sages" herein, as it does not relate to what we are talking about. It is believed that a Giant was double the size of modern man in dimension, so, whether this is true, a myth or just an allegory for perhaps something else, the numbers may have been calculated accordingly during the construction of the Seven-Pillared Temple. Hence, the arms-length of the Kabbirim is double the arms-length of modern men. For that matter, archeologists measured their total lengths to vary between 28 and 49 meters maximum, while their widths and heights range between 10 and 14 meters each. That said, the partial length would vary between 21 and 42 meters for each, the *Outer Circle Court* and the *Inner Circle Saint* parts of the Temple, whereas the length of the *Holy of Holies* would usually be around 7 meters or so.

Naturally, Temples or *lodges* to borrow a Masonic term used for the Phenokian Tradition would have to typically mirror the *Temple of Initiation* in everything, thus being exact replicas for better performing the *Phoenician Rite*. We will not elaborate more on that in this book, and all rules and regulations for admittance and Initiation, etc., will have to be reserved for another future specific work.

Now, along with our research, we have found that Great White Fraternity adepts were divided into three degrees. First, *Listeners* who receive teachings from Initiates, Masters, or High Priests. This degree could take many years of labor before an adept can thus advance to the next one. Second, *Initiates* who receive Divine teachings through Rituals (sacred practices, religious ceremonies, etc.). Last, *Sacred Builders* who were once Listeners then Initiates and have become afterward builders of special consecrated sacred places worldwide. Thus, fundamentally, the Phenokian Fraternity was conceived as a disciplinary, esoteric, religious, and mystical system that builds and elevates humans and prepares them to receive the Divine in Temples it erects!

However, while keeping that spirit alive, we have envisioned its functionality through the subsequent below method since we have already found its *Initiatic Mysteries* at the heart of the Great Five Masters' teachings. Let us have a peek at the *5 Degrees Initiatic System* that we would implement in our Phenokian Fraternity, as per the Tradition communicated to us throughout the ages.

Should we present it in Chronological Order of time, we would thus start with—

- *Royal Arch of Enoch* (Origin)
  1 Degree and 3 Levels: Perceiving—Accepting—Teaching/Initiation
- *Order of Milki-Sedek*
  1 Degree and 3 Levels: Initiation—Priesthood—Ritual
- *Council of Hiram*
  1 Degree and 3 Levels: Temple—Sacred Symbols—Cosmic Balance
- *School of Pythagoras*
  Degree and 4 Levels:
  Preparation—Purification—Perfection—Baptism
- *Church of Christ* (Present)
  1 Degree and 3 Levels: Baptism—Perfection—Union

However, we would implement our *Initiatic* system by Order of Function, and it would be transmitted to the *Initiates* in the following manner—

- **1st Degree:** *Council of Hiram* of 3 Levels
  ~ Building the Temple
  ~ Implementing the Sacred Symbols
  ~ Creating the Cosmic Balance that links man/woman with the creator

- **2nd Degree:** *School of Pythagoras* of 4 Levels
  ~ Preparation of the neophyte
  ~ His/Her bodily Purification
  ~ His/Her mental Perfection
- ~ His/Her spiritual Baptism (by Fire, the light of the Sun, symbolizing the Divine Light)

- **3rd Degree:** *Royal Arch of Enoch* of 3 Levels
  ~ Perceiving the Divine Light
  ~ Accepting the Sacred Teachings
  ~ Teaching/Initiating the Inner Circle

- **4th Degree:** *Order of Milki-Sedek* of 3 Levels
  ~ Initiating the Inner Circle into the Priesthood
  ~ Creating the Priesthood
  ~ Performing the Ritual

- **5th Degree:** *Church of Christ* of 3 Levels
  ~ Baptism of Priest/Priestess (by Sacred Water, symbolizing the Essence of Kosmic Life and spiritual Purification, and by the Sacred Fire—the Divine Light of the Most High "EL")
  ~ Perfecting their Spirits
  ~ Rising and Union (with the Father)

Finally, we have learned that *Rituals* were always performed by Initiates or High Priests and were often perceived as supportive elements to the basic imparted religious or Divine Teachings *newly accepted adepts* or *Initiates* would gradually grasp during their development. Rituals, however, were left secret and only enacted in special consecrated sacred places such as Temples, Sanctuaries, etc., originally called *Beth El*, meaning the "House of El," as we have earlier seen. That said, we will reserve the performance of the *Ancient and Primitive Phoenician Rite* inside that very *Temple of Initiation* for yet another particular and detailed title.

Epilogue

The majority of us, Humans, are doped with ignorance and blinded by superficial appearances and illusions. From the beginning of the visions, we may all felt the presence of God. It was so because God is omnipresent, omnipotent, Father of all, and Universal Mind that diffuses *Love and Intelligence* in everything.

There is a big secret everywhere and in everything; hidden in the simplest atom. There is a miracle everywhere and in everything and is hidden in the plainest atom as well. There is even beauty everywhere and in everything; hidden in the ugliest form, and there is intelligence everywhere and in everything, and is hidden in the dullest atom. Everything is sacred under God.

No matter how long the *Sphere of Generation*, Earth, would thence move around itself and the Sun, it will always remain in the *Centre of Space* that we perceive. It is on its circular surface where we live and upon its cubical foundation, we would evolve too. No matter how far our evolution might lead us forward, we will constantly remain in the *Centre of Eternity* . . .

Time and space seem to surround us from all sides and directions, but we share existence with *Time* and are far-reaching, as is the *Space*. So is God. Nevertheless, what differentiates us, creatures from the absolute Creator is that the latter, God, is also beyond both and beyond the dualistic principles. It is true; the Mind of God lives and is immortal.

The very thought of God conducts and controls the Universe, as it does so to every animate and inanimate being. Everything created, everything is, and everything will be. Nothing is lost, but everything is preserved through its continuous transformation. We were all then, we are here now, and we will be there for eternity.

Stars, planets, Earth, and animals that crawl on it, the oceans and its crea-tures, the sky, and the songs of birds that resonate across it are *letters* of the Alphabet. The voice of Nature dispersed within the elements of life, the awful, the words of men, cries of the oppressed, and the whispers of the lover are *letters* of the Alphabet. All are the Sacred *Alphabet*, Occult *Numbers,* and Mystic *Symbols* in which they communicate themselves to us and inform us of the *Will* and *Law* of God—the Universal Mind. To go beyond time and space, and leave the *Circle of Necessity*, or the *Cycle of Death and Rebirth, Man* has to tend towards God, for the end of him or her is to become like God.

Let Man be a living mind, an *Individual Monad* communing with himself, and with God, the *Great Monad*. His visions will be or rather *become* a look into the eternal, his momentary time, that of infinity, and his existential space, a graceful dwelling in the bosom of all-embracing Love. Let Man live an enchanted life, for it is his and his making.

Freedom is always better than disgraceful and conditioned life, for slavery is what makes us lose our dignity, our *Humanity*, which is all that we have.

It is true; everything that surrounds us is born from the very free thought of the absolute Creator. However, everything that exists has nothing hidden or concealed from the knowledge of the Father. Make of God neither specific idols nor images, *so to speak*, as objects of your rituals and ceremonies, though with complete hearted devotions of faithful sons and daughters, build your Father places of worship in the depth of your hearts first, then spread them freely across the Earth. Just remember that *Free and Eternal is El.*

If, however, the *Ineffable Name*, the *Omnific Word,* was or is to be composed of four letters of the Canaanite-Phoenician Alphabet, the best name we would personally give is ABBA our Father. If anyhow, we were to choose a name of four letters from the Latin Alphabet, a descendent of the Phoenician through the Greek, we would certainly vote for LOVE.

Both ABBA and LOVE might probably be equal names for the God we believe in . . .

It is in the Epistle of St. Paul to the Romans that the word ABBA also appeared, in his words, 8:15, "For ye have not received the spirit of bondage again to fear, but ye have received the spirit of adoption, whereby we cry, Abba, Father."

Therefore, free and eternal must Man always be! It could happen only if he could commune with the voice of mind in every sound, or in every thought manifested, could he feel the spiritual scenes around him and see the signs in every passing form of things. Let Man live a life of *Balance*, communing with the Father, as Sons and Daughters, in total silence. God, the Author, would thence speak to their minds, words of Truth, Justice, Mercy, and Wisdom.

It is true; no one has seen the Master of Time and Space, but it is only by merging with *Him* that you may feel His Essence, Invisible Spirit; the Source of Intelligence that exists in the heart of the Macrocosm, and of the Microcosm that you are. Know that the *Individual Spirit* incarnated in each one of you is like water, agitated by the deeds of the mundane world. You are required to soothe it down through the serenity achieved by pure meditation, prayers, and rituals. Thus, you must purify it to make it clean and clear. Then and only then will you achieve the *Great Unity* by simply harmonizing with *Him*. God the Father will thence *Resuscitate* in the depth of your conscious mind, and you will subsequently participate with *celestial grace* in His great powers and enter Perfection to dominate matter by the sole command of your Intellect and Will. Accordingly, and with faith in your heart, you will be active like *Him*.

And . . . the *Word* was made flesh and has dwelt amongst us. It was seeded, grown and lived in very few, the *Initiates* who died, *sacrificing themselves for the sake of Humanity*, but it would live, and die, in the Man to become Divine, where the peace of the world depends on their lives, deaths, and their eternal resurrections.

Behold, we witness the ultimate realization of Man, the Resurrection of the Kosmic Man!

It echoes consciously in our realms, as the day ends and the night becomes silent, still. And the Sun shines again . . . upon a new Cycle!

~ ~ ~

—And there . . . inside the *Sanctum Sanctorum*, the marble statue of the Most High stood in golden ethereal light behind the Altar of life, presiding over the most sacred rituals of all times, that of *Bread and Wine*, observing the journey of *Initiation* of the Human body from *Aleph* till *Tau*, from the moment of Birth to the time of Death and the glimpse of Resurrection into the Spiritual Realm, quenching its thirst from the cup of Immortality, the Holy Grail, all balanced by Him, God the Father, the Universal Mind, the Great Monad, the One.—

Bibliography

ENGLISH

Blavatsky, H.P., *Isis Unveiled*, The Theosophical Publishing House, First Quest Edition, Printed in the United States of America by Versa Press, 1993, Volume I & II.

———, *The Secret Doctrine*, The Theosophical Publishing House, First Quest Edition, Printed in the United States of America by Versa Press, 1993, Volume I, II & III.

Charoux Robert, *Forgotten Worlds*, Popular Library Edition, New York, Printed in the USA, 1973.

Collins, Andrew, *Gods of Eden: Egypt's Lost Legacy and the Genesis of Civilization*, Inner Traditions - Bear & Company, Vermont, USA, 2002.

Duncan, Malcolm C., *Duncan's Ritual of Freemasonry*, Dover Publications, Inc. New York, Manufactured in the United States by Courier Corporation, 2013.

El Koussa, Karim, *Jesus the Phoenician*, published by Sunbury Press, Mechanicsburg, Printed in the United States of America, 2013.

———, *Pythagoras the Mathemagician*, published by Sunbury Press, Camp Hill, Printed in the United States of America, 2010.

———, *The Phoenician Code – Unveiling the Secrets of the Holy Grail*, Ars Metaphysica, an imprint of Sunbury Press, Inc., Mechanicsburg, Product of the United States of America, 2018. (First published by Sunbury Press, 2011)

Enoch, *The Book of Enoch The Prophet*, translated by Richard Laurence, Wizards Bookshelf, San Diego, Printed in USA, 1983

Eusebius (of Caesarea), *Praeparatio Evangelica* (Preparation for the Gospel).

Finkelstein, Israel & Silberman, Neil Asher, *The Bible Unearthed – Archaeology's new vision of ancient Israel and the origin of its sacred texts*, A Touchstone Book, published by Simon & Schuster, New York, Manufactured in the United States of America, 2002.

Gilgamesh, *The Epic of Gilgamesh*, Translated by R. Campbell Thompson, Luzac & Co., London, 1928.

Hall, Manly P., *Melchizedek and the Mystery of Fire*, Published by The Philosophical Research Society, Los Angeles, Printed in the United States of America, 1996.

Hall, Manly P., *The Secret Teachings of All Ages*, Jeremy P. Tarcher/Penguin, a member of Penguin Group (USA) Inc., New York. Reader's Edition. Printed in the United States of America, 2003. (Copyright © 2003 by Philosophical Research Society. Original text published in 1928)

Harnack, Adolf Von, *Marcion the Gospel of the Alien God*, Translated by John E. Steely and Lyle D. Bierma, Wipf & Stock Publishers, Eugene, Oregon, USA, 2007. (Previously published by the Labyrinth Press, 1990)

Herodotus, *The Histories*, published by Barnes & Noble Books, New York, USA Press Inc, Printed in the United States of America, 2005.

Iamblichus, *Life of Pythagoras*, translated from the Greek by Thomas Taylor, Printed in Great Britain by the Haycock Press Ltd, London, 1965.

Knight, Christopher and Lomas, Robert, *The Hiram Key*, published in the USA by Fair Winds Press, Printed and bound in Canada, 2001. (First published in the UK by Century Books, Random House, 1996. First published in the USA by Elements Books, Inc., 1997)

Pike, Albert, *Morals and Dogma of the Ancient and Accepted Scottish Rite of Freemasonry*, Kessinger Publishing Company, Montana, USA. Originally published in 1871.

Picknett, Lynn & Prince, Clive, *The Templar Revelation*, Corgi Books are published by Transworld Publishers, London, Printed and bound in Great Britain, 1998. (Originally published in Great Britain by Bantam Press, a division of Transworld Publishers, 1997)

Rawlinson, George, *History of Phoenicia*, The Project Gutenberg EBook, 2006. (First Published 1889 by Longmans, Green, and Co.)

Robinson, John, *Born in Blood – the lost secrets of Freemasonry*, M. Evans & Company, New York, Manufactured in the United States of America, 1989.

Smith, Mark S., *The Origins of Biblical Monotheism – Israel's Polytheistic Background and the Ugaritic Texts*, Oxford University Press Inc., New York, Printed in the United States of America, 2001.

Strabo, *Geography*.

Sullivan, Robert W., *The Royal Arch of Enoch*, Published by Rocket Science Productions, August 2011.

Thompson, Thomas L., *The Mythic Past – Biblical Archaeology and the Myth of Israel*, Published by Basic Books, a Member of the Perseus Books Group, Printed in the United States of America, 1999.

Waddell, L.A., *The Phoenician Origin of Britons, Scots, & Anglo-Saxons*, First Published by The Christian Book Club of America, Hawthorne, California, Printed in the USA, 1924.

Webb, Thomas Smith, *Freemason's Monitor or Illustrations of Freemasonry*, Published by Cushing & Appleton, Boston, Joshua Cushing Printer, 1797.

Wilmshurst, W.L., *The Meaning of Masonry*, Gramercy Books, a division of Random House Value Publishing, Inc., New York, Printed and bound in the United States, 1980. (Copyright © 1980 by Crown Publishers, Inc.)

FRENCH

De Nerval, Gérard, *Voyage en Orient*, Éditions Galimmard, 1984, pour l'établissement du texte et le dossier, 1998, pour la préface et la présente édition. Édition dérivée de la Bibliothèque de la Pléaide. Imprimé en France.

Lenoir, Frédéric, et, Tardan-Masquelier, Ysé (Sous la Direction), *Encyclopédie Des Religions*, Nouvelle Édition, Revue, Augmentée et Mise a Jour, Bayard Éditions, Achevé d'imprimé en CEE, Août, 2000.

Renan, Ernest, *Mission De Phénicie*, Michel Lévy Frères Éditeurs, Imprimerie Impérial, Paris, 1864.

————, *Vie de Jésus*, Édition établie, présentée et annotée par Jean Gaulmier, Éditions Gallimard, Imprimé en France, Août, 1974.

Schuré, Édouard, *Les Grands Initiés – Rama, Krishna, Hermès, Moïse, Orphee, Pythagore, Platon, Jésus*, Esquise de L'histoire secrète des Religions, Librairie Académique Perrin, Imprimé en France, Avril, 1997.

ONLINE AND EBOOK

Josephus, Flavius, *The Antiquities of the Jews*, translated by William Whiston, produced by David Reed, and David Widger for Project Gutenberg (License included with this eBook or online at www.gutenberg.org), Release Date: January 4, 2009 [EBook #2848], Last Updated: August 9, 2017.

Julian, *Humyn el King Helios*, wikisource.org (*Hymn to King Helios*). In this work (Introduction to Oration IV), translated by Emily Wilmer Cave Wright. The Works of the Emperor Julian, Volume I (1913), Loeb Classical Library.

About the Author

Born in 1971, Ehden, North Lebanon, bestselling & award-winning author Karim El Koussa started his career with self-publishing four books in Lebanon from 1996 to 2003, before he got the chance to publish the 1st US edition of Pythagoras: The Mathemagician, 2005 (winner of Saïd Akl Prize, 2001, for the Lebanese edition). Besides writing books, he worked and wrote a few articles for magazines in Lebanon, the USA, and Canada.

Since 2010, he was signed by Sunbury Press, a US-based publishing company that released his books: *The KABBALISTIC Visions—And the Secrets of the Phoenician Tradition*, 2021 (1st US edition); *JESUS the Phoenician*, 2013 (1st US edition); *The PHOENICIAN Code—Unveiling the Secrets of the Holy Grail*, 2011 & 2018 (2nd US edition); and *PYTHAGORAS the Mathemagician*, 2010 (2nd US edition).

His thriller, *The PHOENICIAN Code*, was also published in Arabic by the Lebanese publishing house Dar Saer Al Mashrek in 2016 and by the French Éditions Dervy (Groupe Trédaniel) in 2018. Also, in 2018, Northern Star Pictures, a US-based film/TV development & production company, signed him, optioning the rights to *The PHOENICIAN Code* for a TV series.

His work is a mixture of religion, history, philosophy, spirituality, and esoteric inner insights. With over 25 years of extensive research into the religion and history of the world with a special focus on the Canaanite-Phoenician and Egyptian traditions and the Christian religion, Mr. El Koussa has gathered a well-rounded knowledge in the writing of specialized books that are acknowledged, awarded, and widely read.

As author and researcher, he had numerous worldwide book events (lectures & signings), and his presence in media was abundant on radio, TV, press, and Internet, mainly in Lebanon, the USA, and France. In addition, he is a member of many international organizations and is currently working on a few book projects, films, and TV Series..

For more information:
http://www.el-koussa.com

Made in United States
Troutdale, OR
02/04/2024